Commodity Spread Trading
Take Advantage of Seasonality

DAVID CARLI

This book is sold with the understanding that neither the author nor the publisher is engaged in rendering legal, accounting, or other professional services or advice by publishing this book. Each individual situation is unique. Thus, if legal or financial advice or other expert assistance is required in a specific situation, the services of a competent professional should be sought to ensure that the situation has been evaluated carefully and appropriately. The author disclaims any liability, loss, or risk resulting directly or indirectly from the use or application of any of the contents of this book. There is a substantial risk of loss in commodity trading. It is not suitable for everyone.

Copyright © Eleventh edition in September 2024 by David Carli.

All rights reserved. This book or any portion thereof may not be reproduced or used in any manner without written permission of the copyright holder except for the use of excerpts if you are reviewing the book.

First Printing: 2017

ISBN: 9798355760908

Website: www.tradingwithdavid.com
E-mail: info@tradingwithdavid.com

EDITED

Hannah Hermes
hannahhermes@gmail.com

CONTENTS

Introduction – About the Author	1
Introduction – About SpreadCharts	2
Introduction – Preface	3
Chapter 1 – What You will Gain from this Book	4
Chapter 2 – Birth of Commodity Market	6
Chapter 3 – Introduction to Commodity	10
Chapter 4 – Spread trading	15
Chapter 5 – Seasonality & Correlation	22
Chapter 6 – Statistical Databases	26
Chapter 7 – Seasonal Patterns	53
Chapter 8 – Not only Seasonality	60
Chapter 9 – Fundamental Analysis	63
Chapter 10 – Reports	68
Chapter 11 – The C.O.T. Report	77
Chapter 12 – FPD, FND and LTD	86
Chapter 13 – Money Management	91
Chapter 14 – Value-at-Risk (VaR)	95
Chapter 15 – The Term Structure	102
Chapter 16 – Multi-Leg Spreads	109
Chapter 17 – Contango & Backwardation	117
Chapter 18 – The Starting Date	124
Chapter 19 – Exploit the Manipulation	127
Chapter 20 – Ratios	132

Chapter 21 – The Open Interest	139
Chapter 22 – Subjective Probability	149
Chapter 23 – Crop Year	156
Chapter 24 – Intermarket Spreads	158
Chapter 25 – Final Comments	170
Appendix A – Commodity Summary	176
Appendix B – The Unit Move	178
Appendix C – FND and LTD	180
Appendix D – Month Symbols	182
Appendix E – Commodity Reports	183
Appendix F – Web Resources	190
Appendix G – Commodity Glossary	193

About the Author
Introduction

My journey in the investment and trading world started shortly after I graduated from the University of Pisa, Italy. I then travelled to New York City USA., where I attended exclusive courses by Steve Nison who introduced the western world to the art of the Japanese candlestick as a tool for analysing market trends and investment decisions.

I have been working as a full-time trader and an independent financial analyst since 2007 hence I established Trading with David as a niche investment service with the primary focus on FX markets and commodities. During that time, I collaborated with reputable financial trading services and investment magazines. And in 2012-2013 I worked as a hedge fund manager for an Italian investment bank. In 2018, I began providing market analysis and trading ideas for a major European commodity investment company up to this date.

I published several trading and investment books to pass on my knowledge and expertise on how to analyse the financial market correctly and have the odds on your side to become a profitable trader. My approach is based on low-risk investment strategies across all markets to achieve a balanced asset allocation through diversification and risk management.

I have several other books for those who wish to learn more about certain aspects of trading, such as Forex, Commodities Spread Trading, and Options, so you can see how I approach other markets. In my books, I teach interested investors how to correctly and comprehensively analyse financial markets, so that they always have a clear view of the situation and the odds of success in their favour.

You can find out more about my educational library on https://tradingwithdavid.com to develop an extraordinary edge to your trading and investments plan with a deep understanding of the macro environment, along with advanced analysis and risk management they are designed to build or improve your trading skills.

About SpreadCharts

Introduction

~

SpreadCharts is a complete analytical platform for commodity futures and spreads. Find out more on https://SpreadCharts.com.

Seasonality alone is no longer sufficient in today's financial markets. It is like a rear-view mirror: it tells you something about the past but very little about the present. You have to do better to be successful in today's ever-changing markets. You need additional tools that work independently from seasonality and reflect what is happening in the market right now. You need SpreadCharts.

SpreadCharts offers the widest range of functions, which gives you a unique insight into the markets. Technical analysis, seasonality studies, sentiment data, term structure dynamics... these are just a few of the many tools you will find in this app. And they are free for anybody to use, which is especially helpful for beginners. Moreover, all of this is served in a modern, user-friendly environment. You can run the app anywhere and anytime - on your PC, tablet, or phone if necessary.

While the free features are great, the premium features on SpreadCharts will blow your mind. A good example is the trading signals powered by artificial intelligence. The intelligent model generating the signals takes other types of data into account, not just seasonality. It makes predictions in real-time, continually learns from new data, and adapts to the ever-changing market environment.

For those who desire a more personal approach, there is premium research. It is world-class research of the best opportunities in the markets from people with a successful track record in the hedge fund industry.

Although the premium features are exciting, they will not make a successful trader out of you. Their purpose is to save you time analysing tens of markets, finding you only the best opportunities. The rest is, however, up to you. Only hard work and thorough study will bring you success. But you are lucky! This book is precisely the right source for the start of your journey in the markets...

PREFACE
INTRODUCTION

~

Everyone has seen the movie 'Trading Places', at least once in their life; after all, it is a must during the Christmas holidays. The trade on pork bellies at the beginning; the orange juice report, with which the two starring actors, Dan Aykroyd and Eddie Murphy, take revenge on Duke cousins… priceless!

Wheat, coffee, orange juice… not only you can use them to prepare a delicious breakfast, but you can also trade them for profit. Trading with commodities is the most fascinating and intriguing way to trade, as it includes a characteristic uncommon to any other market: seasonality.

Spread trading is the best way to trade commodities and provides an excellent opportunity to diversify your portfolio, reducing the risks. Balancing, covering and protecting the portfolio have to be the trader's first goal.

'*Take Advantage of Seasonality*' is the first volume of the series 'Commodity Spread Trading'. This book is a real and complete course on commodities and spread trading. You will learn aspects that you will not find in any other book or course, and they come from over 25 years of experience in financial markets, even as a fund manager for a small Italian investment bank.

Inside this book, you will find explained not only the statistical databases and software for your analysis but also the main commodity reports, how to read the C.O.T., term structure, and why you have to be careful of the First Notice Day (FND) and Last Trading Day (LTD).

And again, the importance of a correct reading of contango and backwardation, understanding if a movement is driven by speculation or real reasons such as a drought or epidemic, and many other essential aspects.

With '*Take Advantage of Seasonality*' you will learn a new and exciting way to trade. With its modest price, this book is my gift for all those who aspire to become professional traders.

I invite you to visit my website, https://tradingwithdavid.com, where you will find articles, analysis, and other useful resources to support you on your journey of growth in the world of trading.

WHAT YOU WILL GAIN FROM THIS BOOK

CHAPTER 1

~

This book will guide you through the world of commodities: what they are, how they move in the markets, and how to analyse them accurately. The goal is to provide you with the tools necessary to approach spread trading with awareness and rigour. However, you will not find a ready-made strategy in these pages, like those often offered in trading courses. There is no magic formula to apply indiscriminately to the commodities market. If this is what you were expecting, you probably have the wrong book in your hands. I suggest you look elsewhere, perhaps among those 'gurus' who promise easy gains simply by following seasonality, but who, in reality, are more interested in their own profits than in your success. These shortcut sellers have no concern about the risk of you losing your money.

You have probably already come across advertisements or courses claiming that all you need to do is follow seasonal patterns to make profits. Spread trading is often presented as an easy path to success. But the truth is quite different. Spread trading is by no means easier than other types of trading. It requires in-depth knowledge of commodities, experience, and, above all, discipline. You also need a solid analytical plan that allows you to gather all the necessary information to make well-reasoned decisions with a margin of success on your side.

Here, I want to debunk a myth: seasonality alone is not enough to make profits in trading. In fact, with increasingly frequent climate changes and rising geopolitical tensions, relying solely on seasonality could more easily lead to losses than profits. If it were really enough to subscribe to a seasonal statistics database to make money, then no one in the world would have financial problems.

It is true that seasonality is an important factor in commodity trading, but it is never the only aspect to consider. Events such as climate anomalies, epidemics, social unrest, or strikes can drastically alter seasonal patterns. If you ignore these factors, you risk making poor decisions that can damage your results.

This book aims to give you the foundation for a comprehensive analysis of spreads. It will not be limited to explaining seasonality, but it will provide you with all the tools necessary to understand the various factors that influence the commodities market. You will learn concepts that are often not covered in courses or other books, although I expect someone will soon copy them. By the end of the book, you will be able to identify and understand seasonality, knowing what influences it and how to build a solid, detailed analysis that gives you a clear view of the state of the commodities you intend to trade.

However, it is crucial to understand that this book is primarily theoretical. Do not be under the illusion that you will immediately become a profitable trader just by reading these pages. What you learn here, from fundamental analysis to term structure, from the C.O.T. (Commitments of Traders) report to price study, will need to be applied consistently in practice. The theory will provide you with the foundation, but only direct experience will allow you to refine your skills and approach the market effectively.

In my second book on spread trading, you will find numerous practical examples of spread analysis, where I will apply my method based on the concepts explained in this volume. This method will allow you to identify opportunities and risks that often elude those who rely solely on seasonality. You will learn to recognise the right signals and avoid the pitfalls that catch out less prepared traders.

A small spoiler: in the second volume, I will cover more advanced aspects of spread trading, topics that only the most experienced traders tend to consider. These concepts will give you an even more comprehensive understanding of the market, strengthening your analytical capabilities. The goal is to offer you an integrated perspective that allows you to operate with in-depth knowledge, leaving nothing to chance.

Birth of Commodity Market

CHAPTER 2

What is a commodity? It is a natural, transformable, and tradable resource that forms the essential basis for industrial and food production. Commodities are the fundamental elements on which entire production chains depend, representing a global market of significant economic importance.

The production and consumption of commodities depends on several factors, such the weather, with the seasons, but also by natural and artificial resources. The demand for commodities is influenced by several factors, such as economic, but also by consumer habits.

The Commodity market is the oldest in the world. It was born when ancient peoples began to barter: ten oil amphorae for five measures of wheat in ancient Rome.

In all the squares of the world, until the nineteenth century, the farmers (Producers) met the artisans and entrepreneurs (Hedgers) who bought the wheat for the mills, negotiating the price based on the quality and quantity offered.

Commodities now are traded on the physical market and, more frequently, through exchanges. The first financial contract dates back to around 1700, to the Dōjima Rice Exchange in Osaka, Japan. It was a necessity that began in the 1730s when the price of rice plummeted across Japan. Samurai, who were paid entirely in rice, needed a stable conversion into money.

Today's commodity markets have originated from agricultural trade in the 19th century (the first contract to the Chicago Stock Exchange dates back to 1864 with a contract on wheat).

Both buyers and sellers wanted to limit the risks to which they were subjected during the harvest. The buyers tried to defend themselves in case crops were scarce, and therefore the prices were high; while sellers wanted a guaranteed price to sell their goods, protecting themselves in case of oversupply and low prices. However, the level of standardisation concerning the quality and delivery of products was very scarce, and there was no centralised storage location.

It was founded rounded in 1848 by the Chicago Board of Trade (CBOT), who played an intermediary role between farmers and traders in the trade of grains. It determined procedures for weighing and grading of grains and was created a centralised market. It established in advance the prices of deliveries to be made in the future, and this allowed buyers and sellers to limit the risk of price changes.

The tulip mania

However, the trading of commodities has not always been pursued solely with the intent of mitigating risks, but has often taken on speculative connotations. Even unusual goods, such as tulips in the Netherlands, became the subject of speculative phenomena. At the end of the 16th century, tulip bulbs became the centre of an unprecedented economic bubble, one of the earliest documented examples of mass speculation.

The cultivation of tulips in the Netherlands began in the late 1500s, when bulbs, imported from Turkey, demonstrate toleration for Dutch weather conditions. The combination of a new investment available on the market and a particularly prosperous and flourishing era that allowed the continued expansion of the Dutch economy, very quickly propelling investors into entering this new market.

Very rapidly tulips became a real asset, so much so that they were traded on the exchanges of many Dutch cities and pushed investors towards this investment; the demand for tulips grew to such an extent that they began to be considered luxury goods, a status symbol that could not be renounced.

The speculative bubble, however, unlike what is commonly believed, did not actually start from the tulips, but their bulbs. The tulip bulbs began to be seen as safe future investments, and many investors started to sell properties to buy them, giving rise to a dramatic increase in their price (and, by default, even that of tulips). It was reported that an Utrecht brewer reached the point of exchanging his brewery for three tulip bulbs.

The so-called 'futures' began to make their way in the financial world. Not being the tulips in themselves to arouse the greatest interest for investors, but their bulbs, the merchants began to sell the bulbs that had just been planted, and in this way the 'right on the bulbs' was negotiated.

The buyer paid, therefore, a sum as an advance on the final price, paying the balance only upon delivery of the flowering bulb; this phenomenon did not go unnoticed, so much so that in 1610 a royal edict tried to prevent the trade of bulbs, but failed to stop it.

Their trade became, therefore, a 'trade under-the-table' that took place mainly in taverns, where all that was required from traders was to pay a 'wine money', a commission of 2.5% a trade, for a maximum of three florins.

All of this was, therefore, external to the exchange (precisely since they were considered non-legal) and took place between the individual counterparties. The trade in tulip bulbs continued to grow inexorably until 1636, a date that may be representative of the culmination of the bubble.

You can see in Figure 1 below the price chart of the tulips from November 1636 to February 1637.

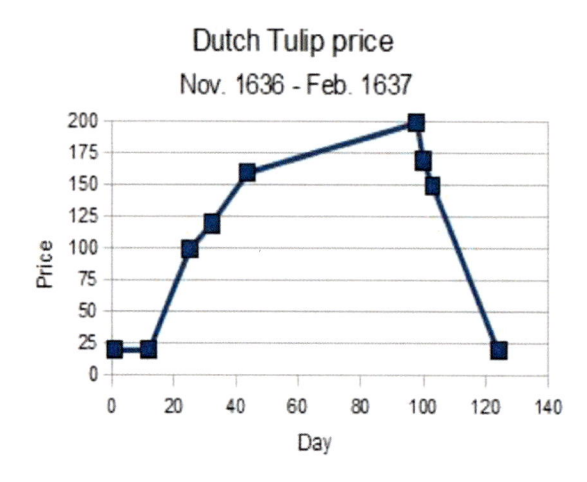

Figure 1 - Price chart of the tulips from November 1636 to February 1637

In 1636, an auction sold a tulip bulb at 6,000 florins (an unreasonable figure considering that the average income of a Dutch family at the time was about equal to 150 florins per year). Like any speculative bubble, the price increase was bound pretty soon to end with a wave of sales and a strong price fall.

The bubble of tulips burst at the start of 1637 and in this case the historical context also influenced a trend in the economy. The bubble burst, in fact, following an auction in Haarlem with no bids, probably due (although there are still numerous debates on this topic), to a possible outbreak of bubonic plague that frightened the population making it stay in their homes.

From that moment on, euphoria gave way to panic, and investors began to sell tulips for fear that they would no longer be required as before, thus trying to make profits before it was too late.

The wave of sales was such that the price of the bulbs and tulips collapsed dramatically, leading to the bankruptcy of numerous speculators. The busted bubble had left behind it a panorama of financial devastation and an economy now in ruins.

Buyers were forced to honour tulip purchase contracts at prices ten times greater than market ones, while sellers held rights on bulbs with the value of one-tenth of the original.

To avoid the worst, on February 24, 1637, the Dutch florist corporation decided to convert all futures contracts (i.e., futures regarding tulip bulbs) into options contracts. In this way, the buyer was no longer legally obligated to buy the bulbs but could also choose not to buy them by paying, in place of the final price, only a penalty.

No one knows today exactly how many people were involved in this market, but there is no doubt that a value well beyond the reasonable physical value was attributed to tulips, with this episode having a considerable impact on the local economy.

The commodity markets today

Markets can be used to reduce the risk of price fluctuations to which you may be exposed, or, on the contrary, to exploit these price movements to your advantage. What was once considered coverage for suppliers and dealers in commodities, today enables more people to have access to these markets.

In recent decades, the commodities market has expanded, involving not only producers and traders but also hedge funds, investment banks, and pension funds, making this sector a crucial tool for diversification and risk management in investment portfolios. The increasing investments in commodities over the years have led to the introduction of an ever-wider range of tradable commodities and a greater variety of investment methods.

Today, commodities represent not only a fundamental market for global economies but also a strategic resource for traders and investors. Many commodities are also used in ways other than traditional ones. Corn, for example, has traditionally been used in the production of food and animal feed. But with the growing awareness of the possible adverse effects on the environment produced by the consumption of fossil fuels, the so-called 'soft commodities' such as corn are increasingly used in the production of biofuels.

These new uses and decreases in the supply of some commodities can create interesting dynamics of supply and demand, influencing prices.

Introduction to Commodity

Chapter 3

Commodities are an integral part of your daily life. From the food on your table to industrial activities, these natural resources play a fundamental role. Unlike stocks, whose value can drop to zero, the price of commodities will never fall to zero: there will always be a need for essential goods like wheat, coffee, and cotton.

The cost of production determines the first fascinating aspect of commodities. I will give an example. Let's take the wheat; it is a commodity widely spread all over the planet. You consume it every day; you find it, in the form of bread (stable food) and cereals. That means that there will always be someone willing to produce it for a profit.

Producing wheat, however, has a cost, and if the price of wheat is too low and fails to compensate for costs, the farmer would stop producing it. This would lead to a reduction in supply because there would be fewer farmers in the world willing to produce wheat. As a result, the price of wheat would begin to rise.

So, if you know the production cost of a commodity, you can purchase that commodity at a low price because you know that below a certain level, that particular commodity is no longer convenient to produce. All of this will affect the price, due to the decrease in supply which would lead to a price hike. And it would do so with very low risks - it is worth emphasising this point.

That is the first interesting aspect that only commodities can offer us. Let's see now what the reasons that underlie an investment in commodities are.

1. Inflation. Commodities have, by their nature, a role of hedging and they do it very well against inflation.

Generally, when the demand for goods and services grows, the prices of these goods and services also rise, and, of course, the prices of commodities that are used in the production tend to increase as well.

Since the commodity price increases during periods of prices rise, investment in this asset can provide the investor with coverage of the portfolio against the pressure of inflation. In even more difficult situations, such as during the geopolitical and macroeconomic upheavals, commodities have often proved more robust than other instruments.

2. <u>Diversification</u>. To diversify, protect and balance the portfolio should be the first rule of every investor. Reduction of the risk always passes through the choice of instruments and different markets, and in this, the commodities play an important role.

It is well known that, very often, when the value of certain assets drops (e.g. equities or bonds), commodities provide very interesting returns for investors. That is why it is important to diversify.

3. <u>Seasonality</u>. Only with commodities can you exploit a seasonality, a cycle which repeats year after year. Just think about heating oil. It is clear that you will have much larger consumption of it in winter, while it will be used a lot less during the summer. This is also the case with the production cycle of the crops, with planting and harvesting occurring every year.

That is a statistical advantage that you only have in the commodity market: if you know in advance the seasonality of a commodity, you can anticipate price movement. Just a few data are enough, some analysis, nothing complex and you can make very interesting profits from this market.

Let us now go and see which commodities are the most invested in the market and that you can trade every day. I start by saying that there are two types of commodities:

a) <u>Soft</u>, such as wheat, coffee, sugar and even livestock. Those are commodities more easily influenced by external factors, such as climate or epidemics because they tend to deteriorate. The producers of soft commodities are often involved in this kind of market, with an interest to set the price of their products.

b) <u>Hard</u>, such as crude oil, gas, gold, and copper, are materials that are extracted from the ground or produced by other natural resources. Even the hard commodities may be affected by external factors, although to a lesser degree than soft commodities, such as strikes and wars.

More specifically, the principal commodities can be divided into five categories:

- <u>Grains</u>: corn, wheat (in all its varieties: winter or spring, soft or hard, etc.), soybean, soybean meal, soybean oil, and oats.
- <u>Softs</u>: cotton, cocoa, coffee, sugar, orange juice, and lumber.
- <u>Meats</u>: live cattle, feeder cattle, and lean hogs.
- <u>Metals</u>: gold, silver, platinum, palladium, and copper.
- <u>Energy</u>: crude oil, gasoline, heating oil, and natural gas.

Even with the five categories listed above, you can diversify your portfolio, in different sectors. You should not concentrate on one category, so you don't diminish the risk of a single investment, for example, in multilevel sectors such as energy and meat.

There are other categories and commodities that I have not listed because although investors expect a florid market in the coming years, all the classical instruments needed to invest in these products are not yet available. At the moment, they can be traded only by Funds. An example is the ETFs on water or hydrogen.

You are, therefore, coming to the general control of commodities through financial products.

Now, let's see what the different factors affecting commodity prices are.

1. **Supply and Demand**. The supply/demand relationship determines the price of the exchange of goods and services. The commodities price reflects exactly this law of the market.

If the supply increases, but demand does not change, (think, for example, the harvest of corn that has a higher-than-expected return and then, with a more considerable amount of corn in the market), the price will tend to fall. Many farmers will be willing to undercut the price of their corn to try to find a buyer.

If demand grows but producers are not able to fulfil it (think of the effects of an epidemic on cattle resulting in a sharp decrease of meat on the market), then the price will increase because buyers will be willing to pay a higher price for the amount of product needed.

2. **The weather**. It can influence the price of commodities and affect production a lot. It is, in fact, often the only thing responsible for very strong price movements due to imbalances in the supply/demand relationship.

Adverse weather conditions do not affect only crops such as wheat or coffee, but all commodities. Just think about the price of oil after the passage of a hurricane, or transportation blocked due to heavy snowfall and frost.

3. **Diseases and epidemic**. Some external factors can cause the price of a commodity to skyrocket, such as diseased crop or an epidemic that affects livestock. Same as with adverse weather conditions, diseases and epidemics create imbalances in the supply/demand relationship because of a reduction in supply which, therefore, results in a strong movement of prices.

The reason for this is that buyers predict that the future availability of a commodity could become scarce; thus, they increase the demand for that commodity. They are willing to pay more for it today than in the future, to ensure you never run out of them.

4. **Economic and political factors**. Prices of commodities are also affected by the economic and political events of the countries that are producing or using that commodity. For example, political unrest in the Middle East often causes fluctuations in the futures price of oil due to uncertainties on the supply side.

Think, also, of the strike in the gold mines in South Africa, or the duties in some South American countries on exports of grains. So, the political and economic instability of a country can influence the price of a commodity.

5. **Reports**. They are essential and give you a picture of the situation of commodities in their various phases: production, demand, supply, etc. Even just a change in the size of land cultivated can cause a rise or drop in the price of a crop.

The inventories and stocks showed by the reports affect the price of a commodity a lot. Like, for example, the Weekly Petroleum Status report that every Wednesday is released by the EIA (US Energy Information Administration) and that provides information about the petroleum supply situation. The new inventories can influence the crude oil price strongly.

6. U.S. Dollar. The prices of commodities are in dollars, so, the US dollar is their enemy. A rising dollar is anti-inflationary, so it applies downward pressure on commodity prices. Similarly, a falling dollar will usually apply upward pressure on commodity prices.

Investing in commodities is very different from investing in stocks and other financial assets. With commodities, you are dealing with a physical good, and managing that physical good requires effort that stock investors do not have to worry about.

Another aspect that you can deduce from the list above is that the commodity market is less easily manipulated than other financial markets because price is affected by the weather, diseases, epidemics, political factors, etc. that cannot be artificially induced (unless you can somehow cause a drought...).

At this point, you are probably wondering: how can I invest in commodities? There are several ways to do it:

A) Physical. The most obvious way to invest in commodities is by buying the physical commodity itself. By owning a commodity, you will have direct exposure to increases and decreases in its value, and you can sell it when you want to convert it back to cash.

However, most physical commodities involve significant logistical problems. With commodities like gold or silver, it is relatively simple to find dealers to sell your coins or bars, albeit often at a slight profit margin. Instead, it is a lot harder to take possession of 1,000 barrels of crude oil or 5,000 bushels of soybean. Because of those problems, owning physical commodities works well only in limited situations with specific commodities.

B) Futures. They are derivatives. That is, their value derives precisely from an index, a commodity etc which are linked by something called an underlying asset. Investing in commodities via futures offers investors a way to get exposure to changing prices of commodities without having to take physical possession of them.

Using futures contracts, you will never get to possess a commodity in which you are going to invest. A futures contract is an agreement to buy or sell a certain amount of a commodity in the future, with an established price that can fluctuate with market conditions.

C) Spread trading. With spread trading, you no longer work on single futures, but on the difference between two or more correlated futures. You move from being directional on the market with the futures to non-directional with spread trading. That is a crucial aspect.

With spread trading, investors create a hedge of the position with a significant reduction of the risk. They get several other advantages that trading with futures cannot offer. I will not add anything else; you will see spread trading further in the next chapter.

D) ETCs. The Exchange Traded Commodity (ETC) gives investors exposure to commodities in the form of shares. Traded as a stock, i.e., bought and sold on a stock exchange, ETCs replicate the price movement of commodities, such as oil, gold, silver, etc. and then fluctuate on the basis of the value of those commodities.

An ETCs can invest in either one commodity or in a commodity basket. An example of a commodity basket ETC is one that is composed of multiple metals (not only one), like gold, palladium, copper, etc. In this way, you have invested in metals correlated with the growth of an economy (i.e., copper and aluminium) and, at the same time, you are covered with defensive assets like gold and silver.

E) Equities. With equities, you are going to invest in shares of companies linked to the world of commodities. Mining companies, oil and gas exploration and production companies have direct exposure to commodities prices. Affiliated businesses like heavy-equipment manufacturers and oilfield services companies tend to do better when the underlying asset is performing well.

Unlike an ETC or ETF, you will invest in companies that work as an individual commodity, and this implies substantial differences. Furthermore, often the price of a share of a company can undergo significant fluctuations due to external and economic factors. The price of a commodity cannot fall to zero; the price of a share, on the other hand, can.

F) Options. They are contracts that give the holder the right to buy (call option) or sell (put option) a given quantity of an underlying financial asset (equities, futures, ETFs, etc.) at a specific price (the strike) and a date (or within a date). If I buy an option, I pay a premium; if I sell it, I get a premium.

Just like the futures market, options are also derivatives. But unlike futures with which you promised to fulfil the contract, when you buy options, if you feel that the operation is no longer convenient for us, you are not obliged to fulfil the contract, and you will only lose the premium you paid previously.

For the second time during the reading of this chapter, you are probably wondering: among all these, which is the better way to trade commodities? You can, of course, use all the ways seen above. The best ones to trade commodities, for many good reasons, is through the spread trading and options.

For options, I refer you to my book *'Options Relaxing Trading – From Theory to Practice, A Complete Guide for Beginners'*. It will provide you with comprehensive knowledge about options and the main strategies.

As for spread trading, it is a method that offers numerous advantages compared to direct futures trading. In the next chapter, you will explore in detail how spread trading works and how it can reduce risk and improve your results.

Spread Trading

Chapter 4

Let me start by defining the term spread. In financial terms, a spread is the price or yield differential between two related financial instruments. This concept is the foundation of many trading strategies and is particularly used to reduce risk by exploiting the relative movements between the two instruments, rather than betting on the absolute direction of prices.

A classic example of a spread is the price difference between two stocks within the same sector, such as Goldman Sachs and JP Morgan, both banking stocks. Another example could be the difference between two stock indices, such as the S&P 500 and the DJ30, or the difference between the yields of two interest rates, such as the German Bund and the 10-year US T-note.

In the commodities market, a spread usually refers to the price differential between two futures contracts of the same commodity with different delivery dates, or the price differential between two related commodities, such as corn and wheat. This type of operation allows you to benefit from the relative price movements between different contract maturities or between commodities with similar characteristics but slightly different supply and demand dynamics.

In the context of spread trading, understanding correlation is essential. Correlation is defined as the relationship that describes the degree of connection between two markets. Markets are said to be correlated when, as one market rises, the other also increases, and conversely, when the first market declines, the second also falls. The peaks and troughs of the two markets often coincide.

The correlation coefficient is a measure that determines the degree of association between the movements of two markets. The coefficient can never exceed 1.0 or fall below -1.0; if it does, it is a clear indication that there has been an error in the calculation. A coefficient of -1.0 indicates a perfect negative correlation (inverse correlation), while a coefficient of 1.0 indicates a perfect positive correlation. Let me show you this concept in practice.

In Figure 2 below, you can see the comparison between Goldman Sachs and JPMorgan stocks, both from the banking sector. It is clear how the two stocks tend to move in a very similar manner.

Figure 2 - Goldman Sachs and JPMorgan charts (TradingView.com)

You talk of inverse correlations when the first market ascends whilst the second descends, and vice versa, when the first market decreases and the second increases, most of the time.

You can see an example in Figure 3 with the S&P500 and VIX futures.

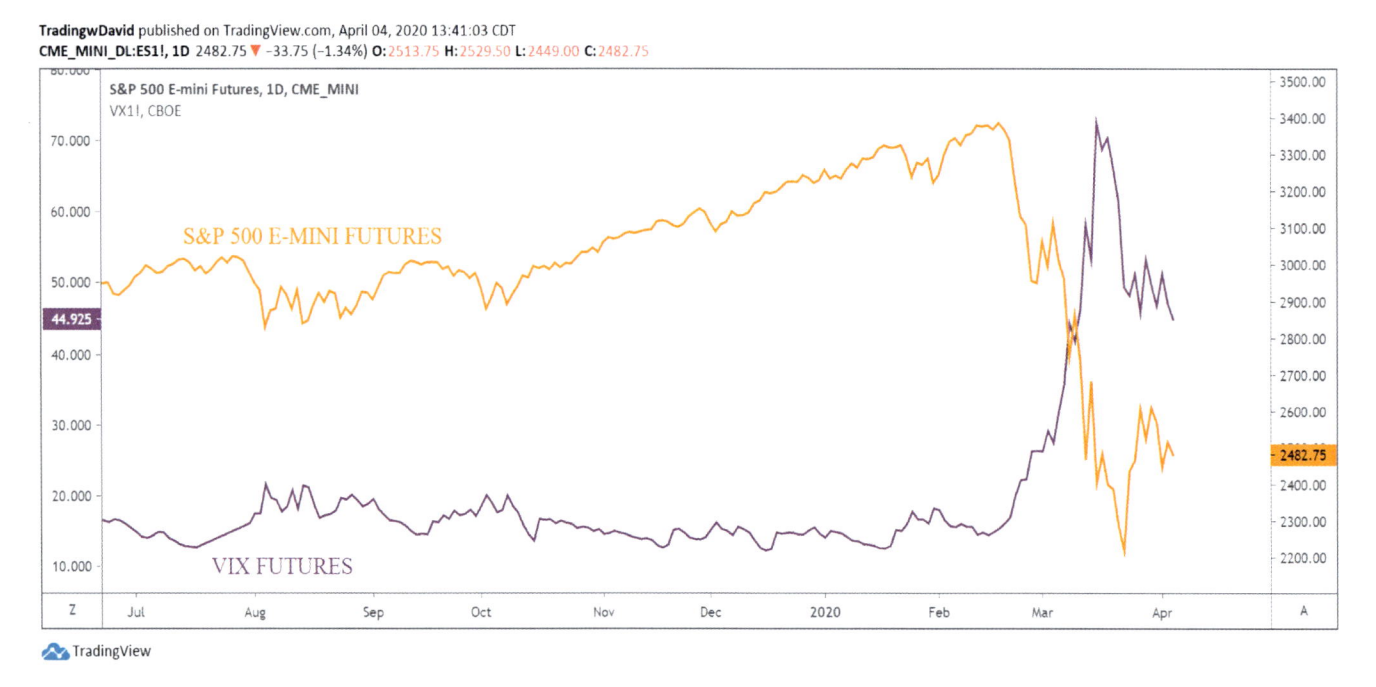

Figure 3 - S&P500 futures and VIX futures charts (TradingView.com)

Decorrelation occurs when two markets move in completely independent directions from each other. An example of decorrelated markets can be seen in Figure 4, comparing Apple and coffee.

Figure 4 - Apple and coffee futures charts (TradingView.com)

     In most cases, correlated markets belong to the same sector or share similar characteristics. This means that factors such as macroeconomic data, global events, corporate news, and monetary policies tend to influence them in a similar way. For example, the two banking stocks, Goldman Sachs and JP Morgan, are subject to similar movements in response to changes in interest rates or news about the global economy. The same applies to commodities such as corn and wheat, which often react in parallel to weather conditions or political decisions regarding agricultural trade.

     So, what is spread trading? Spread trading with commodities is an investment strategy that involves buying a futures contract on a commodity and, at the same time, selling another futures contract on the same commodity with a different delivery date (i.e., expiry), or on another correlated commodity. The aim is to exploit the price difference between the two futures contracts.

     The objective, therefore, is to profit from the relative changes between the two instruments, rather than from the absolute movements of individual prices. With spread trading, you no longer focus on a single price, but on the difference between two prices.

     An example of a spread is SBH18-SBK18, meaning you buy the March 2018 sugar futures contract and sell the May 2018 sugar futures contract. In this case, you build the spread by subtracting the price of the second futures contract (with delivery in May) from the price of the first contract (with delivery in March), as illustrated in Figure 5.

Figure 5 - Spread SBH18-SBK18 (SeasonAlgo.com)

The two (or more) futures that make up a spread are called legs. You can decide to open the position at the same time, or with one leg at a time. It is possible to transform a trade with futures into one of spread trading and vice versa, depending on the time.

There are three types of Spreads.

1. Intramarket, when you buy (go 'long') and sell (go 'short') futures contracts of the same commodity, but with different delivery dates. This type of spread is a *Calendar Spread*.

You can see an example of an Intramarket spread in Figure 6 below with the natural gas, and more precisely, with the spread NGN18-NGU18 (buy natural gas futures delivery July 2018 and sell natural gas futures delivery September 2018). In blue, the 15-year seasonal pattern.

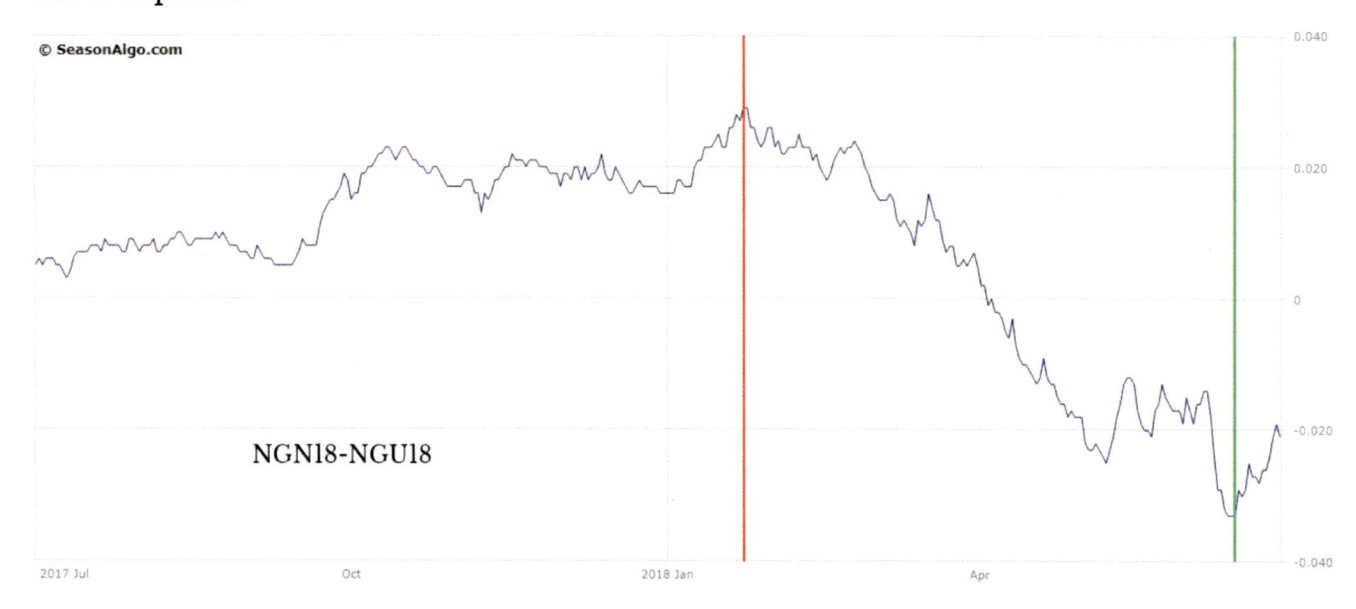

Figure 6 - Intramarket spread NGN18-NGU18 (SeasonAlgo.com)

2. <u>Intermarket</u>, is built by buying a futures contract on one market and selling simultaneously another futures contract on another market with the same delivery. Intermarket spreads can become Calendar Spreads by using futures with different deliveries.

An example of an Intermarket spread is ZCK18-ZWH18 (buy corn futures delivery in May 2018 and sell wheat futures delivery in March 2018) as shown in Figure 7.

Figure 7 - Intermarket spread ZCK18-ZWH18 (SeasonAlgo.com)

3. <u>Inter-exchange</u>, a less commonly known method of creating spreads is via the use of contracts in similar markets, but on different commodity exchanges. In this case too, if the two legs have different deliveries, it is called a Calendar Spread.

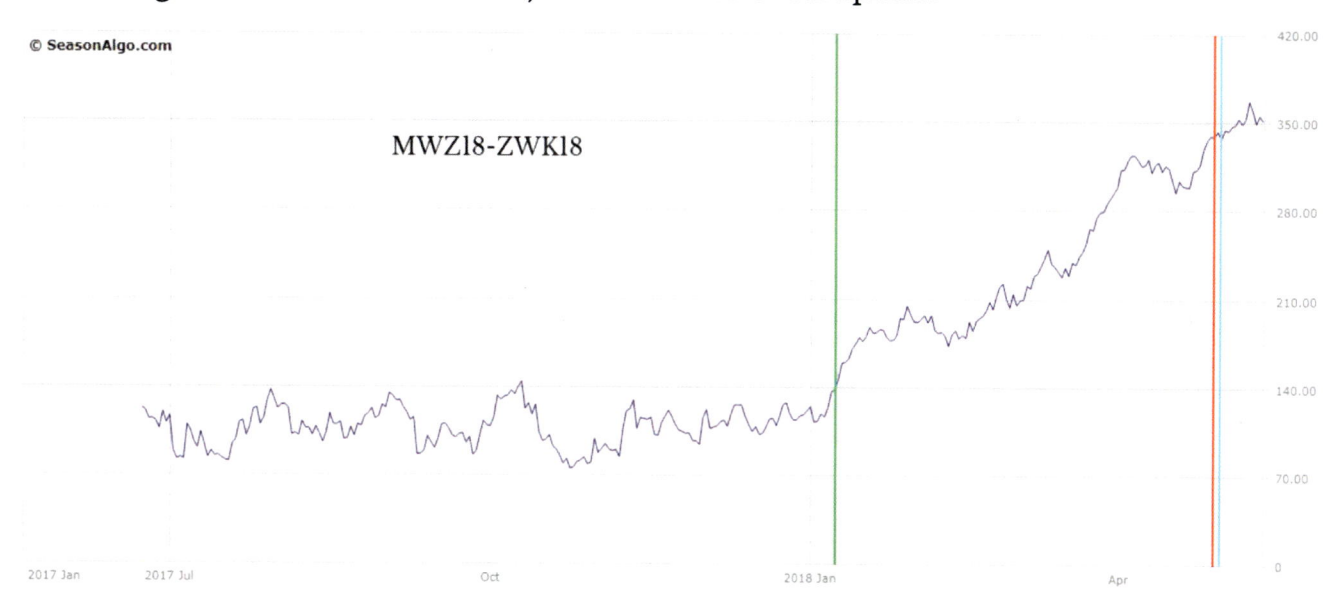

Figure 8 - Inter-exchange spread MWZ18-ZWK18 (SeasonAlgo.com)

An example of an Inter-exchange spread in Figure 8 with the chart of MWZ18-

ZWK18 (buy wheat futures delivery in December 2018 at the Minneapolis Grain Exchange and sell the wheat futures delivery in May 2018 at the Chicago Board of Trade).

Spread trading offers a number of significant advantages. First of all, it eliminates the need to focus on the market's direction. It no longer matters whether a futures contract rises or falls; what truly counts is the price difference between the two legs of the spread. For example, if you buy corn and sell wheat, you can profit whether corn rises and wheat falls, both rise but corn increases more than wheat, or both fall but wheat declines more than corn.

Another important advantage is the lower correlation of spread trading with other financial markets. This makes it an excellent opportunity to diversify your portfolio and reduce overall risk. Trading with correlated but opposing contracts creates a kind of natural hedge for your position, reducing the risk compared to trading individual futures. Furthermore, spread trading tends to be less volatile, offering better protection against fluctuations caused by macroeconomic news or unexpected events.

Spread trading also allows for potential profits during sideways phases, when individual futures do not show a clear trend. Spreads tend to follow more stable and lasting trends compared to individual futures, making trading less stressful.

Another interesting aspect is that spread trading does not require the use of stop-losses for each individual future. This makes your position less visible to other operators and thus less subject to manipulation or stop-hunting. Although spread trading has received more attention from large traders in recent years, it remains less common compared to futures.

You can select and filter spreads based on various factors, such as seasonality, backwardation (which I will cover in the next chapter), and transportation costs, using the same filters applied in futures analysis. You will explore these aspects in the following chapters.

Finally, spread trading requires less active monitoring time. You do not need to be glued to the screen to follow real-time market movements. By using End of Day (EoD) data, you can manage your trading activity efficiently, making it ideal even as a part-time activity. Additionally, working with end-of-day data provides an extra cost advantage, as you do not have to pay for real-time data access.

Many brokers recognise the lower volatility of spreads and offer reduced margin requirements, especially for Intramarket spreads, compared to individual futures. This allows you to operate even with smaller accounts.

Here are a few of the disadvantages of spread trading. When you trade spreads, you are not working with a single futures contract, but with the differential between two or more futures. This means you will need to pay commissions on each leg of the trade, increasing overall costs. However, with online brokers now offering low and competitive commissions, this factor has become less relevant, especially when considering the numerous advantages of spread trading.

Initially, it may seem complicated to understand and create spreads. Prices can be positive or negative depending on how you build the spread, and you will be trading on the narrowing or widening of the spread itself, not on the individual futures prices. Additionally, some commodities have different units of measurement and contract values, so you cannot calculate the spread simply by subtracting the prices of the two legs. You will need to adjust your calculations using the 'Unit Move' (which I will explain in Chapter 6), although most modern brokers and statistical databases have already integrated this function.

Although spread trading requires more practice than trading individual futures or stocks, experience will help you overcome these initial challenges. Commodities, and spread trading in particular, offer many opportunities and advantages compared to other markets. You can exploit unique features such as seasonality and correlation to enhance your performance, as you will see in the next chapter.

However, it is important not to fall into the trap of thinking that spread trading is simple. As with any form of trading, there are no shortcuts, and spread trading is no exception. While it presents many advantages, there are also several factors you must consider: time, economic decisions, and even a country's political situation can influence your success.

Finally, I want to leave you with a fundamental piece of advice, which you will explore in detail at the end of the book: always follow your trading plan and manage your money appropriately. It is easy to fall into the trap of over-trading due to the lower margins offered by brokers, something that happened to me in the early days.

Seasonality & Correlation
Chapter 5

In this chapter, you will begin to explore the fundamental aspects of commodities and understand how these factors directly influence your trading decisions. This section represents one of the most engaging and crucial parts of the book, as it provides the necessary foundation for correctly analysing a spread. In the following chapters, I will delve deeper into each concept to offer you a clear and comprehensive understanding of these essential elements.

A key starting point is the structure of futures contracts associated with each commodity. For every commodity, there are several futures contracts, each with a different delivery month. This means that the same commodity can have varying prices depending on the specific delivery date specified in the contract.

In general, futures with nearer expiry dates tend to have a lower price compared to those with more distant expiry dates. This phenomenon occurs because the further away the delivery, the higher the costs the producer must bear to store, insure, and maintain the commodity over time. These additional costs, known as storage or 'carrying costs', are reflected in the price of futures with longer maturities.

Understanding this dynamic is essential for correctly analysing commodity markets, as the price differential between contracts with different expiry dates can offer you spread trading opportunities, as you will see later on.

Summarised below, you have two different possible situations.

1. Supply and demand are balanced, the market is in a normal situation, so you say it is in contango. If the demand is weak, and the supply is excessive, the market tends to amplify the contango (Figure 9).

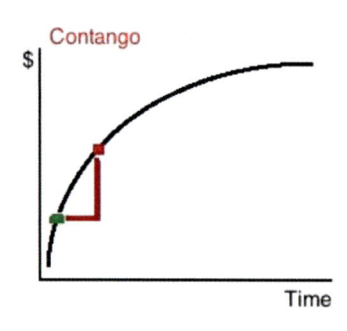

Figure 9 - Contango curve

2. In the case of excess of demand compared to supply, the market tends to reduce the contango and even to reverse the curve bringing it in backwardation (Figure 10).

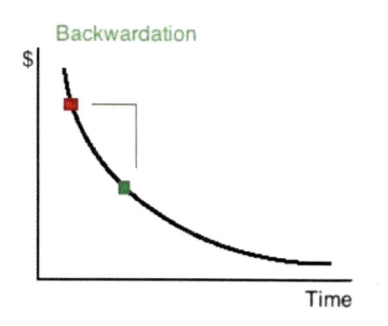

Figure 10 - Backwardation curve

A backwardation occurs when futures contracts with nearer expiries are priced higher than those with later expiries. This happens because buyers are willing to pay more to obtain the commodity immediately, rather than waiting for a future delivery, fearing that availability may decrease over time.

Backwardation often occurs in the presence of external events that threaten the supply of a commodity. For example, an unfavourable climate change, such as a drought that jeopardises crops, or an epidemic affecting livestock, can create a temporary imbalance between supply and demand. In such circumstances, demand increases, driving up the prices of short-term futures.

The imbalance between supply and demand, caused by external events, can last for varying periods depending on the severity and duration of the event. It is crucial to monitor these dynamics carefully, as they directly influence trading opportunities. As you will discover, anomalies are among my favourite situations, as they can offer excellent profit opportunities.

Now, let's move on to the most exciting aspect of commodity trading, a unique characteristic that is not found in any other market: seasonality. Seasonality is a cyclical phenomenon that repeats every year, just like the change of seasons. This recurring pattern is clearly reflected in commodities, where factors such as planting and harvesting occur regularly at the same times of the year. Industrial production cycles also often follow predictable seasonal patterns, offering a particularly interesting trading opportunity.

Take, for example, heating oil: its consumption rises significantly during the autumn and winter months, when temperatures drop, and declines in spring and summer, when the demand for heating decreases. These seasonal cycles are reflected in the price movements of associated futures contracts, and here lies the unique advantage of commodities. By observing price behaviour during specific times of the year, you can notice the repetition of similar patterns that can be exploited in spread trading.

One particularly interesting aspect of seasonality is that by knowing the seasonal cycles of different commodities in advance, you can anticipate price movements. In theory, this gives you a significant advantage; however, in practice, the process is a bit more complex than what is often presented on the internet.

You are probably wondering: "*How do I identify these seasonal cycles?*" Do not worry, you do not have to do everything on your own. There are statistical databases that collect and analyse this data for you, providing detailed and precise information.

Some of the main tools available for seasonal analysis are Moore Research, SeasonAlgo, and SpreadCharts, all of which specialise in providing historical data and suggestions on the best seasonal windows for different commodities. In the next chapter, you will see how to use these tools to integrate seasonality into your trading strategy.

It is important to always remember, however, that seasonality is only one of the factors to consider when analysing a spread. Although it represents an excellent starting point or idea for identifying trading opportunities, it should never be the sole reason for opening a position. After selecting a spread based on seasonality, it is essential to filter and evaluate it through other criteria, which will be explained in detail in the following chapters and put into practice in the second volume, '*Commodity Spread Trading – The Correct Method of Analysis*'.

As you have seen, it is crucial for a commodity's futures to be in a contango phase, as a backwardation situation could compromise seasonality. However, this is not the only aspect to consider. In addition to seasonality, another key factor to consider is the correlation between commodities, which can provide further insights for building effective strategies.

In the previous chapter, you learned that correlation measures the degree of relationship between two markets. Two markets are considered correlated when the movement of the first, whether upward or downward, is followed by a similar movement in the second. The highs and lows of the two markets often coincide, creating a mirrored behaviour.

When working with correlated commodities, you will not only notice that their price movements tend to synchronise, but also that news and macroeconomic data will have a similar impact on both. This is a crucial aspect in spread trading, as it reduces the risk of unpredictable fluctuations that could lead to sudden losses.

A less relevant aspect, in my opinion, is the correlation of a spread with past years' trends. For example, knowing that your Intramarket soybean spread is following exactly the same path as in 2012 may seem interesting, but it does not offer a real advantage. Always remember a fundamental concept: if no external factors intervene to change the dynamics of a commodity, seasonality tends to repeat itself. Therefore, the correlation with a past year merely indicates that the market conditions were similar. However, if an unexpected event were to occur tomorrow, such as a hurricane severely damaging crops, the historical correlation would become irrelevant.

In summary, seasonality and correlation are two key elements that make commodities and spread trading particularly unique. However, when analysing a spread, it is important to also consider other factors in order to build a robust strategy.

In the next chapter, you will delve deeper into these aspects, exploring the main statistical databases and learning how to effectively use them for your analyses.

Statistical Databases

CHAPTER 6

~

Statistical databases are fundamental for those who utilise spread trading because they provide seasonal windows within which a spread usually tends to move, under certain conditions but always in the same way. However, there is additional information you can gather.

The three most known and used statistical databases are SeasonAlgo, Moore Research and SpreadCharts. In Appendix F, at the end of this book, you can find their websites and other interesting news about these three companies. Starting with SeasonAlgo. Once you are logged into the site, it prompts you to this window (Figure 11).

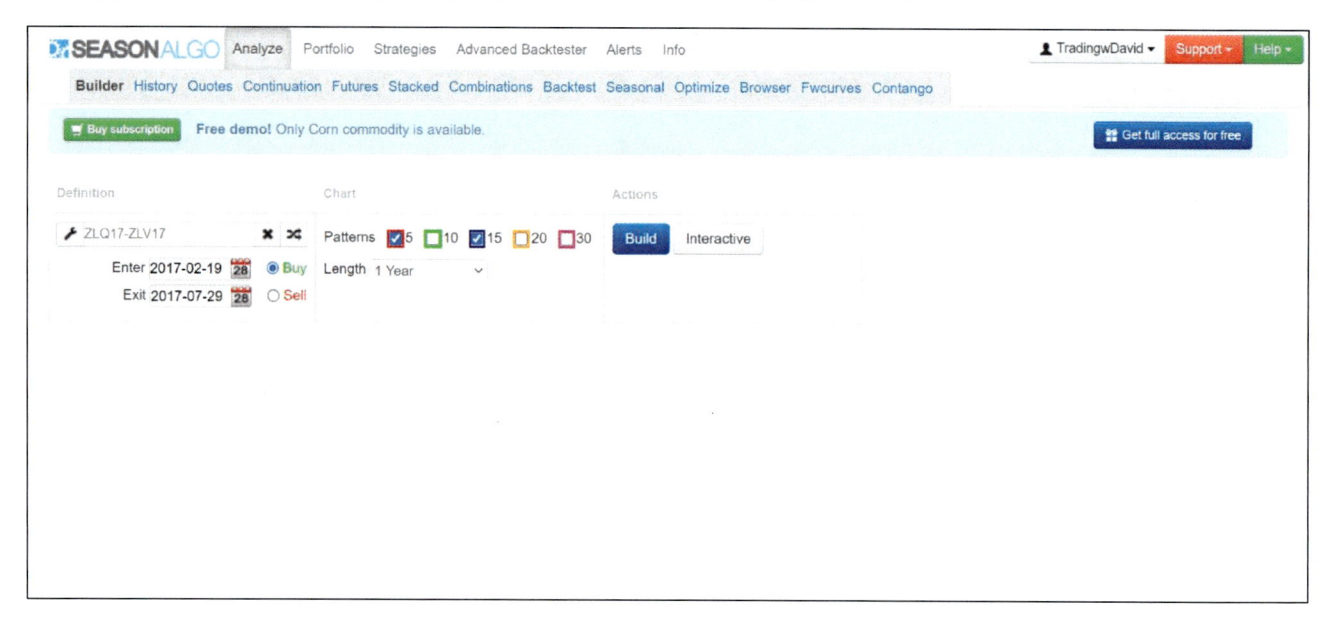

Figure 11 - SeasonAlgo login (SeasonAlgo.com)

In the top menu, you find several items. First, you need to check which seasonal windows SeasonAlgo suggests as the best for you.

Clicking on Strategies, and then on Recommend, you get the proposals of the month both on the individual futures and on the spreads, with two legs and multi-legs, recommended by SeasonAlgo, as shown in Figure 12.

Name	Side	#Legs	Category	Tickers	Enter	Exit	Win	Win%	APW%	Days#
ZLU17	Buy	1	Grain	ZL	2017-02-01	2017-04-11	14/15	93%	67%	70
ESM17	Buy	1	Index	ES	2017-02-05	2017-04-25	14/15	93%	53%	80
HEQ17	Buy	1	Meat	HE	2017-02-16	2017-03-10	14/15	93%	47%	23
NGX17	Buy	1	Energy	NG	2017-02-27	2017-06-17	14/15	93%	53%	111
RBJ17	Buy	1	Energy	RB	2017-02-04	2017-03-09	14/15	93%	53%	34
RSX17	Buy	1	Grain	RS	2017-02-12	2017-06-20	14/15	93%	87%	129
ZSQ17	Buy	1	Grain	ZS	2017-02-01	2017-07-10	14/15	93%	60%	160
ZMV17	Buy	1	Grain	ZM	2017-02-12	2017-07-16	14/15	93%	60%	155
GOM17	Buy	1	Energy	GO	2017-02-02	2017-02-19	13/15	87%	80%	18
SBK17	Sell	1	Food	SB	2017-02-25	2017-04-15	13/15	87%	33%	50
ZLQ17-ZLV17	Sell	2	Grain	ZL-ZL	2017-02-19	2017-07-29	30/30	100%	40%	161
HON17-RBQ17	Sell	2	Energy	HO-RB	2017-02-15	2017-03-28	29/30	97%	50%	42

Figure 12 - Futures and Spreads recommended (SeasonAlgo.com)

Among all the spreads that SeasonAlgo proposes for us, you choose ZLQ17-ZLV17. It means selecting the spread that was built buying soybean oil futures with the delivery of August 2017 (ZLQ17) and selling the soybean oil futures with delivery October 2017 (ZLV17). The seasonality is bearish, running from 19 February (entry date) to 29 July (exit date) for a total of 161 days, meaning you should sell the spread, as advised by SeasonAlgo.

You can find all the commodity tickers in Appendix A and the month symbols in Appendix D at the end of the book. Clicking on icon at the end of the row, you can access the chart and, by selecting Interactive, you can add indicators, as shown in Figure 13.

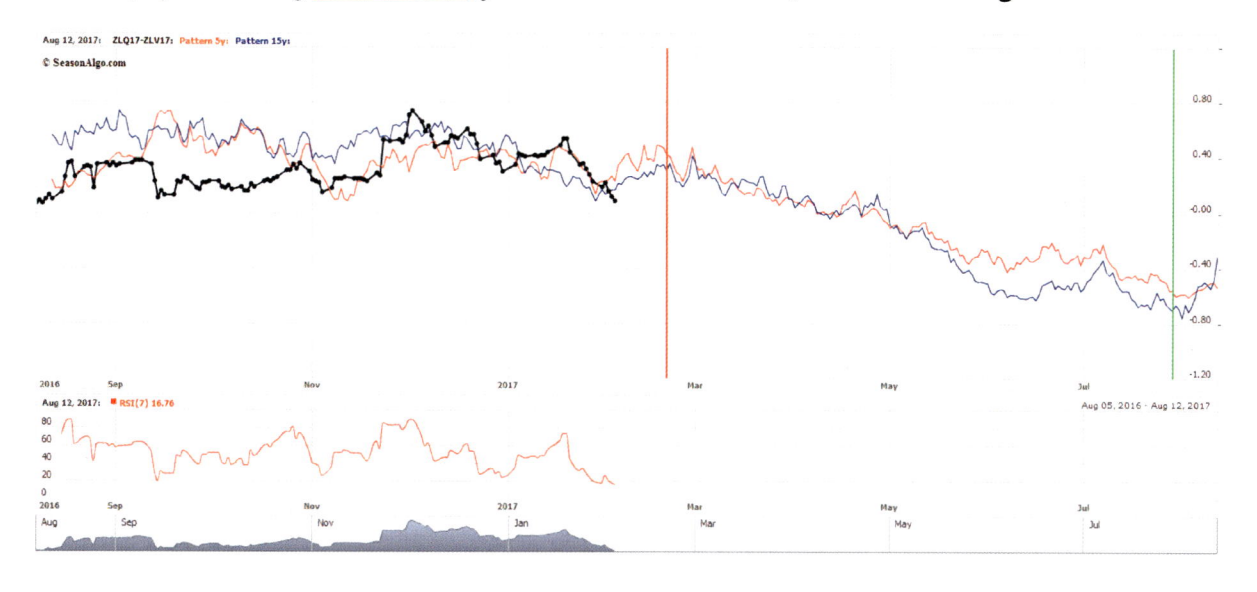

Figure 13 - ZLQ19-ZLV17, the chart (SeasonAlgo.com)

You can also build the spread manually by clicking on Builder, entering the futures tickers, the enter and exit dates of the seasonal window, and all the parameters of your interest. Then, at the end, you click on Build (and then on Interactive) as in Figure 14.

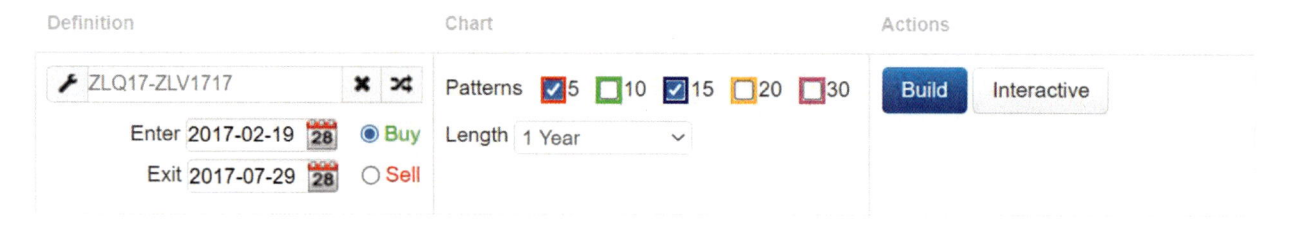

Figure 14 - The Builder (SeasonAlgo.com)

The first step, is to check the previous years' results by clicking on Backtest (Figure 15).

Year	Enter date	Enter price	Exit date	Exit price	Points	Profit	Days#	Best Date	Best	Worst Date	Worst	Drawdown
2016	2016-02-19	-0.04	2016-07-29	-0.24	0.20	120.00	162	2016-06-14	150.00	-	0.00	-78.00
2015	2015-02-19	0.25	2015-07-29	-0.21	0.46	276.00	161	2015-07-29	276.00	2015-02-27	-18.00	-114.00
2014	2014-02-19	0.53	2014-07-29	-0.13	0.66	396.00	161	2014-06-02	408.00	2014-03-07	-396.00	-408.00
2013	2013-02-19	1.04	2013-07-29	-0.20	1.24	744.00	161	2013-07-29	744.00	-	0.00	-474.00
2012	2012-02-21	-0.13	2012-07-27	-0.38	0.25	150.00	158	2012-05-30	180.00	-	0.00	-78.00
2011	2011-02-22	-0.02	2011-07-29	-0.35	0.33	198.00	158	2011-06-09	336.00	2011-03-03	-36.00	-138.00
2010	2010-02-19	-0.23	2010-07-29	-0.32	0.09	54.00	161	2010-06-02	132.00	2010-03-01	-18.00	-108.00
2009	2009-02-19	-0.34	2009-07-29	-0.35	0.01	6.00	161	2009-06-04	12.00	2009-05-15	-66.00	-72.00
2008	2008-02-19	0.03	2008-07-29	-0.64	0.67	402.00	162	2008-06-30	462.00	2008-03-05	-192.00	-360.00
2007	2007-02-20	-0.35	2007-07-27	-0.52	0.17	102.00	158	2007-07-23	156.00	2007-03-26	-18.00	-90.00
2006	2006-02-21	-0.28	2006-07-28	-0.46	0.18	108.00	158	2006-06-30	162.00	2006-03-01	-18.00	-108.00
2005	2005-02-22	0.05	2005-07-29	-0.10	0.15	90.00	158	2005-06-27	204.00	2005-03-17	-540.00	-576.00
2004	2004-02-19	2.79	2004-07-29	0.76	2.03	1218.00	162	2004-07-29	1218.00	2004-04-29	-792.00	-1248.00
2003	2003-02-19	0.58	2003-07-29	0.13	0.45	270.00	161	2003-07-29	270.00	2003-04-07	-234.00	-372.00
2002	2002-02-19	-0.21	2002-07-29	-0.21	0.00	-0.00	161	2002-03-18	66.00	2002-06-11	-36.00	-102.00
2001	2001-02-20	-0.33	2001-07-27	-0.35	0.02	12.00	158	2001-02-28	66.00	2001-05-16	-48.00	-114.00
2000	2000-02-22	-0.28	2000-07-28	-0.42	0.14	84.00	158	2000-05-31	96.00	2000-03-17	-18.00	-96.00
1999	1999-02-19	-0.26	1999-07-29	-0.29	0.03	18.00	161	1999-03-12	42.00	1999-02-22	-42.00	-78.00
1998	1998-02-19	0.40	1998-07-29	-0.28	0.68	408.00	161	1998-06-30	504.00	1998-03-26	-288.00	-288.00
1997	1997-02-19	-0.32	1997-07-29	-0.33	0.01	6.00	161	1997-03-27	24.00	1997-05-05	-198.00	-222.00
1996	1996-02-20	-0.32	1996-07-29	-0.40	0.08	48.00	161	1996-07-18	78.00	1996-04-26	-162.00	-204.00
1995	1995-02-21	0.43	1995-07-28	0.09	0.34	204.00	158	1995-05-19	270.00	1995-03-02	-60.00	-168.00
1994	1994-02-22	1.31	1994-07-29	0.28	1.03	618.00	158	1994-06-29	660.00	1994-04-29	-252.00	-498.00
1993	1993-02-19	0.00	1993-07-29	-0.29	0.29	174.00	161	1993-07-12	210.00	1993-03-01	-6.00	-102.00
1992	1992-02-19	-0.26	1992-07-29	-0.34	0.08	48.00	162	1992-05-07	90.00	1992-03-20	-60.00	-84.00

Figure 15 - Backtest (SeasonAlgo.com)

Here are summarised the previous years, with all the statistics and the equity line. For example, it can be useful to compare historical exit prices with current ones.

The table provides a wealth of data, but two particularly useful metrics are the '*drawdown*' and the maximum loss incurred by the spread each year.

You can also optimise the seasonal window based on the patterns. By default, it is optimised for the 15-year pattern, but if for example, you want to optimise the window of your spread for the 5 or 10-year patterns, just clicking on Optimize you get the data of interest to you (Figure 16).

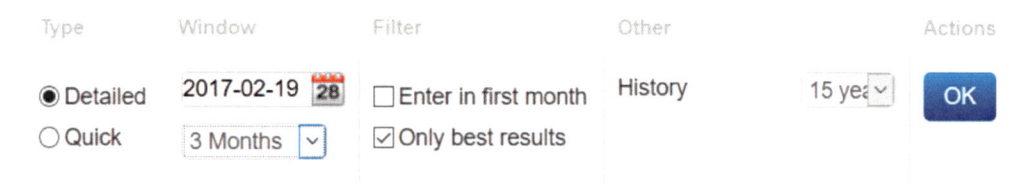

Figure 16 - Optimize the spread (SeasonAlgo.com)

You can also set parameters such as the seasonality period (up to three months) and the historical data (the seasonal pattern to optimise). By selecting Price & underlyings, instead, you can see the spread chart and compare it with that of the sugar futures contract with the closest delivery, as you see in the chart in Figure 33. It can also be useful if you are searching for a new seasonality.

At this point you need to compare the spread with results from past years. You can do this by clicking on Continuation, which gives you the continuous chart of the spread in recent years, just like in Figure 17.

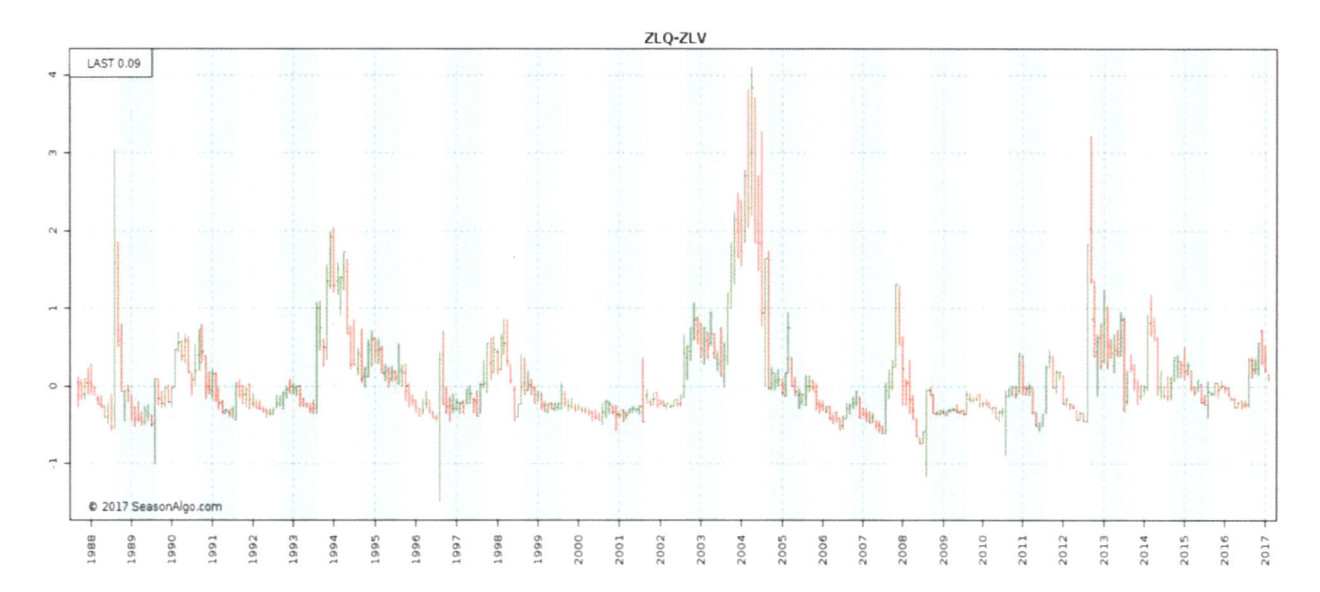

Figure 17 - Continuation chart (SeasonAlgo.com)

You can select the chart duration (from 5 to over 30 years), the time frame (weekly or monthly), and the type of graphical representation (bar, candlestick, or line).

This chart is essential for understanding if the current price of a spread is low, high, or at an average level compared to past years.

By clicking on Stacked (Figure 18), you find another way to assess the spread in relation to its past. Here, you can compare the current spread with every single past year.

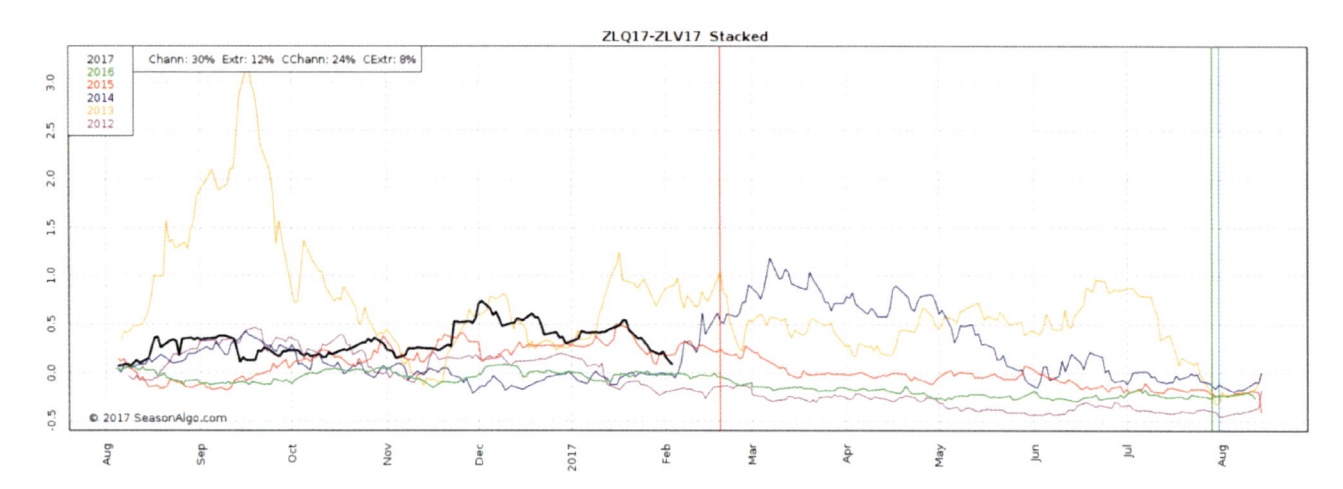

Figure 18 - Stacked (SeasonAlgo.com)

I put just the last five years on the chart (to make it more readable), but you can insert up to 20 previous years.

The next chart is very interesting for studying the correlation. You can find it on Seasonal (Figure 19).

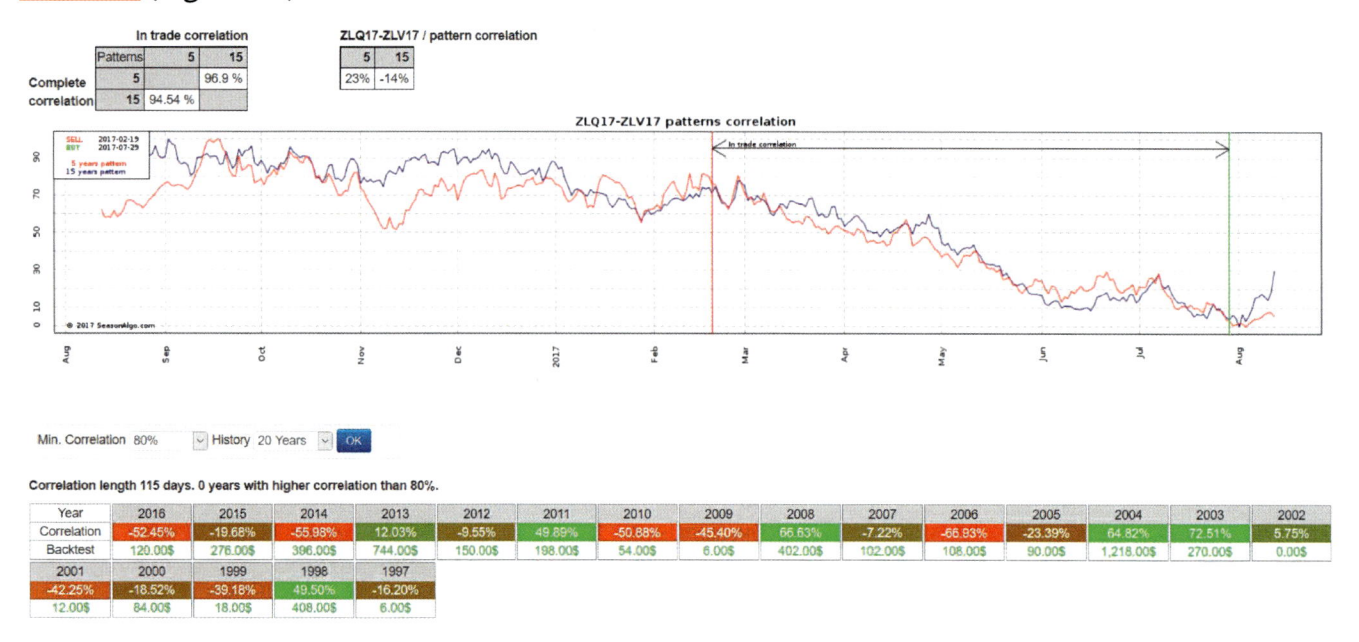

Figure 19 - Seasonal (SeasonAlgo.com)

Here, you can see how much your spread is correlated, and whether or not it has a similar trend to past years. By default, the correlation has to be at least 80%, and I find this quite correct because, with a lower percentage, you would risk losing its importance.

It is helpful (though not essential) to find a year in the past that correlates with the current one. If this happens, it is possible that the correlation could continue during the current seasonal window, and this is another valuable insight you gain from your analysis.

History is very useful because it shows you the chart of the spread of every single year in the past (Figure 20).

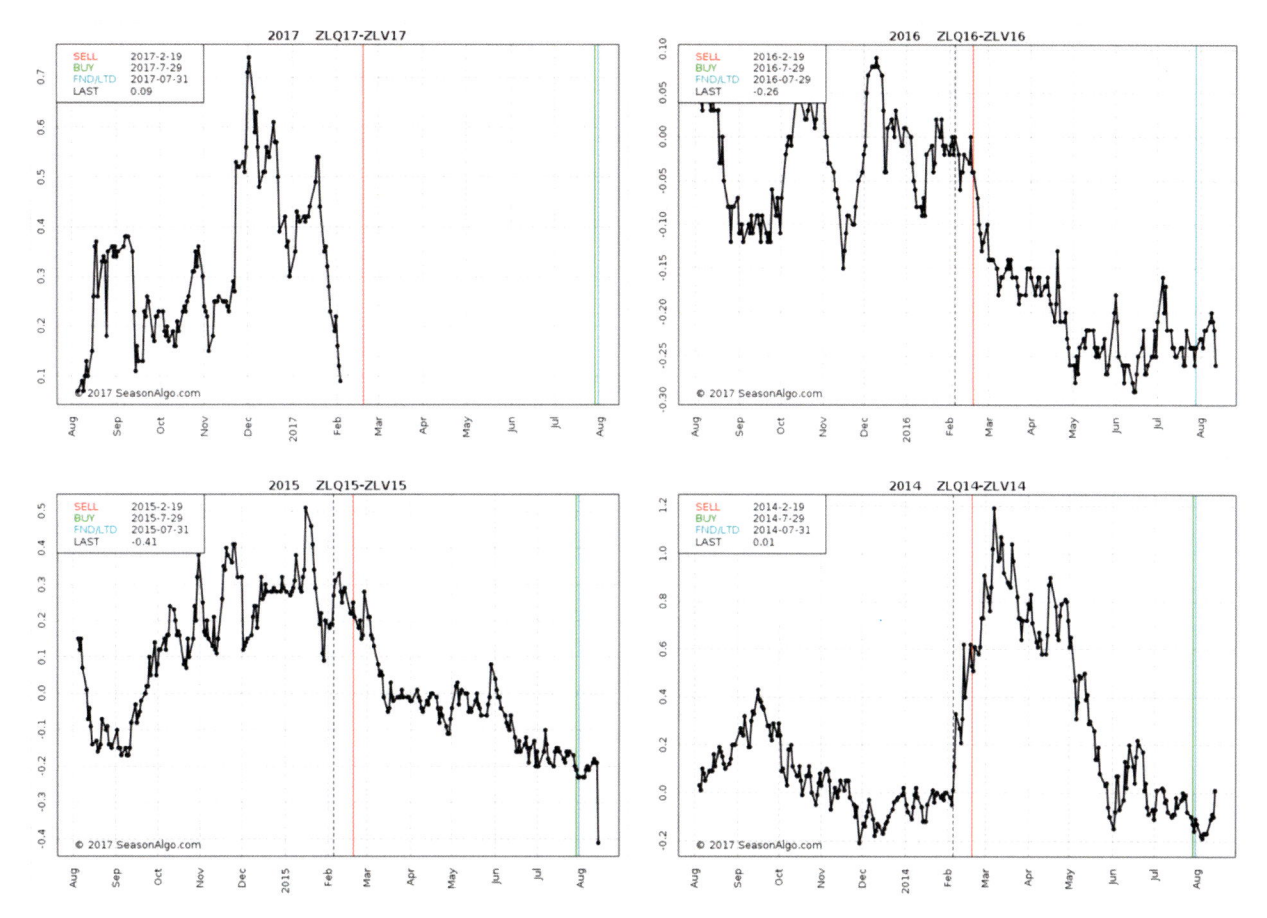

Figure 20 - History (SeasonAlgo.com)

Figure 21 - Futures (SeasonAlgo.com)

And Futures because it makes you see the chart of the individual legs, gives you the open interest, C.O.T. and other parameters (I used volume and C.O.T.) as shown in Figure 21 with ZLQ17 (soybean oil delivery August 2017). About the C.O.T. (Commitments of Traders), it is a weekly report released by the CFTC (Commodity Futures Trading Commission). I will explore it more fully in Chapter 11.

So, you have seen how, with the statistical database SeasonAlgo, you can analyse a spread (but also futures for those who work with them) in all respects. But it is not the only statistical database. A second company that offers this type of service is Moore Research.

Before proceeding, it is important to talk about the Unit Move. The Unit Move represents the dollar value for each point movement of a futures contract. This concept is fundamental when constructing a spread, as both legs of the spread must have the same Unit Move to ensure that price movements are comparable and properly balanced.

In the case of a calendar spread, or spreads between similar commodities like corn-wheat or live cattle-lean hogs, the Unit Move is already aligned, so you will not need to worry about making adjustments. However, when working with more complex spreads such as soybean meal-soybean oil, feeder cattle-live cattle, or gold-silver, you need to ensure that the values of the two legs are balanced, as differences in the Unit Move for each commodity can affect the outcome of your trade.

Fortunately, many advanced seasonal analysis tools like SeasonAlgo and Moore Research offer charts that are already adjusted for the Unit Move, and the process is fully automated. You will not need to perform any manual calculations, as the system will automatically adjust the values for both legs of the spread. However, if you are using tools like SpreadCharts, which do not automatically include this function, you will need to perform a simple calculation to align the two legs.

The calculation is quite simple: you need to multiply each leg of your spread by its specific Unit Move. Here are some examples of how to do it:

- 100ZM - 600ZL for the soybean meal-soybean oil spread;
- 500GF - 400LE for the feeder cattle-live cattle spread;
- 100GC - 50SI for the gold-silver spread.

If you do not make this adjustment, you might mistakenly think that the spread has not moved, even though both legs have actually moved. For example, if both legs of the spread move by one dollar but have different Unit Moves, it will appear that the spread has remained unchanged (the difference between the two legs does not change). In reality, your account will experience a change, as a one-dollar movement has a different financial impact on each leg.

To make your work easier, I have included a summary table with all the main futures contracts and their respective Unit Moves in Appendix B at the end of the book. This will allow you to always have the correct values at hand, ensuring that you construct well-balanced spreads and avoid mistakes that could compromise your trading results.

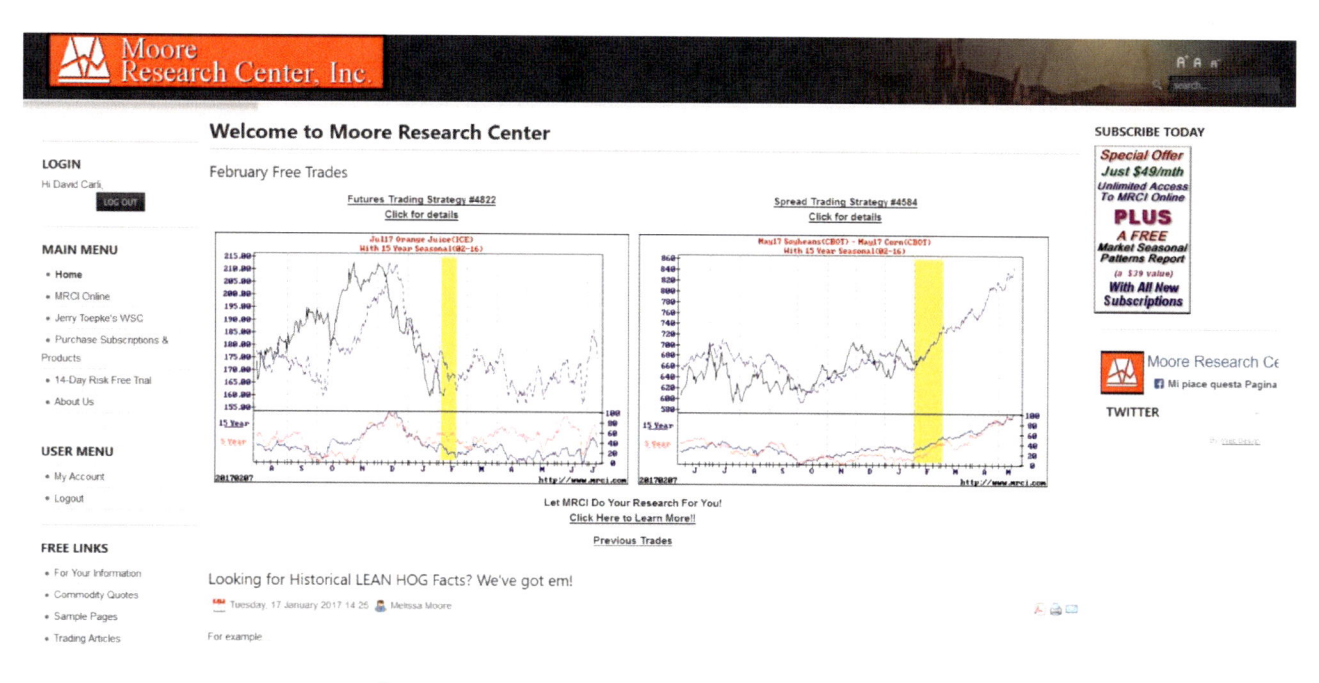

Figure 22 - Moore Research login (www.mrci.com)

After taking a look at this aspect, I want to introduce you to the seasonal database of Moore Research. Once you are logged into the website, it takes you to this page (Figure 22 above).

A click on MRCI Online (left column) and it will open this page (Figure 23).

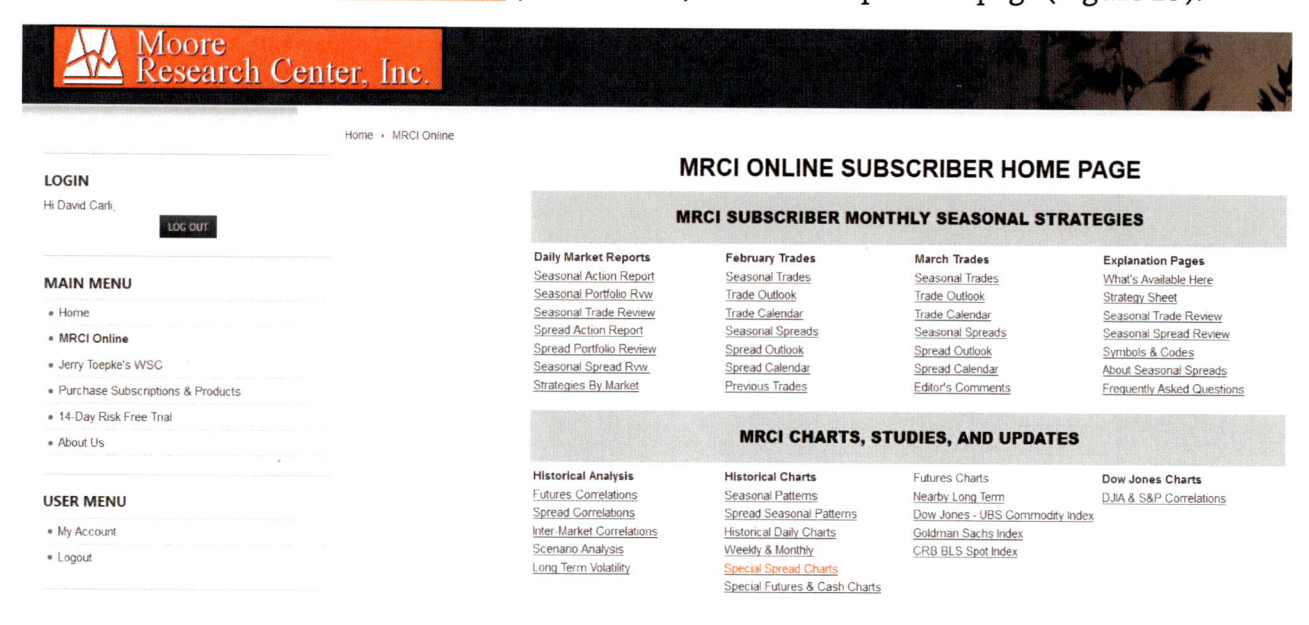

Figure 23 - MRCI Online (www.mrci.com)

Here you can find recommendations of Moore for the current month and the next one (at the time of writing this chapter, for February and March 2017), along with several other reports and reviews that I invite you to read as they are very useful and interesting.

33

By clicking on Previous Trades, you find the previous three months (Figure 24).

MRCI PREVIOUS TRADE STRATEGIES

November	December	January
Seasonal Trades	Seasonal Trades	Seasonal Trades
Trade Outlook	Trade Outlook	Trade Outlook
Trade Calendar	Trade Calendar	Trade Calendar
Seasonal Spreads	Seasonal Spreads	Seasonal Spreads
Spread Outlook	Spread Outlook	Spread Outlook
Spread Calendar	Spread Calendar	Spread Calendar

Figure 24 - Moore Research Previous Trade (www.mrci.com)

In most cases, they are seasonality that have already been completed, but it can happen occasionally that a spread may still be within its wide seasonal window. You could have trades that are still open, and in this way, you have the possibility of returning to see and analyse them again.

February 2017 Trades

	Seasonal Strategy	Entry Date	Exit Date	Win Pct	Win Years	Loss Years	Total Years	Average Profit	Avg PPD/Days
4822	Sell Jul Orange Juice(ICE)-JON7	2/4	2/19	93	14	1	15	522	33/16
4823	Buy May RBOB Gasoline(NYM)-RBK7	2/4	2/26	93	14	1	15	4668	203/23
4824	Buy Dec Natural Gas(NYM)-NGZ7	2/5	4/16	80	12	3	15	2954	42/71
4825	Buy Mar Australian Dollar(CME)-ADH7	2/10	2/24	100	15	0	15	835	56/15
4826	Buy Apr Platinum(NYMEX)-PLJ7	2/10	3/4	87	13	2	15	1756	76/23
4827	Buy Jun S & P 500 E-Mini(Globex)-ESM7[1]	2/10	4/6	93	14	1	15	2258	40/56
4828	Buy Jun Crude Oil(NYM)-CLM7	2/11	3/7	93	14	1	15	3994	160/25
4829	Buy Jul Soybean Oil(CBOT)-BON7	2/12	4/10	87	13	2	15	934	16/58
4830	Sell May Cocoa(ICE)-CCK7	2/14	4/6	80	12	3	15	981	19/52
4831	Buy Jul Copper(CMX)-HGN7	2/16	3/5	87	13	2	15	1703	95/18
4832	Buy Aug Lean Hogs(CME)-HEQ7	2/16	3/8	93	14	1	15	899	43/21
4833	Buy Jun Canadian Dollar(CME)-CDM7	2/22	4/7	100	15	0	15	1123	25/45
4834	Buy Mar Feeder Cattle(CME)-FCH7	2/23	3/2	80	12	3	15	752	94/8
4835	Sell May Sugar #11(ICE)-SBK7	2/25	4/13	93	14	1	15	1415	29/48
4836	Sell Jul Wheat(KCBT)-KWN7	2/25	4/28	80	12	3	15	1214	19/63

[1]Note: due to number of years trading historical research is performed on a blended full size/mini contract.

Figure 25 - Moore Research Futures Seasonal Trades (www.mrci.com)

By clicking again on MRCI Online, you get back to the previous page, and in the first line, by clicking on Seasonal Trades, you can see the 15 proposals by Moore in February for individual futures (Figure 25 above).

By clicking on Seasonal Spreads, from the MRCI Online page, you have the 15 recommendations by Moore in February, but this time, related to spreads (Figure 26).

February 2017 Spreads

Seasonal Strategy	Entry Date	Exit Date	Win Pct	Win Years	Loss Years	Total Years	Average Profit	Avg PPD/ Days
4584 Buy May Soybeans(CBOT) - SK7 Sell May Corn(CBOT) - CK7	2/1	3/3	87	13	2	15	1914	62/31
4585 Buy May Soybean Meal(CBOT) - SMK7 Sell Dec Soybean Meal(CBOT) - SMZ7	2/1	3/8	87	13	2	15	1126	31/36
4586 Buy Aug Lean Hogs(CME) - HEQ7 Sell Aug Live Cattle(CME) - LCQ7	2/2	4/20	87	13	2	15	1152	15/78
4587 Buy Jun Crude Oil(NYM) - CLM7 Sell Dec Crude Oil(NYM) - CLZ7	2/5	3/7	93	14	1	15	1001	32/31
4588 Buy Jul RBOB Gasoline(NYM) - RBN7 Sell Dec RBOB Gasoline(NYM) - RBZ7	2/6	3/11	100	15	0	15	1223	36/34
4589 Buy Jun Australian Dollar(CME) - ADM7 Sell Jun Japanese Yen(CME) - JYM7	2/7	4/22	100	15	0	15	4857	65/75
4590 Buy Jul Soybeans(CBOT) - SN7 Sell Jul Wheat(CBOT) - WN7	2/9	4/30	93	14	1	15	4350	54/81
4591 Buy Jun Swiss Franc(CME) - SFM7 Sell Jun British Pound(CME) - BPM7	2/15	3/17	93	14	1	15	1985	64/31
4592 Buy Oct Sugar #11(ICE) - SBV7 Sell Jul Sugar #11(ICE) - SBN7	2/16	4/29	93	14	1	15	506	7/73

Figure 26 - Moore Research Spreads Seasonal Trades (www.mrci.com)

There are not only commodities but also T-Bond and currencies. Personally, I do not have a great experience with them. Not in general terms, obviously, but in connection with spread trading. I never traded them because I believe far less in their seasonality. They are not affected by natural or production cycles but are conditioned by other factors such as central bank decisions on rates and inflation, which have nothing to do with seasonality.

To see more details on a spread, simply move the mouse over the spread number for a preview of the chart, allowing for a quick view.

By clicking on the number, you have all the charts and tables relating to the spread that is of interest to you. Let's see them in detail; I use as an example the spread number 4592 SBV7-SBN7 (buy sugar delivery October and sell sugar delivery July).

The first table that appears relates to the results of the past years, and it shows you how many winning trades there were over the last 15 years (Figure 27). If you would like to expand this statistic, you need to click on the upper right box 30-Years Max Results. In this way, the table shows you the same statistic over the past 30 years.

A statistic closest to the current year is more important than, for example, the one from the year 1988 because market conditions have surely changed over the years. The closer the year is to the current one, the more significant the statistics become. Moreover, recent years usually yield more information.

You should take into account profits (but also losses and the drawdown), as they can be highly indicative. They are the result just in the seasonal window (entry date – exit date) optimised by SeasonAlgo and Moore Research. However, relying exclusively on entry and exit dates given by two statistical databases, in my opinion, is not the right way to work.

Buy Oct 17 Sugar #11(NYBOT) / Sell Jul 17 Sugar #11(NYBOT)

Enter on approximately 02/16 - Exit on approximately 04/29

Cont Year	Entry Date	Entry Price	Exit Date	Exit Price	Profit	Profit Amount	Best Equity Date	Best Equity Amount	Worst Equity Date	Worst Equity Amount
2016	02/16/16	0.22	04/29/16	0.27	0.05	56.00	04/28/16	145.60	03/22/16	-201.60
2015	02/17/15	0.38	04/29/15	0.40	0.02	22.40	03/02/15	380.80		
2014	02/18/14	0.36	04/29/14	0.67	0.31	347.20	04/17/14	369.60	02/27/14	-145.60
2013	02/19/13	0.38	04/29/13	0.39	0.01	11.20	02/25/13	100.80	03/14/13	-123.20
2012	02/16/12	0.33	04/27/12	0.42	0.09	100.80	04/19/12	100.80	03/22/12	-694.40
2011	02/16/11	-1.68	04/29/11	0.40	2.08	2329.60	04/28/11	2340.80	02/18/11	-33.60
2010	02/16/10	-1.96	04/29/10	0.59	2.55	2856.00	04/16/10	3080.00		
2009	02/17/09	0.37	04/29/09	0.66	0.29	324.80	04/07/09	548.80	02/26/09	-44.80
2008	02/19/08	0.23	04/29/08	0.90	0.67	750.40	04/29/08	750.40	02/21/08	-44.80
2007	02/16/07	0.20	04/27/07	0.32	0.12	134.40	04/16/07	235.20	02/22/07	-11.20
2006	02/16/06	-0.24	04/28/06	0.27	0.51	571.20	04/26/06	649.60	02/22/06	-33.60
2005	02/16/05	-0.10	04/29/05	-0.03	0.07	78.40	03/28/05	336.00	02/17/05	-22.40
2004	02/17/04	0.12	04/29/04	0.17	0.05	56.00	04/28/04	123.20	03/24/04	-235.20
2003	02/19/03	-0.29	04/29/03	-0.07	0.22	246.40	04/29/03	246.40	03/06/03	-11.20
2002	02/19/02	0.20	04/29/02	-0.06	-0.26	-291.20			04/22/02	-324.80

Percentage Correct		93					Protective Stop			(658)
Average Profit on Winning Trades					0.50	563.20	Winners			14
Average Loss on Trades					-0.26	-291.20	Losers			1
Average Net Profit Per Trade					0.45	506.24	Total trades			15

Figure 27 - Moore Research SBV7-SBN7 Past Years (www.mrci.com)

Firstly, it is normal for seasonality to vary slightly from year to year due to factors like changing weather conditions and other influences such as the US dollar or supply levels, which can affect the statistical movement of a spread. And then, you take, as reference, the seasonal windows, but you can also look for a graphical signal, which is an opportunity, before or after the starting date, that you can attempt to exploit. How much, before or after? All manuals say up to 2 weeks but from my experience even a month or longer. It depends on seasonality, the situation of the spread, and fundamental analysis.

However, they give you an idea of what could be your gain or loss and they provide you with useful indications. However, it is always preferable to choose your stop-loss first, according to your money management and other aspects, just in case.

Now, by clicking on Cont Year (first column), you can see in a chart if there are correlations with past years (Figure 28). If in the chart, there is only a 15-year pattern (like in this case), it means that there are no correlations with past years.

Going back to the previous page (the one with the table of results from past years) if you click on the box Sugar Quotes at the top, you can see the volume for each sugar futures contract. It would be preferable to have a daily volume of at least 1,000 contracts because if there are contracts too low in volume, a big institutional investor might 'shake up' the market, and you could be affected by that abnormal situation.

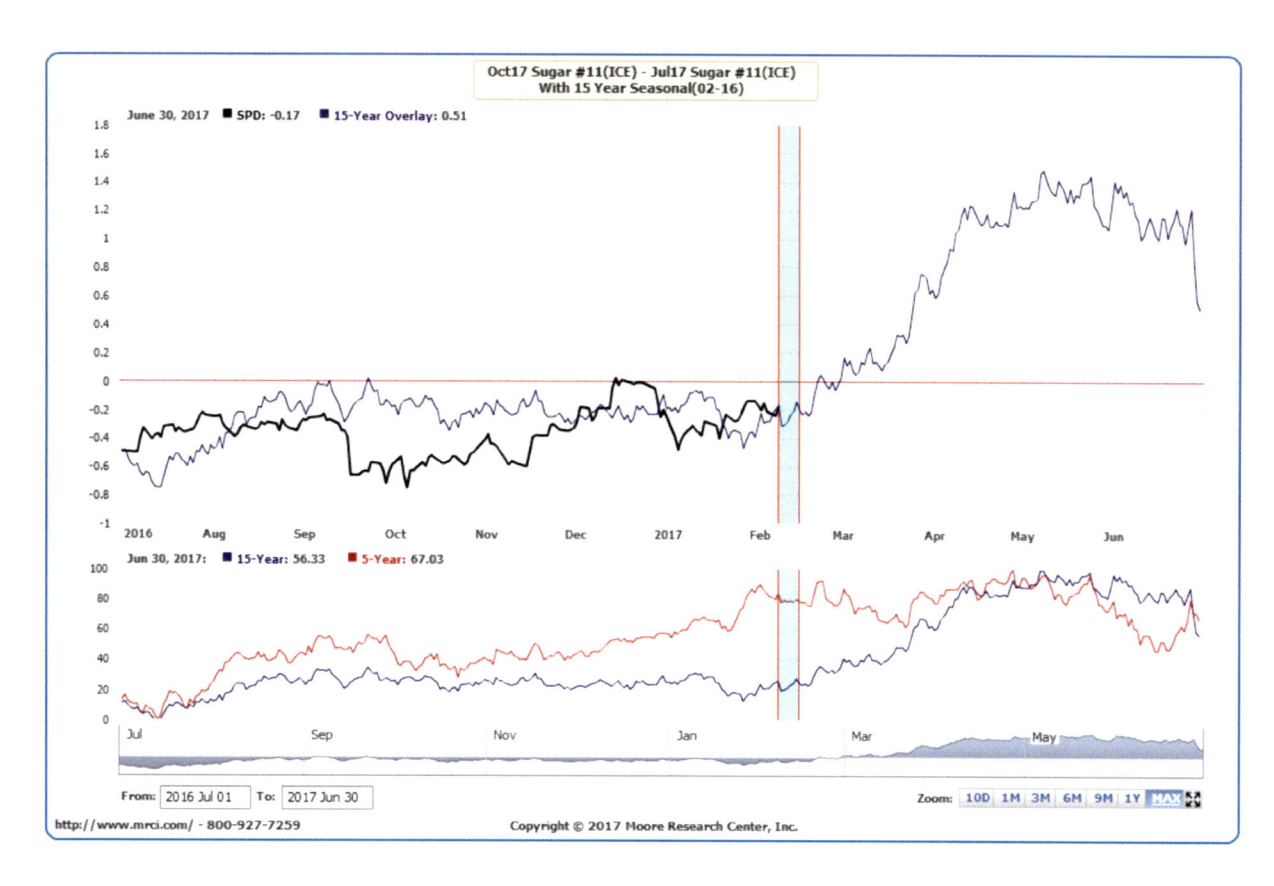

Figure 28 - Moore Research Cont Year (www.mrci.com)

By clicking now in the top box on Daily Chart w Studies, you can see the interactive chart where you can put your studies such as Relative Strength Index or the Bollinger Bands (Figure 29).

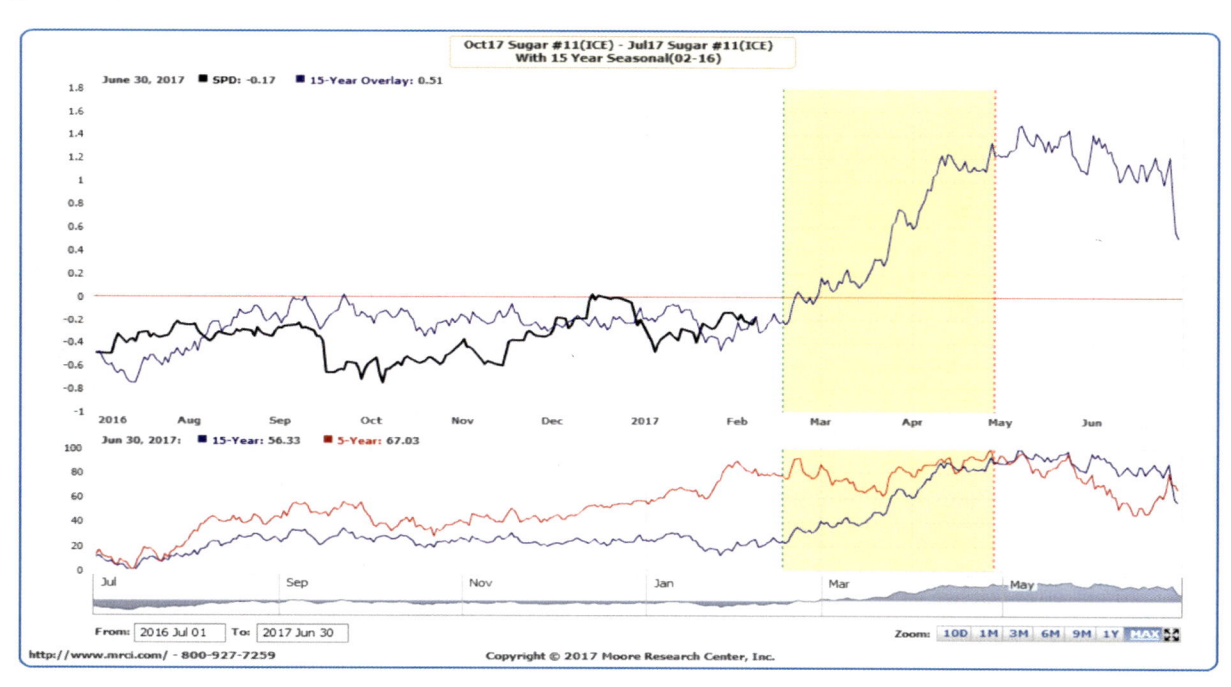

Figure 29 - Moore Research chart (www.mrci.com)

Indeed, clicking on Weekly Continuation, you can see the weekly continuous chart of the spread in recent years (Figure 30).

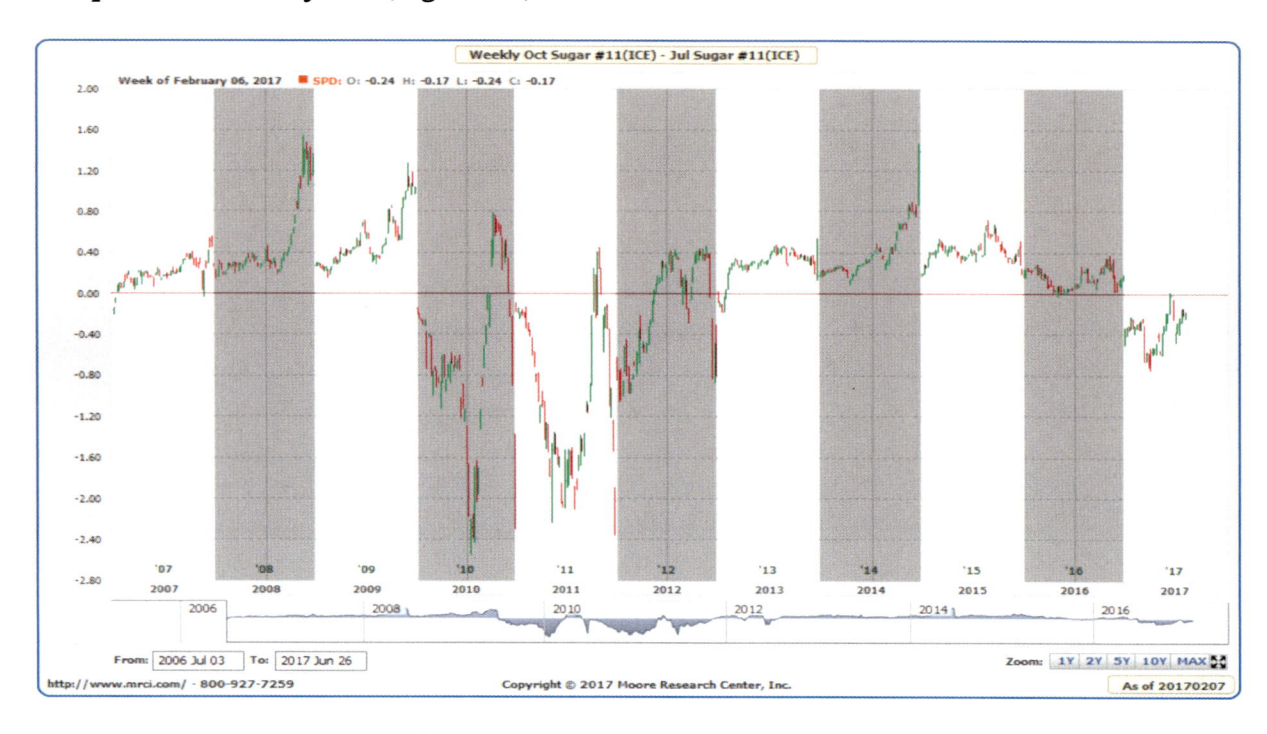

Figure 30 - Moore Research Weekly Continuation chart (www.mrci.com)

While by clicking on Monthly Continuation, you can see the same chart but with the monthly time frame (Figure 31).

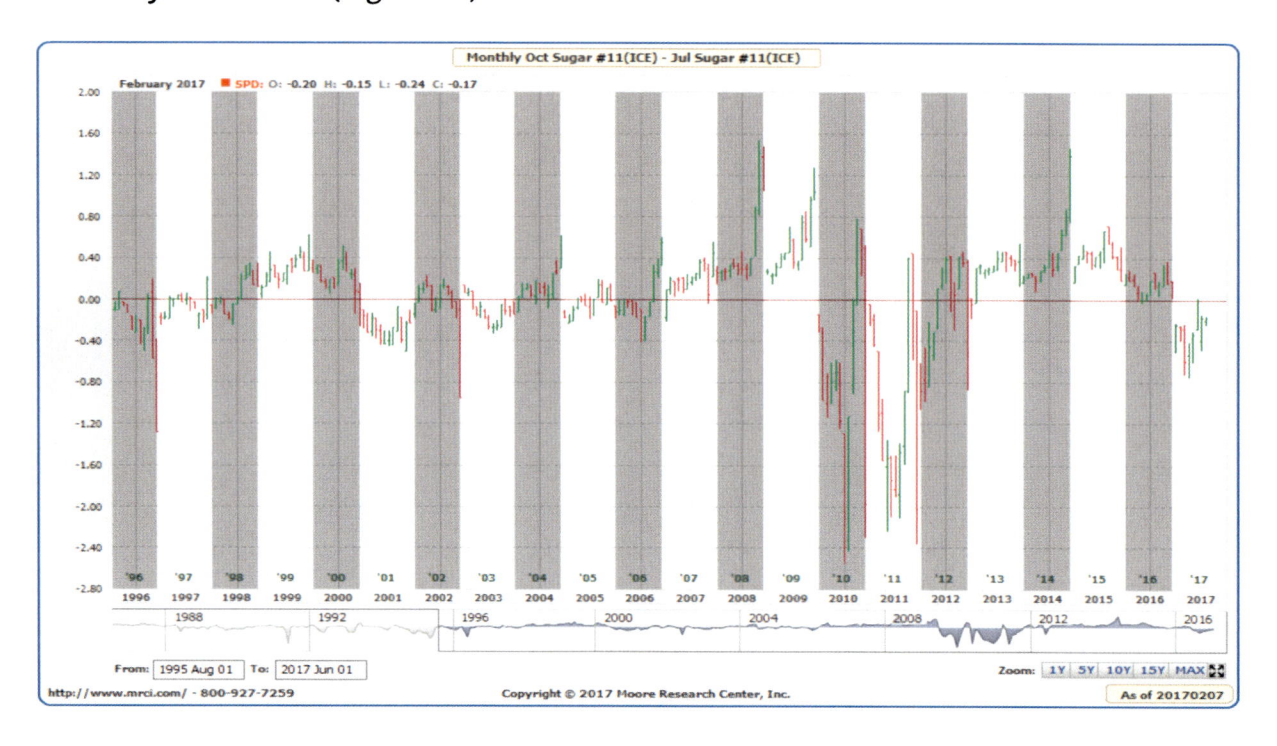

Figure 31 - Moore Research Monthly Continuation chart (www.mrci.com)

Both charts are useful for comparing the current price of the spread with past ones. You have to figure out if it is close to the highs and if there is still room to rise further, also to evaluate any resistance levels that could curb the spread.

Now an important clarification: in the charts of SeasonAlgo and Moore Research, the red and blue lines you see, which represent the 5-year and 15-year seasonal patterns, are not to scale. These lines are 'pasted' onto the charts purely as visual references. Therefore, they should only be considered for the general trend of the seasonal development and never for price levels.

To determine the value of the spread, you need to refer to historical prices, assessing whether the spread you are analysing is overvalued or undervalued compared to previous years. Do not worry, I will explore this aspect in more detail in the next chapter dedicated to seasonal models.

One final point to clarify is the difference between SeasonAlgo and Moore Research in the construction of spreads. SeasonAlgo uses an approach where the price of the nearer delivery futures contract is subtracted from that of the farther delivery contract. Based on this calculation, the spread can be bought or sold depending on seasonality. When the spread price is below zero, you are in a contango situation; when it is above zero, you are in backwardation.

Moore Research, on the other hand, adopts a different method: it subtracts the futures contract that is sold from the one that is bought. Consequently, its spreads are always constructed to be bought and never sold. If the nearer delivery contract is the one being bought, as with SeasonAlgo, you will have contango when the price is below zero and backwardation when it is above zero. However, if the farther delivery contract is the one being bought, the reverse occurs: contango when the price is above zero and backwardation when it is below.

So, you have seen in general terms (a complete and detailed description would require another book) what two of the main statistical databases can offer you. Now, the last but not least, I am going to introduce you to the third statistical database: SpreadCharts.

SpreadCharts is different from the two statistical databases seen above. It does not provide a list of futures and spreads seasonality, but the best trading opportunities. It is a fantastic analysis software, with features that no one else has.

SpreadCharts offers the widest range of tools for analysing commodity futures and spreads, providing not only a comprehensive view of historical trends but also advanced metrics that allow you to predict market movements with greater precision. This extensive toolkit gives you a unique insight into the market, enabling you to identify opportunities that may otherwise go unnoticed.

The software has a free version and a subscription one. In the free version, anyone who signs up can access the app to analyse a commodity or a spread. Here, by selecting Seasonality - average, you can see any futures or spread chart with the 5-, 15- and 30-year seasonal patterns. You can see an example, with the chart of the spread SBN21-SBV21 (Figure 32).

Figure 32 - SBN21-SBV21 chart (SpreadCharts.com)

By selecting Price & underlyings, instead, you can view the spread chart and compare it with the sugar futures contract closest to delivery, as shown in Figure 33.

Figure 33 - SBN21-SBV21 spread and SBN21 futures chart (SpreadCharts.com)

For an analysis of the volume and open interest, you have to select Volume & OI comparison, and in a chart, you can clearly see what the situation is. You can see this with the spread SBN21-SNV21 in the chart above (Figure 34).

40

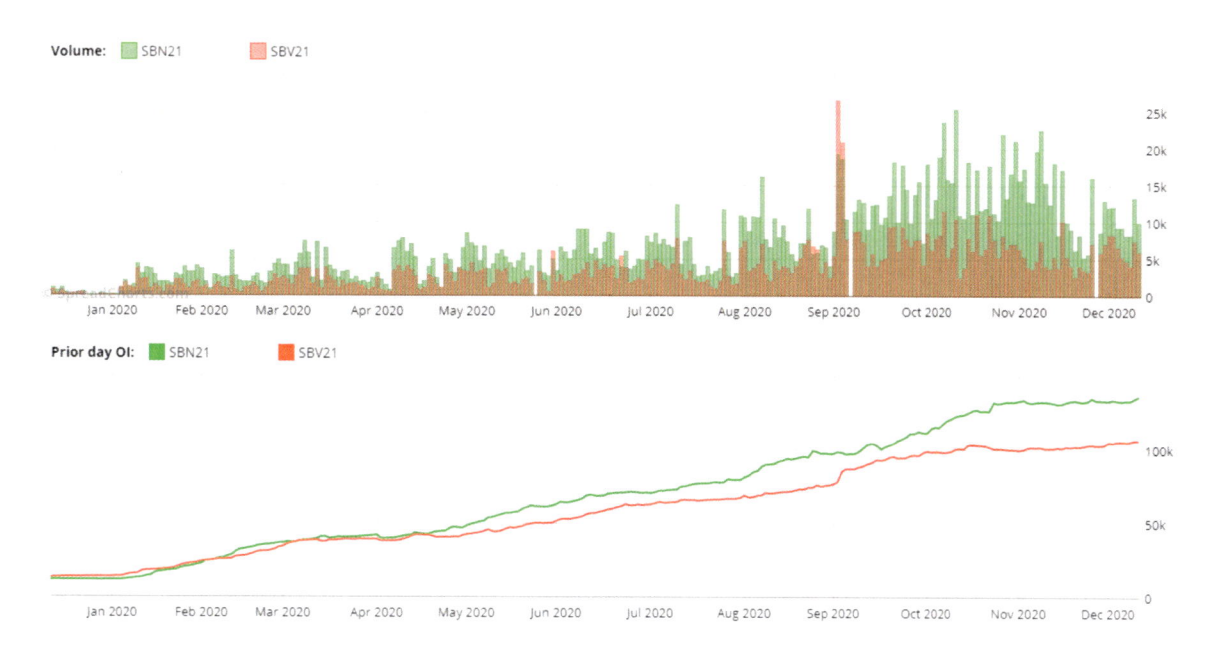

Figure 34 - SBN21-SBV21 spread, Volume & Open Interest (SpreadCharts.com)

When you analyse futures or spreads, it is essential to compare the current chart with that of past years. This is what the Seasonality - stacked function does. Here you can see the previous nine years altogether or select only those that interest you most. You can see an example of this in the chart in Figure 35.

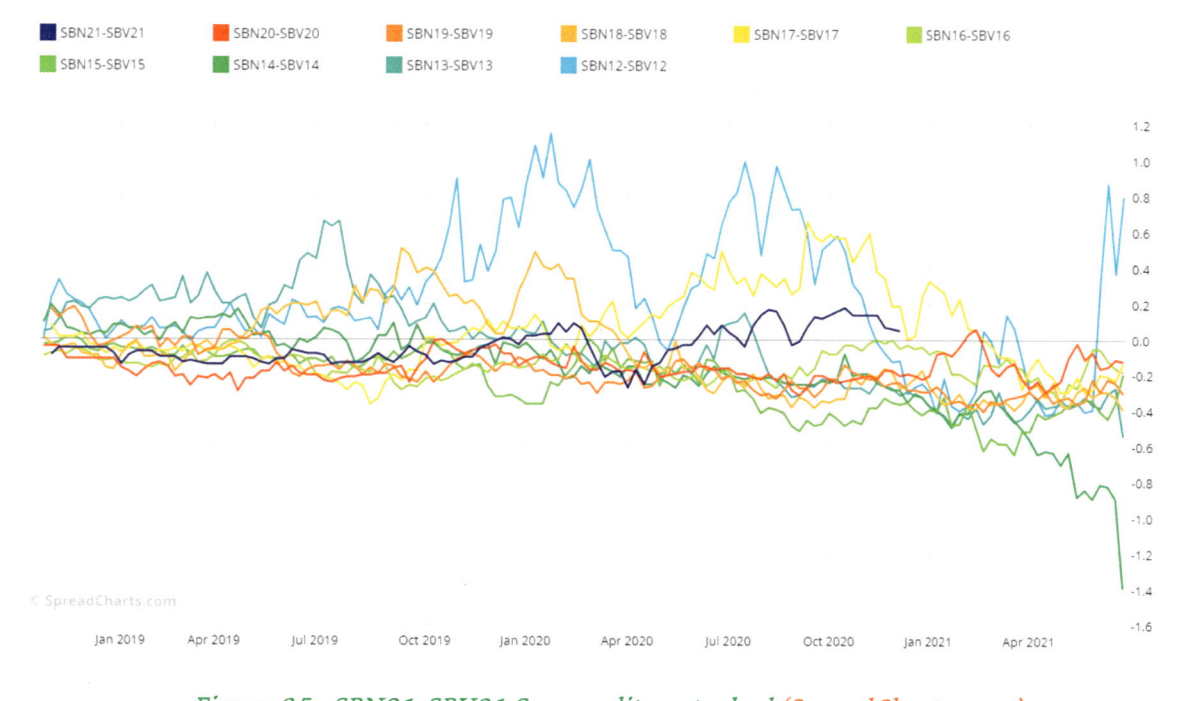

Figure 35 - SBN21-SBV21 Seasonality - stacked (SpreadCharts.com)

Let us now take a look at two new features of SpreadCharts in 2020: Continuous Price and Seasonality - by month.

Until now, if you wanted to analyse the long-term behaviour of a spread, you would use the stacked seasonality chart. This, however, has some drawbacks. First of all, individual years are stacked on top of each other. This is great for analysing seasonal patterns but less convenient for getting the dynamics of the spread over the years.

Secondly, you are limited to just the past ten years. Otherwise, the stacked chart would become unreadable.

That is inconvenient and prevents comparison between various decades.

These drawbacks are now overcome with the Continuous chart. The continuous price chart shows the evolution of the price of your contract or spread over many decades. Although the default zoom is set to the last 2 years, you can easily display a longer period using the zoom panel on the right side.

The contracts are placed one after another once the active contract expires. Only the last year of data for every contract (expiration) is used, even though the life of the contract is greater than one year. On the daily time frame, each contract is highlighted by a different colour that repeats itself after a decade.

The current contract is always blue which is the only colour that is not repeated in the palette. You can easily identify the ticker for historical contracts by moving the cursor over the desired line. If you display a longer period (more than 2 years of data), the chart will switch to candlesticks which offers better readability for very long periods (years up to decades).

An example of this can be seen in Figure 36, using the SBN21-SBV21 spread.

Figure 36 - SBN21-SBV21 spread (SpreadCharts.com)

You will notice a difference between the Continuous price of some spreads and the price chart for the continuous contract. Let me make this clear.

42

The continuous contract is composed of a commodity symbol and a number determining the order of the selected contracts at the time they were plugged into the series, for example, NG1-NG2. There is no expiration month on the ticker. It is an artificially created time series. You cannot trade a continuous contract unless you roll over your futures position every month. Doing that would cost you additional broker commissions, due to contango which is not reflected in the continuous contract.

Moreover, continuous contracts in every charting service will look slightly different as there is no preferred roll methodology (i.e., the rule determining the exact time to switch to the next contact). Therefore, continuous contracts are useful for long term analysis of a particular commodity and are not intended for trading decisions. In other words, there are other charts that can be used for entering this type of spread.

On the other hand, the new Continuous price chart can be displayed only for an actual spread, i.e., something you can really trade. Although even the Continuous price is an artificial time series made of many contracts connected together, it is more relevant for making trading decisions on particular spread combinations as only the contracts with the same expiration month are plugged into the Continuous price.

Let me demonstrate this on the following chart (Figure 37).

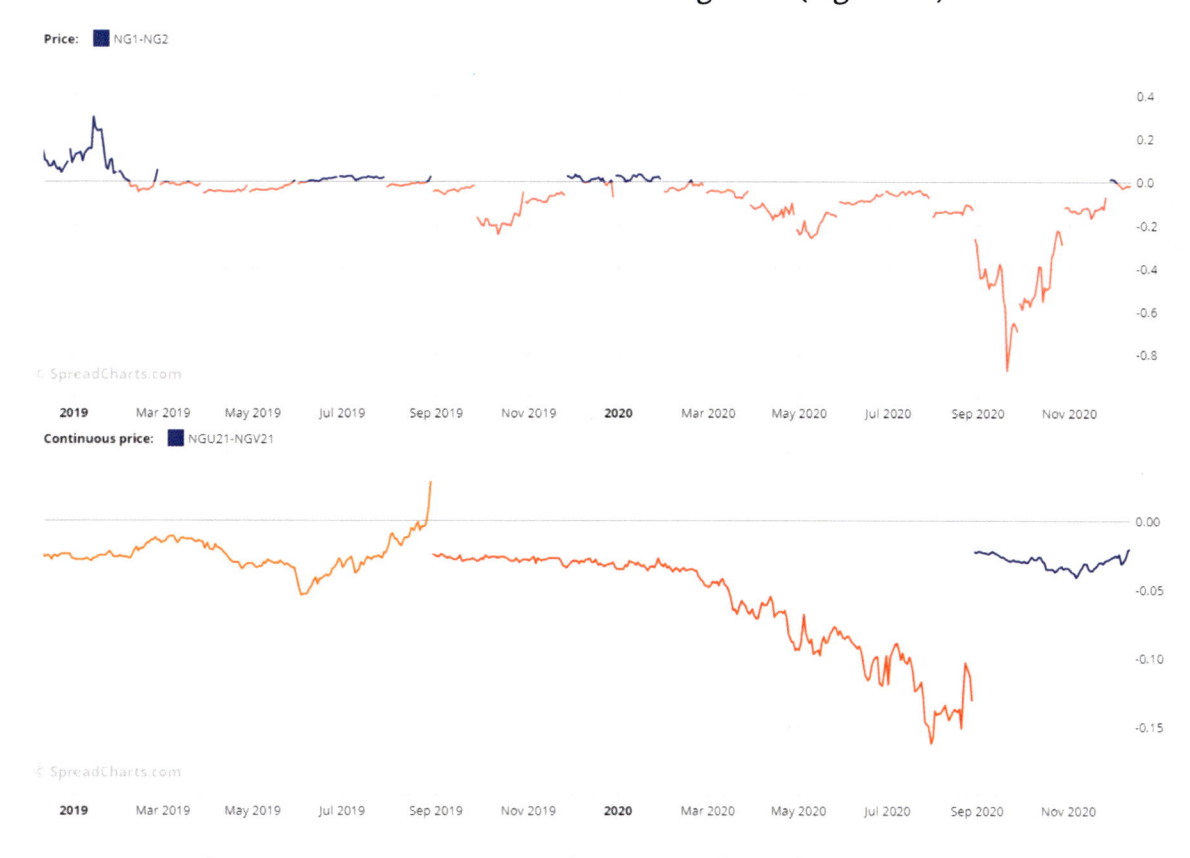

Figure 37 - NGU21-NGV21 and NG1-NG2 charts (SpreadCharts.com)

Here is the comparison between the Continuous price of NGU20-NGV20 and NG1-NG2. Although technically they are both 1-month wide bull spreads, they look dramatically different.

Let's see the second new feature of SpreadCharts. Until now, you used to have two types of seasonality charts, the Seasonality - average that give you a quick overview of the seasonal trend, and Seasonality - stacked which is great for a more detailed analysis. Now, there is a third type: Seasonality - by month.

Let's find out what this is all about, looking at the chart below, again using the SBN21-SBV21 spread (Figure 38).

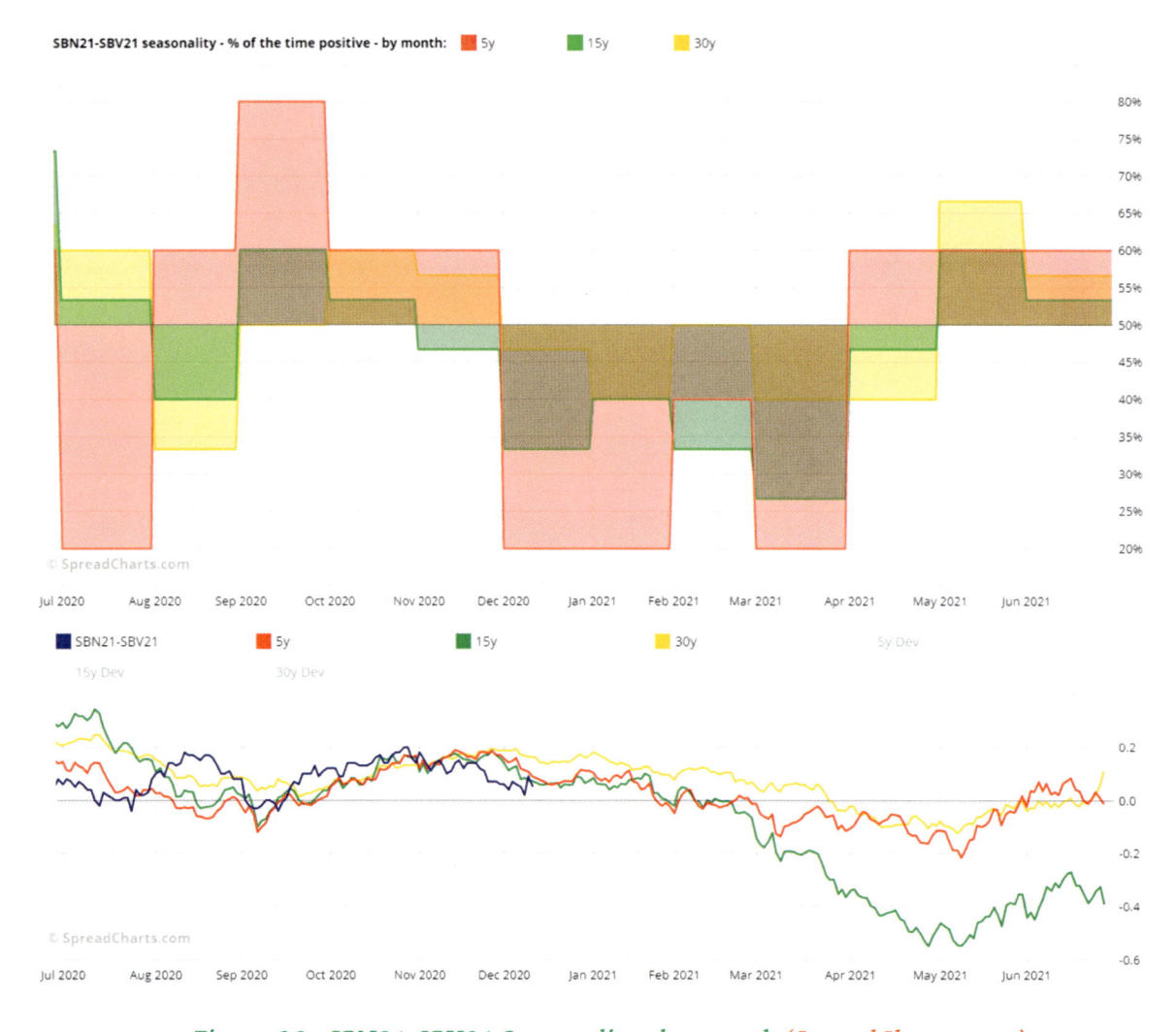

Figure 38 - SBN21-SBV21 Seasonality - by month (SpreadCharts.com)

The chart shows how many times (in percentage terms) the spread moved up in each month over the past 5-, 15-, and 30-year periods. Let's focus, for example, on the red curve. Its value in July is exactly 20% which means the spread has moved higher in July one out of five times in the last five years.

It might look like a negative seasonal trend. However, the 15-year value for July (green) stands at 53% which means the price moved lower only in 7 years out of the past 15 years.

44

This means that in recent years the seasonality of the spread in July has changed to negative (you cannot see this with the seasonal patterns in the chart below, only with the Seasonality - by month does it become clear).

I think the logic is clear. The chart provides you with additional information about the reliability of the seasonal trend broken down by month. Keep in mind it says nothing about the magnitude of the seasonal trend, just the frequency at which it occurs. It certainly complements the averages or stacked seasonality charts well.

Now let's take a look at the term structure of the underlying asset by selecting SB - Term structure. SB because the underlying of the spread SBN21-SBV21 is sugar. Here you can compare the current term structure with that of a day, a week or a month ago, and with the 5- and 15-year seasonal patterns.

In Figure 39, you can see an example with the current term structure of sugar (in blue), that of a month ago (in grey), and the 5-year seasonal pattern (in red).

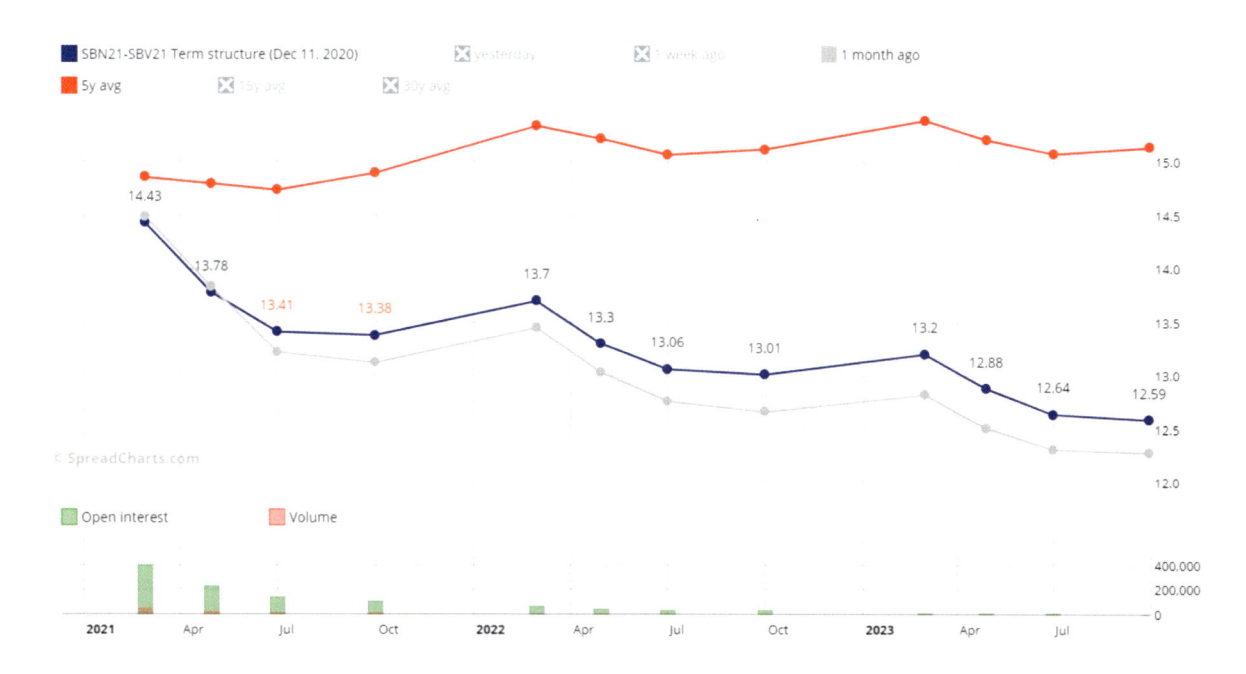

Figure 39 - Sugar Term Structure (SpreadCharts.com)

Thus, you have the opportunity to fully analyse the term structure, which is fundamental for understanding many aspects of futures or spreads. You will see the term structure explained in detail in Chapter 15.

Another very helpful tool is the C.O.T. (Commitment of Traders). It allows you to see what the big players are doing so that you can manage your positions accordingly. SpreadCharts has developed its own Commitment of Traders data processing methodology and uses disaggregated data. We will study C.O.T. in more detail in Chapter 11. In Figure 40, you can see the Sugar futures and below the C.O.T. net position.

Figure 40 - Sugar C.O.T. net position (SpreadCharts.com)

There are two more advanced features that SpreadCharts offers us: Continuous histogram and Carrying charges analysis for grains.

The intention of Continuous histogram remains the same as with the old Contango histogram, that is, it visualises the distribution of market data using the histogram chart. However, the calculation itself has been reworked from the ground up. I will present to you its features one by one.

Here is the contango distribution in the coffee spread KCH21-KCN21 over the past 20 years (Figure 41). First, there is the distribution itself (blue columns) and the last value (vertical blue line) centred on the nearest column. Together, they allow you to compare the current contango value to the historical distribution. The levels of high density (clusters of tall columns) tend to act as an attractor to the price.

You have surely noticed the red and green areas. These are very helpful and will help you to speed up your analysis. The red-coloured area shows the 25th to 75th percentile range. It means 25% of the lowest values are located to the left side of it and 25% of the highest values to the right side of it. The red area basically highlights the region where the contango tends to return because it is mostly made up of 50% of the most common observations.

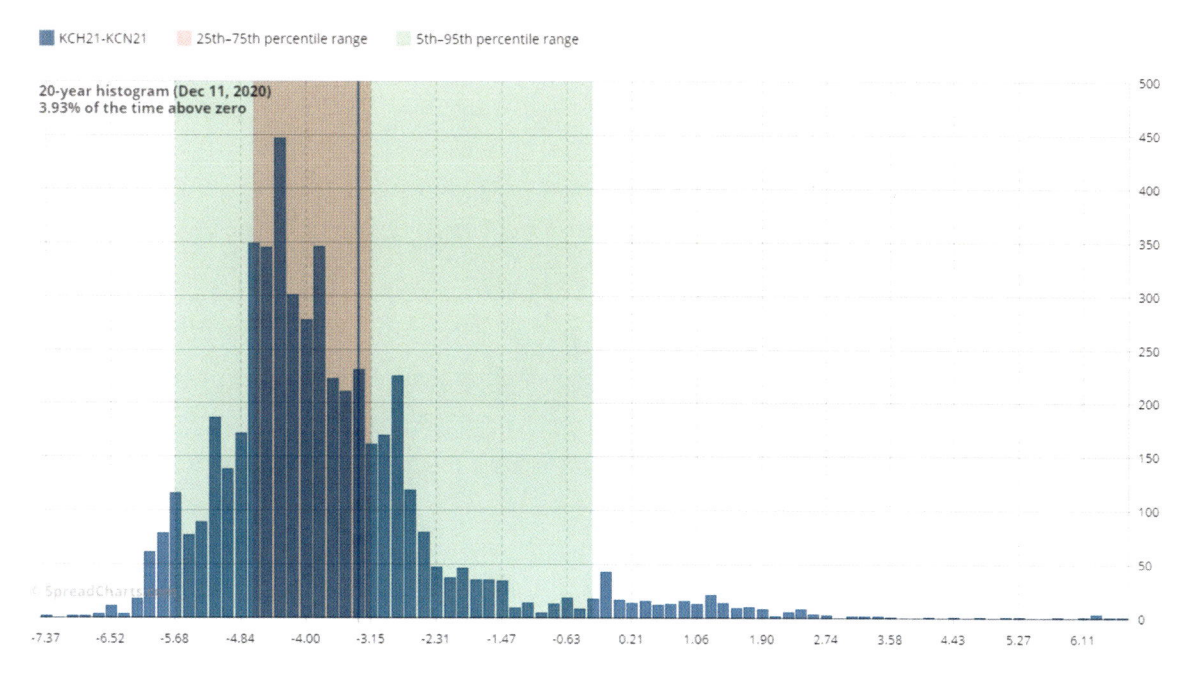

Figure 41 - KCH21-KCN21 Continuous histogram (SpreadCharts.com)

The green-coloured area shows the 5th to 95th percentile range. The logic is the same as before, but the application is different. You have to use this green range to identify extremes. Seeing the contango out of the green region is very rare. So, if that happens, the market is likely overbought or oversold, increasing the chances of a mean reversion. This is because only 5% of the highest values and 5% of the lowest values fall outside this range. This visual cue helps you assess potential corrections or trend reversals in a quick and efficient manner.

Another handy tool is the frequency of positive values in the data set. You will find this in the top left-hand corner of the chart and only if there are negative values in the data (otherwise it is omitted). In the example above, there is '3.93% of the time above zero'. This information helps provide a clear picture of the overall market trend.

These statistics can prove highly useful. In this particular example, it can tell you which spread strategy has a better chance of being successful. Contango has been overwhelmingly dominant in the coffee market and that is a great environment for bear spreads.

What about fundamental ratios? Here is the 46-year distribution of gold/silver ratio (Figure 42) which is carefully watched by precious metals investors. This study is perfect for this kind of data.

There are no limits to what you can visualise. An extreme example is the one below in Figure 43 with the Crack spread.

To get better insight into the data, you can plot the histogram together with any other chart. It makes the most sense to display the histogram together with the underlying data.

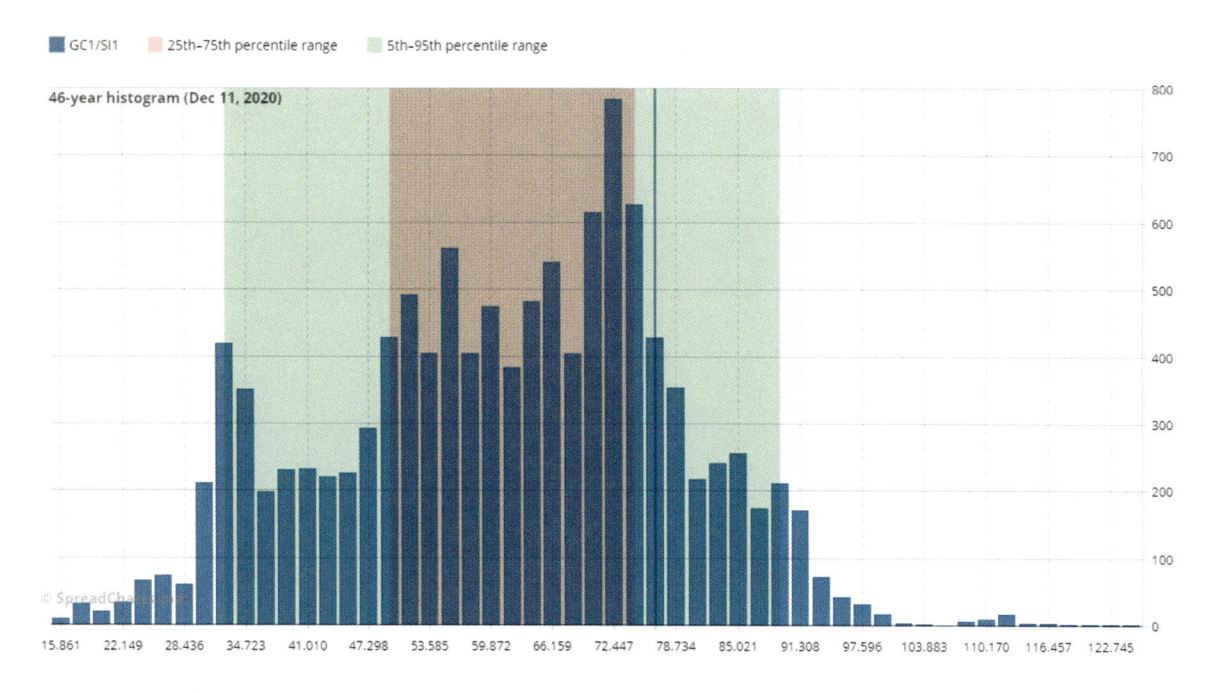

Figure 42 - Gold/Silver ratio Continuous histogram (SpreadCharts.com)

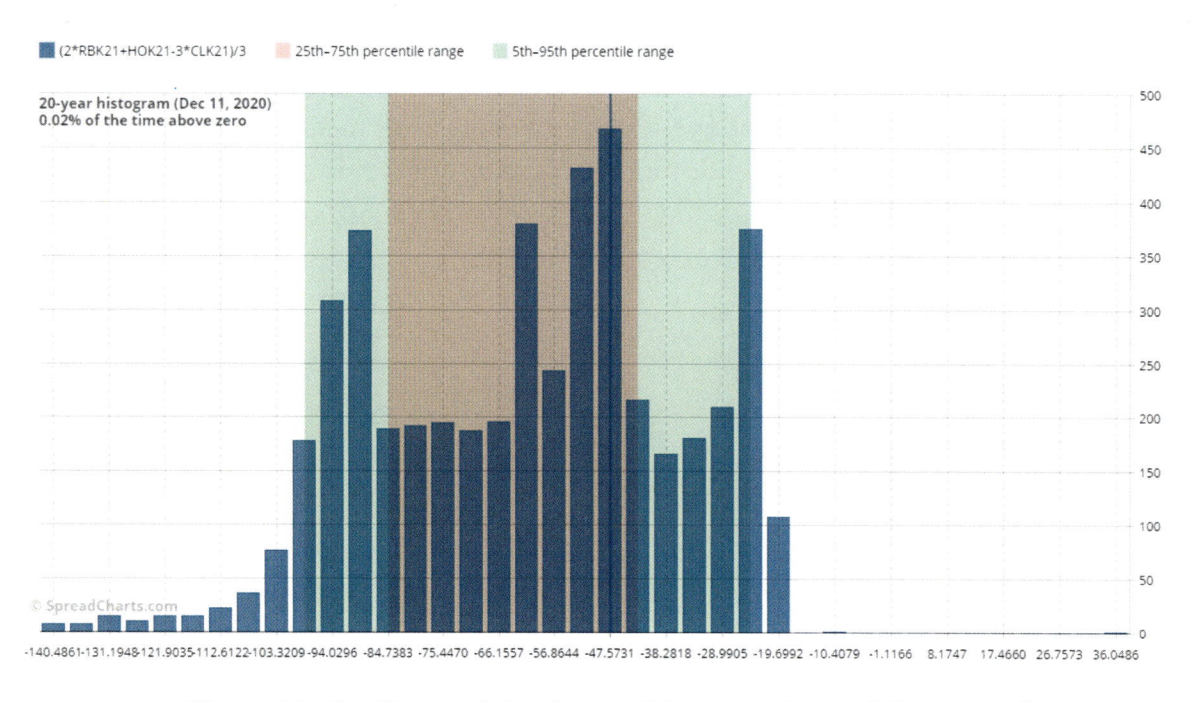

Figure 43 - Crack spread Continuous histogram (SpreadCharts.com)

An example is in the next chart. The top sub-chart is the Continuous histogram for ZSH21-ZSN21 wheat spread. Just below it is the continuous price for the same spread (Figure 44).

The charts are synchronised. If you change the zoom, the bottom continuous price sub-chart will scale accordingly, and the histogram will immediately show you the distribution of the data. To keep the data synced, the mouse zoom is disabled, so you must use the buttons in the right zoom panel.

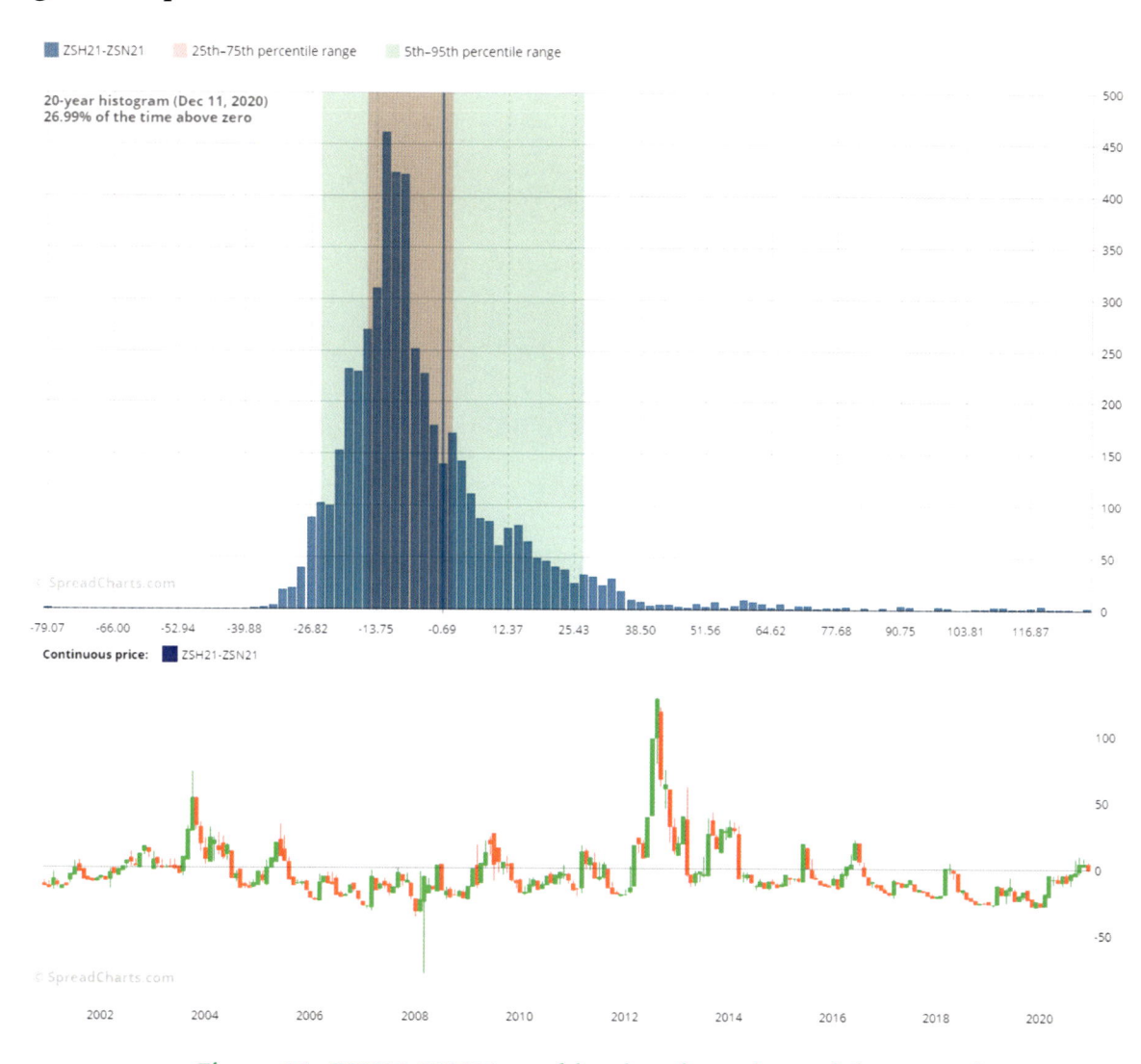

Figure 44 - ZSH21-ZSN21 combination charts (SpreadCharts.com)

    The histogram gives you statistical properties of the data set with the price chart being helpful for analysing the finer details. This setup can help you immediately identify the periods of the extremes from the histogram. These two charts are a perfect fit.

    The new Continuous histogram is a ground-breaking feature. It won't just save your time but also reveal important data properties you would otherwise miss. Now, the bad news. Due to the advanced character of this study and the computational time involved, the new histogram chart will be available only to premium users. The only exception is CBOT Corn contracts (including Intramarket spreads) for which you can use it freely to get a taste of this powerful chart.

    The carrying charges analysis for grains is another important source of information. The SpreadCharts software gives you the opportunity to analyse the Full Carry and the Full Carry Ratio. This is a new aspect for many of you and a slightly difficult one, at least at first glance, so before I continue, I will give a brief explanation.

The cost of transporting physical commodities is one of the main reasons why their term structure curves are not flat. In the grains markets, the precise determination of transportation costs plays a central role for farmers. Instead of selling the harvest immediately after it is gathered, farmers often prefer to sell the carry, keeping the grains stored on their farms. This allows them to profit from the price difference between the futures contract with the farther delivery date and the current price at harvest time.

However, this strategy also involves additional costs, such as storage expenses and the need to finance the new crop without receiving income from the previous one. For the operation to be profitable, the profit generated by the spread must exceed these costs. This condition frequently occurs in years of abundant harvests, where futures show a strong contango, making it more favourable for farmers to hold grains in storage.

As I said, SpreadCharts allows you to see both the Full Carry and Full Carry Ratio; let you start by looking at the first of these. When you build a calendar spread in grains, you can display the Full Carry under 'Price & underlyings' tab by clicking on the 'Full Carry' button (the grey/green square in the chart's legend). Full Carry is an arbitrage level, the price of the spread cannot exceed it. This level determines your maximum risk when you open a bull spread, and maximum profit in a bear spread trade.

You can see an example of this with the spread ZCN20-ZCK20 in Figure 45, in blue the spread and green the Full Carry.

Figure 45 - ZCN20-ZCK20 spread with Full Carry (SpreadCharts.com)

Normally, the price of a spread cannot exceed the full carry value under stable market conditions. However, there are some exceptional circumstances in which this limit can be surpassed, for example, when the physical market becomes disconnected from the futures markets. During these periods, poor convergence occurs between the futures price and the spot market price, a phenomenon that exchanges actively seek to prevent. Poor convergence is problematic as it discourages the main users of futures, hedgers, from using these instruments to cover their operations.

To mitigate this risk, CME Group, the leading US commodity exchange, has adopted specific measures. It introduced the VSR (Variable Storage Rate) mechanism for wheat listed on the CBOT and KCBT, and increased the maximum storage rate for soybeans and corn. The VSR is a system that dynamically adjusts the storage rate based on market conditions, improving price convergence between futures and the physical market. All of these models, including the VSR, have also been implemented on SpreadCharts, allowing you to better analyse market dynamics.

More important than the Full Carry itself is the ratio between the price of the spread and the Full Carry, that is, the Full Carry Ratio. Even farmers prefer to follow this value. It is located under the 'Full Carry' tab, and it shows what percentage of Full Carry the spread made in previous years.

This is very helpful because this metric shows the true value of the spread. You can compare the spread's value over the years and decide whether it is currently undervalued or overvalued. To understand better how to use it, look at an example with the spread ZCZ21-ZCZ20 (Figure 46).

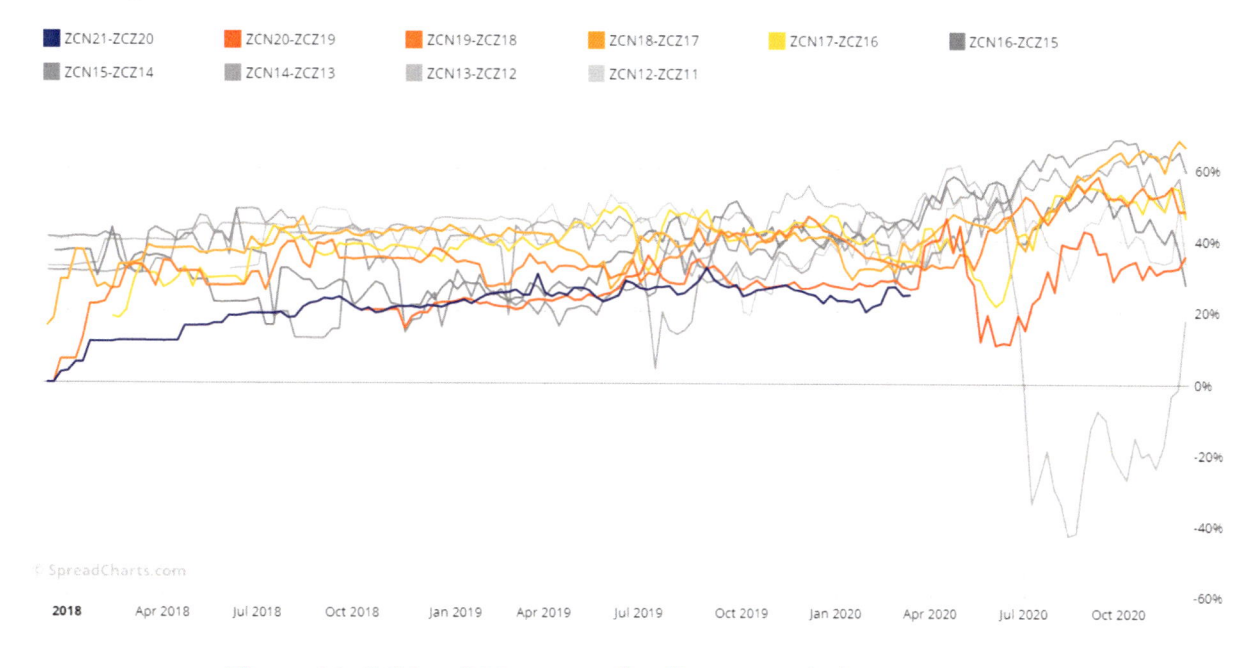

Figure 46 - ZCN21-ZCZ20 spread Full Carry Ratio (SpreadCharts.com)

One way of looking at the Full Carry Ratio is by estimating whether the current spread is cheap or expensive. Looking at the chart, you can see that the current spread (in blue) is lower than all the previous spreads from recent years, making it appear undervalued. So, from this aspect, it is convenient to buy the spread.

A second way of looking at the Full Carry Ratio is by taking a look at the future to see the potential of the spread. In the chart above, you can see that these spreads tend to reach up to 60% of Full Carry. So, in the future, the current spread is expected to reach a higher value.

These rules are valid for all grains and oilseeds except for CBOT wheat (ZW). Because of the Variable Storage Rates concept, the Full Carry in ZW is no longer an unbreakable barrier. It can rise or decline substantially in a short period of time. It could be at a wildly different level several months from now.

They can reach or even exceed the Full Carry. That is because the Variable Storage Rates brings uncertainty into the equation. The market does not know how high the storage rate will be at expiration and may be pricing a different degree of Full Carry from today's level.

You can see an example of this with the chart ZWZ20-ZWK20 (Figure 47).

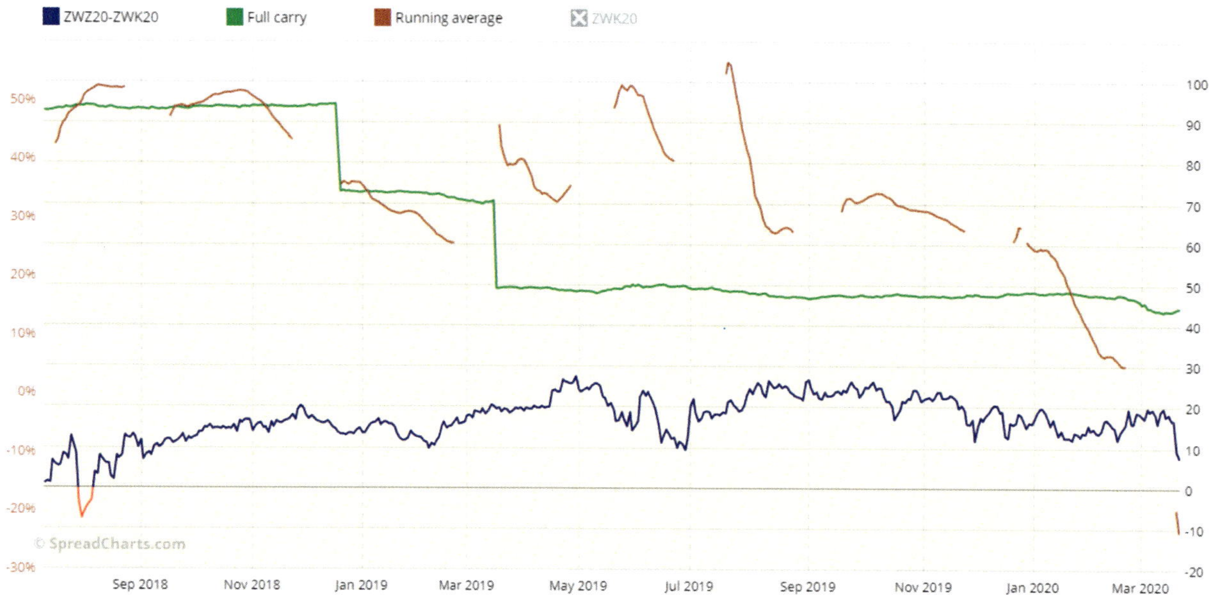

Figure 47 - ZWZ20-ZWK20 spread Variable Storage Rates (SpreadCharts.com)

This complexity brings you new opportunities. Spreads can depart too far from the current Full Carry, indicating a huge discrepancy between the expected outlook and reality. Or the Full Carry can start to move, but spreads can take their time reacting, etc. Besides, you can measure the probability that the maximum storage rate will move in advance. This is what the so-called 'Running average' study is intended for.

So, are you now attracted to spread trading? I bring you the bad news: seasonality is not everything, as you will see for yourself in the Chapter 8. If subscribing to a statistical database was enough to make money, would not you think everyone would do it?

Seasonal Patterns

CHAPTER 7

As you have seen, there are several websites that, with a subscription, allow you to access the best seasonality patterns for futures and spreads. You can open the chart and observe the 'seasonal averages' of a futures contract or a spread, calculated over periods like the last 5 or 15 years.

However, it is precisely this term, 'seasonal average', that tends to create confusion. Many traders are inclined to consider it as a regular moving average, applying the same logic and analysis used in technical analysis. This can lead to incorrect interpretations and, consequently, to poor trading decisions.

In reality, what are called 'seasonal averages' are not averages in the conventional sense of the word, but true seasonal models. Their construction is very different from that of a moving average, which is based solely on historical price data. Seasonal models, on the other hand, take into account recurring patterns tied to specific annual cycles in the market. Therefore, you cannot apply the same analysis and conclusions that you would with a moving average.

To help you better understand this distinction, I will explain how seasonal models are constructed, aiming to make everything as clear and simple as possible, without delving into unnecessary technical details.

Let's say you want to build the 5-year seasonal pattern of the futures contract ZCK22 (using SeasonAlgo, I chose the corn because I am not a subscriber). In Figure 48 you can see the stacked chart of ZCK22 for the last 5 years (2017 to 2021).

Figure 48 - ZCK22 stacked chart (SeasonAlgo)

Now, I want to show you the creation of the 5-year seasonal model. The first thing you need to do is normalise the values of the individual futures contracts from the last 5 years. But what does 'normalise' actually mean? Essentially, it means converting the values from absolute to relative. Instead of seeing, for example, the corn futures contract at $600 or $650, you will see the values transformed on a scale from 0 to 100.

This normalisation process serves to make prices from different periods comparable, eliminating the influence of absolute price variations and allowing you to focus solely on recurring seasonal patterns. In other words, the actual price level no longer matters; what matters is how prices moved during that period.

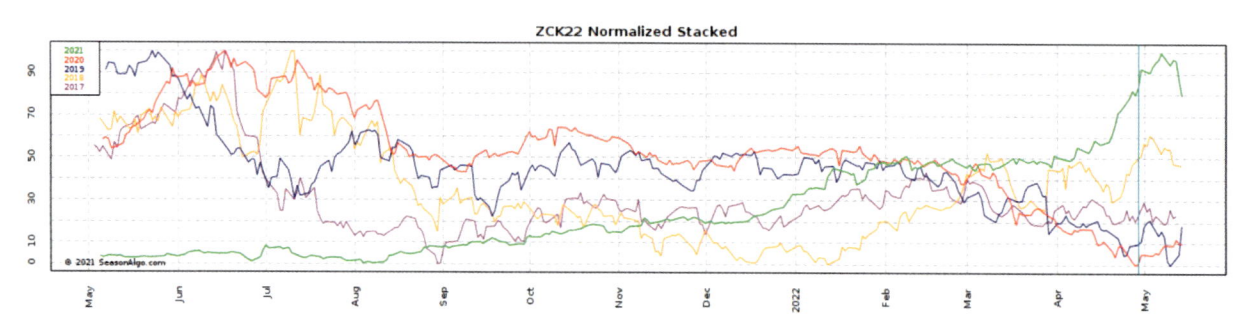

In Figure 49, you can see the same stacked chart of ZCK22 as above but normalised.

Figure 49 - ZCK22 stacked chart normalised (SeasonAlgo)

As you can see, the chart shows all 5 normalised years of ZCK22. Where 0 corresponds to the minimum level touched by each futures contract and 100 corresponds to the maximum level. I do this because what interest me, is the movement of the seasonal pattern, not its dimension.

All you have to do at this point is an arithmetic sum of the five years, and normalise the values again, as shown in the chart below of the ZCK22 5-year seasonal pattern (Figure 50).

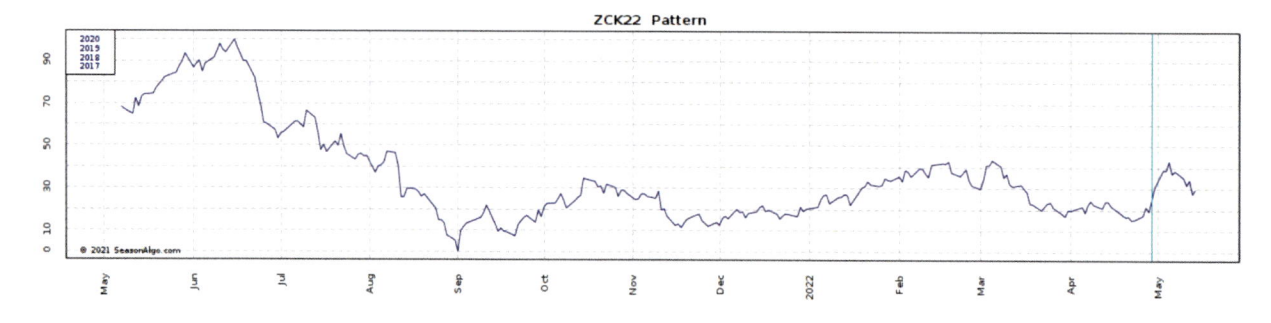

Figure 50 - ZCK22 seasonal pattern chart (SeasonAlgo)

The seasonal pattern is then 'stuck' into the chart of the futures contract as you can see in Figure 51.

Figure 51 - ZCK22 chart (SeasonAlgo)

This, then, is how I or any of you can build a seasonal pattern. Obviously, nobody does all these steps since statistical databases like SeasonAlgo or SpreadCharts do that. Now that you understand how seasonal patterns are constructed, it is equally crucial to know how to interpret them correctly. Misinterpretations can lead to poor trading decisions. Let us now explore some common mistakes traders make when using these patterns.

I have read, and some traders have reported to me that in some courses it is explained, that it is advisable to enter long on a spread only if it is below the seasonal patterns and short only if it is above them. This is completely incorrect, and I strongly advise against taking such advice seriously.

Just as it is wrong to use seasonal patterns to calculate supports and resistances, stop losses, or target profits. As I have shown you, seasonal patterns are calculated in a different way and then stuck onto another chart, so the values shown on the y-axis are only to be considered for the current spread, not the seasonal patterns.

Another bit of nonsense I have read is, "*the seasonal pattern has gone up of x points, so the spread has a wide margin*". As I said, the seasonal pattern should only be considered for its movement, not its dimension.

The following observational points are from my own experience.

In addition to its movement, the seasonal pattern is also useful for understanding its volatility. Indeed, the closer the 5- and 15-year seasonal patterns are, the less volatile the futures contract or spread analysed. However, this statement is not always true. As well as that there should be, during the seasonal window, a strong correlation between the 5- and 15-year seasonal patterns.

The problem with these considerations is that it only takes one of the last 5 years with a strong movement against seasonality that the 5-year seasonal pattern will be significantly affected. Let me show you this with an example. Below you can see the CLZ22-CLM23-CLZ23+CLM24 spread chart (Figure 52).

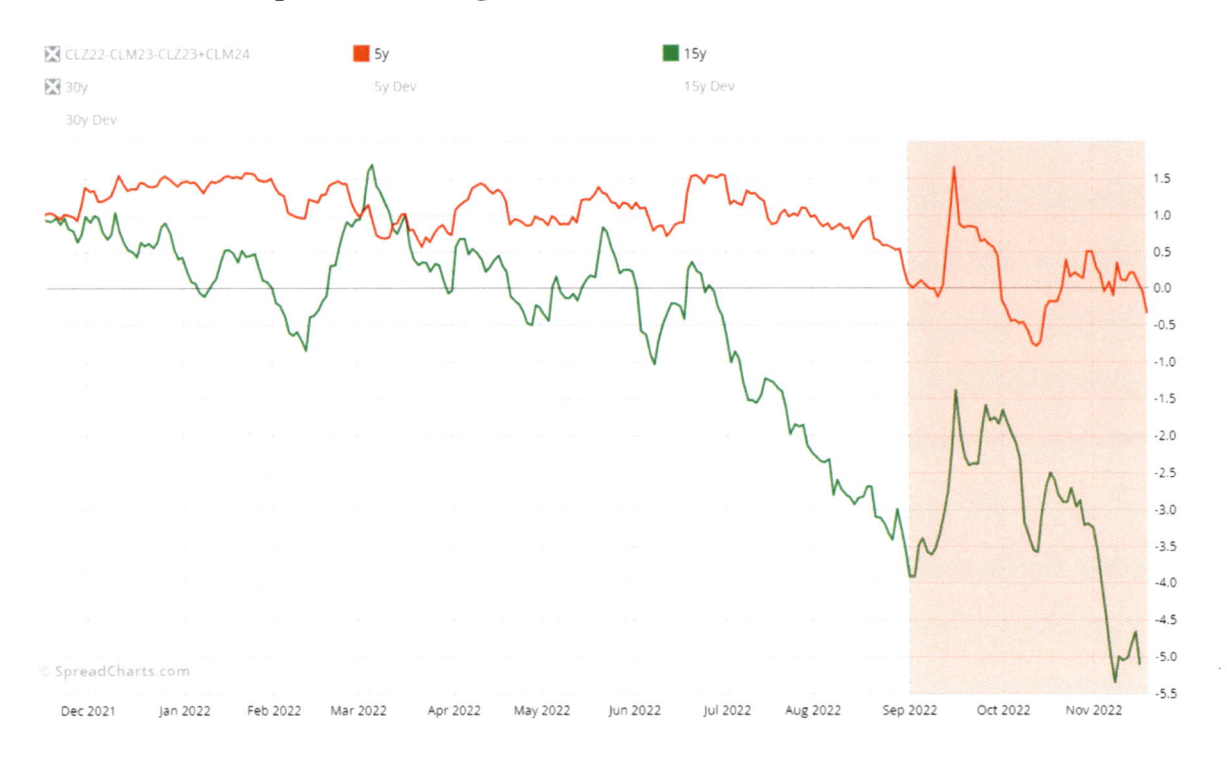

Figure 52 - Spread CLZ22-CLM23-CLZ23+CLM24 (SpreadCharts.com)

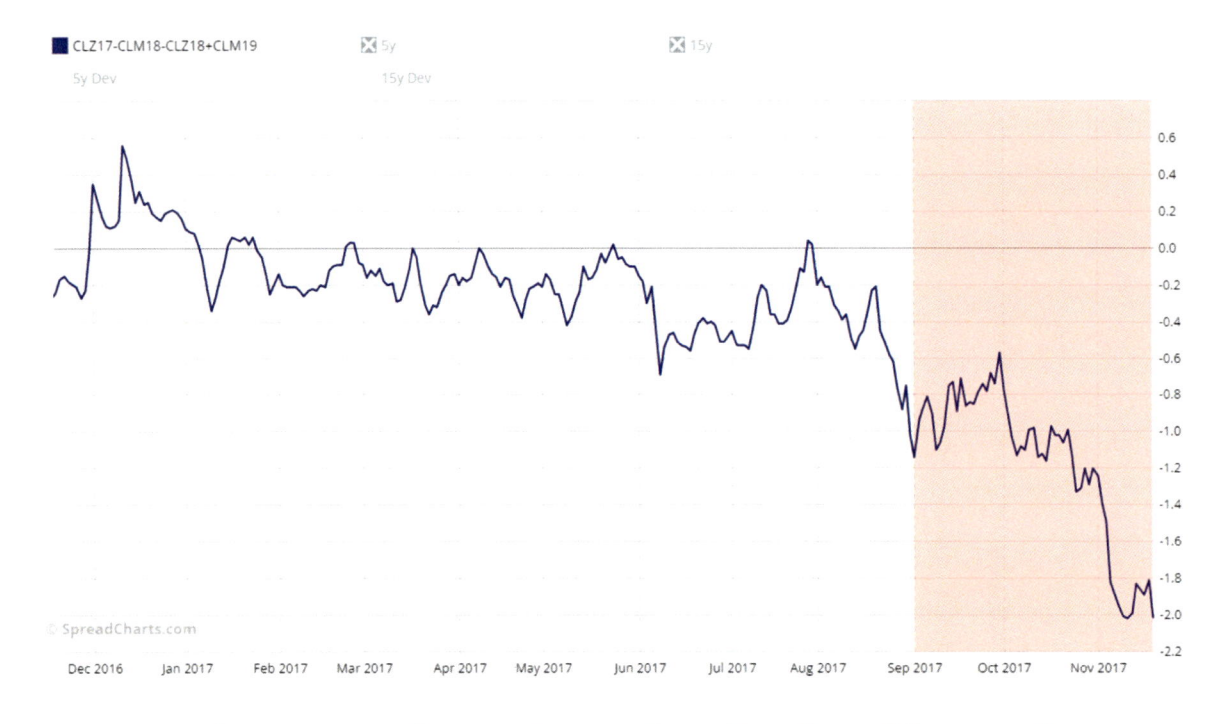

Figure 53 - Spread CLZ17-CLM18-CLZ18+CLM19 (SpreadCharts.com)

If you focus on the trend of the two 5- and 15-year seasonal patterns within the seasonal window, you can easily see that until mid-October the movement is very similar, then the 15-year seasonal pattern goes down while the 5-year seasonal pattern is lateralised. I now show you four charts relating to the spread in 2017 (Figure 53 above), 2018, 2019 and 2020 (Figures 54, 55, 56).

Figure 54 - Spread CLZ18-CLM19-CLZ19+CLM20 (SpreadCharts.com)

Figure 55 - Spread CLZ19-CLM20-CLZ20+CLM21 (SpreadCharts.com)

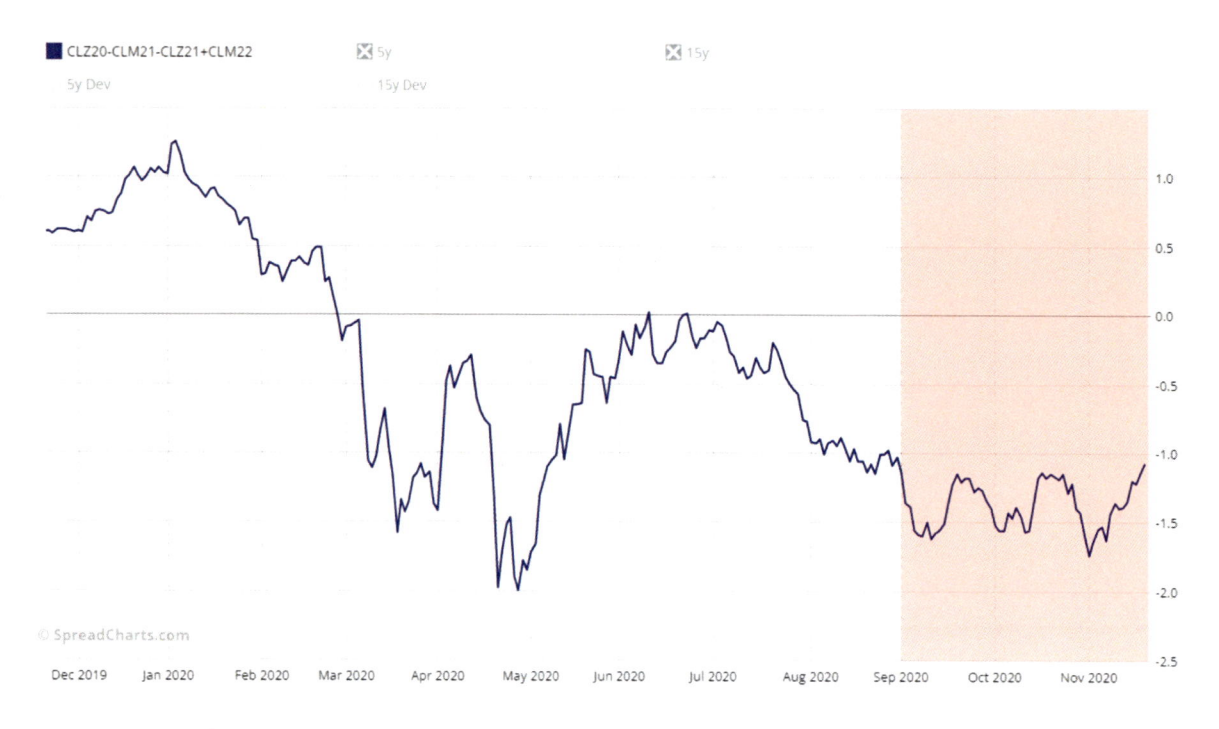

Figure 56 - Spread CLZ20-CLM21-CLZ21+CLM22 (SpreadCharts.com)

As you can see, seasonality has been respected. Naturally, the entry and exit levels should always be optimised to achieve the best results. The lack of correlation between the two seasonal patterns in the second half of the seasonal window is due to the impact of the spread in 2021 on the 5-year seasonal pattern, which you can see below (Figure 57).

Figure 57 - Spread CLZ21-CLM22-CLZ22+CLM23 (SpreadCharts.com)

The sharp rise in the spread this year, driven by strong speculation in the underlying asset, has significantly impacted the 5-year seasonal pattern.

Therefore, when the two seasonal patterns are not well correlated, it is essential to investigate the underlying reasons. Sometimes you will find that, as in the case above, it is due to an 'abnormal' year, other times that the spread is losing its seasonality.

In this chapter, I wanted to show you how seasonal patterns are calculated, how they should be used and the most common mistakes that are made. Take these seasonal patterns for what they are, just lines showing the performance of a futures contract or spread over time. Also, because, contrary to what is advertised, seasonality is not everything as you will see in the next chapter.

Not only Seasonality

Chapter 8

The statistical databases seen in Chapter 6 are an important aid to your trading in commodities. They are used to discover recurring seasonal patterns on single commodities or spreads and provide you with useful information on how to take advantage of the best trading opportunities.

They are fundamental for every trader that wants to trade commodities, both with the single futures and through spread trading, in order to exploit the most exciting aspect of this kind of trading: seasonality.

They are not, however, everything you need to know in order to become, month by month, a profitable trader of commodities. Statistical databases can be the starting point or can give you a confirmation about the analysis you have already made, but they are not the only information you have to take into account to open a trade. In fact, problems may arise when you are relying only on this type of software, or information coming from these sites, without adequate experience and preparation.

If you have attended courses, you have probably been told that you must follow seasonality because it predicts the future behaviour of a spread. That you should base your entire analysis on seasonal patterns. It may seem strange, but following this advice will most likely lead you to lose money.

You need to understand right away that no one gives money away; thinking you can make a profit and achieve consistent returns over time simply by possessing statistical information is unrealistic. Do you not think that everyone would do it if merely subscribing to these websites and basing their analysis solely on seasonality meant easy money?

I will show you this through some examples (although there are many others). I start with a spread on cotton; more precisely CTZ21-CTN22 and constructed by buying the cotton futures contract with delivery in December 2021 and selling the cotton futures contract with delivery in July 2022 (Figure 58).

Highlighted in red is the bearish seasonal window which runs from mid-August/mid-September until November. As you can see, the current spread (blue line) instead of falling, as has been the case in past years, and as suggested by the 5- and 15-year seasonal patterns, continued a bullish movement that started already in late May. In this case, if you had based your trade only on seasonality, this would have resulted in a loss.

Figure 58 - Spread CTZ21-CTN22 (SpreadCharts.com)

The next example concerns the ZLQ21-ZLZ21 spread, constructed by buying the soybean oil futures contract with delivery in August 2021 and selling the soybean oil futures contract with delivery in December 2021 (Figure 59).

Figure 59 - Spread ZLQ21-ZLZ21 (SpreadCharts.com)

The seasonality is bearish, as evidenced by the red band, and runs from December to May. Throughout the period the spread has moved in the opposite direction to what the two seasonal patterns at 5- and 15-year have done.

The next and final example concerns coffee with the KCH22-KCN22 spread, constructed by buying the coffee futures contract with delivery in March 2022 and selling the coffee futures contract with delivery in July 2022, and with a bearish seasonality running from mid-August/mid-September until January (Figure 60).

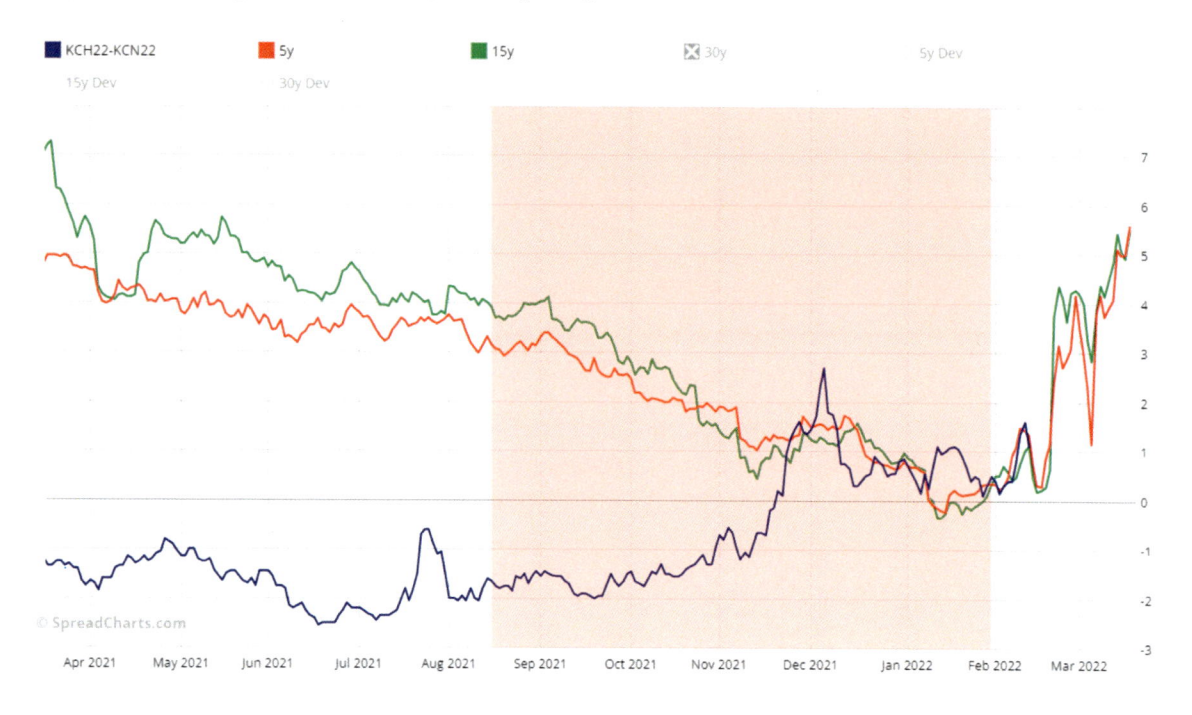

Figure 60 - Spread KCH22-KCN22 (SpreadCharts.com)

Again, the spread moved in the opposite direction to the two seasonal patterns at 5- and 15-year.

In conclusion, you have seen three examples of seasonality that were not respected, and I could give many more. Especially in the years 2020 and 2021, due to the pandemic and strong speculation on commodities, many seasonality have been disregarded. The same applies to 2023, due to ongoing climate changes and numerous geopolitical events.

Statistical databases can (and should) be considered as good suggestions and starting points (or confirmations), to understanding seasonality, to keep an eye out at certain times of the year.

However, the climate and other aspects like the demand and supply can be slightly shifted year by year, if not changed compared to previous years. So, it is essential to apply fundamental in your study for optimising not only the market entry but also the entire analysis.

Do not think that Moore Research and SeasonAlgo are the magic solution; they are just tools that can support your trading. Now, here is the fundamental analysis.

Fundamental Analysis

CHAPTER 9

~

While statistical data provides a solid foundation for opening a trade, it is often insufficient on its own. It is therefore essential to seek further confirmation. And where can we find it? Through technical analysis? The answer is no. Surely, technical analysis certainly provides clear signals, but unfortunately, most of the time it leads to a loss.

In my years of experience as a trader in an Italian investment bank, I learned to use subjective probability. You will see what this is all about in Chapter 22, let me now introduce another key aspect of spread trading: fundamental analysis.

While fundamental analysis plays a limited role in trading in general, with traders almost exclusively focused on measuring price trends (with indicators, oscillators, price action, and so on), commodity markets do tend to incorporate a significant amount of fundamental analysis.

Fundamental analysis is a method used to assess and predict the forces that may impact the future supply and demand of a commodity or other financial instruments.

Hence, the basis for fundamental analysis is supply and demand. When examining the prices of a commodity, the concept of supply and demand is reduced to a simple equation. However, things are a bit more complicated when you try to forecast future prices trend.

In fundamental analysis, commodity price movements can be broken down in two simple formulas:

- Demand > Supply = Higher Prices
- Supply > Demand = Lower Prices

Supply and demand are key economic concepts that attempt to explain what the market is willing to pay for a given product, where the quantity produced is equal to the quantity demanded. This interaction is key to the analysis of the price of a futures contract.

Fundamental analysts will use their knowledge of supply and demand factors to create their opinion of whether the futures contract is fairly valued, or if price will increase or decrease.

The supply of a commodity is the quantity of product that is carried over from the previous year of production (ending stocks) plus the quantity that is produced in the current year. For example, the current supplies of wheat include the crops in the ground and the ending stocks from the previous year. In general, the greater the quantity of product from the previous season (ending stocks), the more prices tend to fall.

Many factors impact the supply of commodities like weather (e.g., a drought or frost), the total amount of acres planted and their yield, crop diseases, production strikes, etc. The main thing to remember when using fundamental analysis is that high commodity prices will lead to increased production. Everyone wants to make a profit, so it is more profitable to produce a certain commodity when prices are higher.

The demand for commodities is the quantity that is consumed at a given price level. The general rule is that demand increases when the price of a commodity falls. Conversely, demand decreases when the price of a commodity rises. An old saying among commodity traders is that 'low prices cure low prices'. It means that a larger quantity of a commodity will be consumed at lower prices, which reduces supply, thus prices will eventually rise.

Fundamental analysis of commodities is simple economics. Consumption patterns change as the prices of commodities move higher and lower.

Now that you have explored the concepts of fundamental analysis, supply, and demand, how can you apply these concepts practically in your trading analysis?

A basic concept that you will find in all my books, and more than once, is that in the short-term it is speculation that moves prices but in the medium to long-term it is fundamental analysis. That is why my trades (not only in spread trading) have a time span of at least one month. Rarely, very rarely, and for very specific reasons, I would consider trades with a shorter time span.

Once again, you must use fundamental analysis to forecast future commodity prices. You have to look for trends that are developing which will cause a shift in supply and demand factors. To begin your fundamental research of commodities, there are numerous reports that are compiled by government sources such as the USDA (United States Department of Agriculture) and the EIA (Energy Information Administration).

Two of the most important reports are explained in the next chapter. <u>In Appendix E you will find a list of all the main reports with the links where you can consult them.</u>

The aim of the analysis is to compare the current data with that of the previous weeks, months and year to understand how prices reacted under those conditions. The goal is to forecast the supply and demand scenario for the future.

In essence, what you want to do is look for trends in production and consumption and trade with that bias. For example, if a record number of acres of wheat have been planted for this season, it is likely that wheat futures will trade with a downward bias.

As mentioned, the factors that affect supply and demand are numerous and highly interrelated. Some of these factors include:

- Unique factors for a specific market. Some markets have factors that will affect supply and demand uniquely for that market and have little to no effect on another market.

For example, weather plays a very important role on the supply side of agricultural commodities, like soybeans, but may not be as relevant for markets like gold or crude oil where mining and drilling activities are less affected by the weather. The same, a swine epidemic will greatly affect the supply of hogs while it will have no effect on natural gas or coffee.

You will become familiar with the specific factors that impact their industry and keep track of these factors as you trade.

There are contributing factors in key times where Crops have during their growing cycle where weather can have a major effect on harvest yields; planting, growing, and harvesting. If the climate is too wet or too dry during these times, supply might be adversely affected. But if conditions are favourable through the entire cycle, yields might increase. In some years there might be excess supply, and, in some years, there might be low supply.

- Correlations with other markets. Supply and demand can also be connected; there are times when one futures contract might represent an input for another. The futures markets are interrelated, and this relationship can be calculated and analysed by the fundamental analyst.

Let's take corn for an example, it can be used as livestock feed and in the production of ethanol. A corn trader might look at the corn market and its relationship to cattle, as well as its relationship to ethanol.

Another example is crude oil and gasoline futures. Where the price of gasoline futures can be influenced by the supply and demand of gasoline and the price of the input commodity.

If you only focus on supply and demand for one market, you might miss an important effect from a related market.

- Interactions with the economy. Economic data, albeit to a lesser extent than financial futures, can also influence the demand for commodities. Just think of the inflation figure, which in this precise historical context (spring 2022) is the one most closely followed.

Traders should be aware of economic release dates and their related market impact, as not all data will always have the same impact. It is important to understand how the data fits into the current economic landscape and whether the market has determined that it is important or not.

All futures contracts will have an economic release that is specific to their sector.

Such as the USDA crop reports are specific to agricultural futures, and detail plating conditions, progression of growth and harvest results. They are updated through the agricultural season, and futures prices react to the data, moving up if forecast crop yields are down and moving down if crop yields are higher than expected.

Another unique report for agricultural traders is weather reports, as overly wet or dry conditions can impact crop yields and ultimately price.

- **Natural cycles**. Since many futures represent commodities that do not have a continuous, supply like corn, or commodities that are in higher demand at a certain time of the year, like heating oil, these seasonal patterns of supply and demand create natural cycles that influence the price of futures contracts.
  For example, crops are grown and harvested during specific months of the year, once harvested, supply will not increase until the next harvest.
  Fuel-related commodities, like heating oil, have a naturally higher demand at certain times of the year. During the winter months, heating oil has more demand because people use the fuel to heat their homes.

During the year, commodity prices can deviate from what we might consider an equilibrium based on supply and demand. This offers traders the opportunity to capitalise on this imbalance, if one can call it that, by riding the wave towards a return to what are theoretical equilibrium values.

No one, however, can know with certainty what the final value of the futures contract will be, what the spot market will be like at expiration, or what will it be tomorrow or next week. This uncertainty is what spread traders and commodity speculators try to take advantage of by trying to predict its effects.

The reality is despite the importance of fundamental analysis in commodity markets to successfully predict price movement, it remains a daunting task, and whether, corn or oil will move is another matter.

In Chapter 11, which discusses the C.O.T. report, you will see that several participants operate in the commodity market. One of these is Commercial. The Commercial are those who actually produce or use the commodities, tends to be based upon a more intimate knowledge of the supply and demand for the commodity than speculators would generally have access to.

Always remember that when you trade commodities, you are dealing with very large companies, which include not only the end users and producers of those commodities, but also large institutional investors, and these participants have much broader skills, knowledge and resources than individual traders to be able to perform fundamental analysis and use it to their advantage. I know this very well from working with a top Swiss investment company which counts several important companies among its clients.

You must also bear in mind that there is also the possibility that the current state of fundamental knowledge about the market has already been priced in or, more correctly, is about to be priced in. Since positions are built by large investors over time (and not in a day like those of traders), it is possible that what you know has already been incorporated into current commodity prices; however, positions may take days or weeks to be fully implemented.

If this was not the case, the opportunities for small individual traders would be much more limited. If large traders, whose outlook changes with new information, were to execute all their orders at once, commodity markets would be somewhat more efficient, but also much more volatile, where the gains would be far worse than if large orders were executed more patiently.

It is the smart money that drives all markets and their positions greatly influence prices, even though they choose wisely to trade more patiently, trying to minimise these effects.

Along the way, traders can try to profit from this situation. If these price adjustments happened all at once, without warning, this would not be possible. For example, if the price of a commodity is $8 and due to changes in fundamentals it should be priced at $5, in most cases this change will happen over a period of time, with entry and exit of positions.

In this way, small traders can try to take advantage of market fundamentals, not by trying to discover them, but instead by trying to discover when the market itself suggests a change in beliefs.

This strategy is similar to, but distinct from, purely technical analysis, in that it seeks to identify not the price trend, but rather when prices have a significant trend due to a large accumulation or distribution of contracts.

Therefore, it is important to keep up to date not only by reading reports but also news regarding the commodity you are interested in. How do you stay up to date? There are many sites on the Internet where you can find news about commodities. But you do not have to worry about doing research. In Appendix F, I have compiled a comprehensive list of sites you can use to stay up to date with the latest commodity news; these are the same sources I rely on in my own analyses.

In conclusion, each futures market will have its own supply and demand factors, a trader will want to determine the most important factors and carefully piece together the data to build their analysis and trading decisions.

As anticipated, in the next chapter you will see two of the most important commodity reports.

COMMODITY REPORTS

CHAPTER 10

In the commodity market, reports play a crucial role in helping you understand the status and trends of commodities in all their phases, from production to demand and supply. These reports can be published at different frequencies, weekly, monthly, quarterly, biannually, and annually, and each one provides key information that can directly influence trading decisions.

In Appendix E, you will find a comprehensive list of the main reports related to commodities; in this chapter, I want to explain two of the most important ones: the WASDE and the Weekly Petroleum Status Report.

WASDE

The WASDE, World Agricultural Supply and Demand Estimates, is a comprehensive report released by the USDA (United States Department of Agriculture) providing comprehensive forecasts about demand and supply on the crop (USA and world) and livestock (the USA only). The USDA releases the report around the 10th of each month.

On the first pages of the WASDE, you find a synthesis and textual report of all the information, results and numbers that you will see in detail at the heart of the report. The WASDE provides a complete assessment for each commodity by dividing estimates between demand (domestic use, exports and ending stocks) and supply (beginning stocks, imports and production).

WASDE also reports seasonal pricing for most commodities taken into account. Prices tie together demand and supply data and also indicate potential decisions on future plantations. Here is an example of the summary of the corn's report in July 2017.

"*COARSE GRAINS: This month's 2017/18 U.S. corn outlook is for larger supplies, greater feed and residual use, and higher ending stocks. Corn beginning stocks are raised 75 million bushels reflecting lower feed and residual use in 2016/17 based on indicated disappearance during the first three quarters of the marketing year in the June 30 Grain Stocks report. Corn production for 2017/18 is projected 190 million bushels higher based on increased planted and harvested areas from the June 30 Acreage report. The national average corn yield is unchanged at 170.7 bushels per acre.*

During June, harvested-area weighted precipitation for the major corn-producing states was below normal but did not represent an extreme deviation from average (See Westcott and Jewison, Weather Effects on Expected Corn and Soybean Yields, USDA-ERS, FDS-13g-01, July 2013). For much of the crop, the critical pollination period will be during middle and late July.

Projected feed and residual use for 2017/18 is raised 50 million bushels on a larger crop and lower expected prices. With other use categories unchanged, corn ending stocks are raised 215 million bushels from last month. Small revisions are made to historical trade and utilisation estimates based on the 13th-month trade data revisions from the Census Bureau. The season-average corn price received by producers has lowered 10 cents at the midpoint for a range of $2.90 to $3.70 per bushel with the larger carryout.

This month's 2017/18 foreign coarse grain outlook is for higher production, reduced trade and increased stocks relative to last month. EU corn production is down reflecting a lower projection for Spain, where heat and dryness during grain fill hurt yield prospects.

Historical revisions are made to Kenya's corn production estimates to better reflect statistics published by the government. Barley production is lowered for Argentina, the EU, and Ukraine, but raised for Turkey and Russia. For 2016/17, Argentina corn production is raised based on the latest information indicating a higher-than-expected level of the area.

CORN	2015/16	2016/17 Est.	2017/18 Proj. Jun	2017/18 Proj. Jul
	Million Acres			
Area Planted	88.0	94.0	90.0 *	90.9 *
Area Harvested	80.8	86.7	82.4 *	83.5 *
	Bushels			
Yield per Harvested Acre	168.4	174.6	170.7 *	170.7 *
	Million Bushels			
Beginning Stocks	1,731	1,737	2,295	2,370
Production	13,602	15,148	14,065	14,255
Imports	68	55	50	50
Supply, Total	15,401	16,940	16,410	16,675
Feed and Residual	5,113	5,425	5,425	5,475
Food, Seed & Industrial 2/	6,650	6,920	7,000	7,000
Ethanol & by-products 3/	5,224	5,450	5,500	5,500
Domestic, Total	11,763	12,345	12,425	12,475
Exports	1,901	2,225	1,875	1,875
Use, Total	13,664	14,570	14,300	14,350
Ending Stocks	1,737	2,370	2,110	2,325
Avg. Farm Price ($/bu) 4/	3.61	3.25 - 3.45	3.00 - 3.80	2.90 - 3.70

Figure 61 - Corn table from WASDE July 2017 (www.usda.gov)

Major global trade changes for 2017/18 include lower barley exports for Argentina and reduced corn exports for the EU and Tanzania. Foreign corn ending stocks are raised from last month, with the largest increases primarily for Vietnam, Mexico, and Argentina."

In the second part, usually from page 12, you can find the table with all the data relative to each crop. Now I will analyse the table of corn that you can see in Figure 61 above.

The purpose of the table above is to determine demand and supply. First, let's focus on the first column on the left where you find the following fields:

- Area Planted
- Area Harvested
- Yield per Harvested Acre
- Production.

These belong to the supply section.

- Feed & Residual
- Exports

These belong to the demand section.

In the other columns, you find the data for the different years of harvest. The second shows the data for the season 2015/16, and the third is the crop estimate for the season 2016/17. The fourth column relates to the data of the previous WASDE report (June), while the fifth contains the new data (July).

Now that you have seen how the table is built, you can focus on the study of the two sections I mentioned before: supply and demand.

As for the offer, the most important item is Production, that is, the amount of corn produced in a given year. The data is the result of this calculation:

Production = Area Harvested * Yield per Harvested Acre

I will give an example by considering the last column, i.e., the month of July 2017, for which:

Area Harvested = 83.5

Yield per Harvested Acre = 170.7

Production = 83.5 * 170.7 = 14,255 million bushels

The second important item is Beginning Stocks. For 2016/17 this figure is equal to Ending Stocks of the previous year (as you can see, they are both 1,737 million bushels) while for new harvests we talk about projection.

Beginning Stocks = Ending Stocks of the previous year

That is, for July:

Beginning Stocks = 2,370 million bushels (projection)

This means that if the estimate for the Ending Stocks changes, then the estimate for the Beginning Stocks of the following year will change as well.

The third and final item you need to consider about the offer is the Total Supply.

Total Supply is determined by the sum below:

Total Supply = Beginning Stocks + Production + Imports

So, always relating to July:

Total Supply = 2,370 + 14,255 + 50 = 16,675 million bushels

Going to the demand, the first item you take into account is the Use Total. To find the Use Total, you consider Domestic Use and Exports. They are calculated as follows:

Domestic Use = Feed & Residual + Food, Seed and Industrial

That in July was:

Domestic Use = 5,475 + 7,000 = 12,475 million bushels

Use Total = Domestic Use + Exports

Which, always in July, has been:

Use Total = 12,475 + 1,875 = 14,350 million bushels

An important item is the Ending Stocks, because they tell you how many millions of bushels of corn are left over at the end of each year, thus, as you have already seen with the Beginning Stocks, how many bushels of corn will be brought in the next year. Ending Stocks are calculated as below:

Ending Stocks = Total Supply – Use Total

In July the estimate is:

Ending Stocks = 16,675 – 14,350 = 2,325 million bushels

Many traders use this data to get other data, not present in the report, called the Stocks to Use Ratio. This data allows you to have an idea of the relationship between the Ending Stocks and the Use Total. In fact, it is calculated:

Stocks to Use Ratio = Ending Stocks / Use Total

Let's create an example by considering this time the third column, i.e., the year 2016/17, for which:

Ending Stocks = 2,325 million bushels

Use Total = 14,350 million bushels

So:

Stock to Use Ratio = 2,325 / 14,350 = 0.1620 that is 16.2%

And at t the end of the first column in table (Figure 61), is the Average Farm Price. It is a forecast of a price range based on the data you have seen above in the table. The price varies depending on the information in the WASDE report.

For example, if the production increases, supply will also increase whilst the price of corn will decrease, and vice versa. If the planting area increases, the price of corn will drop because you have a greater supply, and vice versa.

If the report shows less use of seed for livestock, the price of corn will fall due to falling demand, and vice versa. And so on, as an outcome of a normal relationship between demand and supply.

In conclusion, you can read the summary of each crop at the beginning of the report and have an idea of the variations of the data in the last month. For more details on the various items, however, you have to read the tables, as you have seen with corn.

Bear in mind, not all tables record the same data, cotton, for example, you will never find Feed and Residual, but the mechanism is the same, and contain the main items that are important for a complete analysis, similar to what you have seen with corn, are also vital in all other crops.

As for livestock, the tables are much simpler. There are only three: U.S. Quarterly Animal Product Production, U.S. Quarterly Prices for Animal Products, and U.S, Meats Supply and Use (here you find: Beginning Production, Imports, Total Supply, Exports, Ending Stocks, Use Total).

Weekly Petroleum Status Report

The [Weekly Petroleum Status Report](#) is a comprehensive and essential report released by the EIA ([US Energy Information Administration](#)), providing detailed information about the petroleum supply situation, framed within historical data and selected price trends. It covers key elements such as crude oil inventories, refinery operations, and production levels. The report is published every Wednesday at 9:30 a.m. (Central Time), offering timely insights into the energy market.

Later in the day, around 1:00 p.m., the [Highlights report](#) is released. This version includes a concise summary page that outlines what occurred over the past week regarding refinery activity, net imports, stock levels, products supplied, and the prices of crude oil and its derivatives. This summary allows traders and analysts to quickly assess the state of the petroleum market.

More specifically, in the upper half of the page, you have a summary like that below shown on the report released on July 26, 2017:

"U.S. crude oil refinery inputs averaged 17.3 million barrels per day during the week ending July 21, 2017, 166,000 barrels per day more than the previous week's average. Refineries operated at 94.3% of their operable capacity last week. Gasoline production increased last week, averaging 10.4 million barrels per day. Distillate fuel production increased last week, averaging over 5.1 million barrels per day.

U.S. crude oil imports averaged over 8.0 million barrels per day last week, up by 48,000 barrels per day from the previous week. Over the last four weeks, crude oil imports averaged over 7.8 million barrels per day, 4.2% below the same four-week period last year.

Total motor gasoline imports (including both finished gasoline and gasoline blending components) last week averaged 723,000 barrels per day. Distillate fuel imports averaged 130,000 barrels per day last week.

U.S. commercial crude oil inventories (excluding those in the Strategic Petroleum Reserve) decreased by 7.2 million barrels from the previous week. At 483.4 million barrels, U.S. crude oil inventories are in the upper half of the average range for this time of year.

Total motor gasoline inventories decreased by 1.0 million barrels last week, but are in the upper half of the average range. Both finished gasoline inventories and blending components inventories decreased last week. Distillate fuel inventories decreased by 1.9 million barrels last week but are near the upper limit of the average range for this time of year.

Propane/propylene inventories increased by 0.2 million barrels last week but are in the lower half of the average range. Total commercial petroleum inventories decreased by 9.4 million barrels last week.

Total products supplied over the last four-week period averaged about 21.2 million barrels per day, up by 4.6% from the same period last year. Over the last four weeks, motor gasoline product supplied averaged over 9.7 million barrels per day, down by 0.3% from the same period last year. Distillate fuel product supplied averaged over 4.2 million barrels per day over the last four weeks, up by 13.2% from the same period last year. Jet fuel product supplied is up 10.7% compared to the same four-week period last year.

The WTI price was $45.78 per barrel on July 21, 2017, $0.75 under last week's price but $2.37 over a year ago. The spot price for conventional gasoline in the New York Harbour was $1.569 per gallon, $0.004 more than last week's price and $0.238 higher than a year ago.

The spot price for ultra-low sulfur diesel fuel in the New York Harbour was $1.516 per gallon, $0.002 over last week's price and $0.185 above a year ago.

The national average retail regular gasoline price increased to $2.312 per gallon on July 24, 2017, $0.034 higher than last week's price and $0.130 more than a year ago. The national average retail diesel fuel price increased for the fourth week in a row to $2.507 per gallon, $0.016 per gallon over last week and $0.128 above a year ago."

In the lower half, instead, you will find tables providing a summary of the items discussed above (Figure 62). However, these tables do not display exactly the same data. In three of them, the figures reported cover the last four weeks ending, rather than just the last two reports. This means the data may differ slightly from what you have already read.

To get a complete and accurate understanding, it is essential to review the specific tables from which the data is drawn: Table 2 for *Refinery Activity*, Table 1 for *Stocks*, *Imports*, and *Products Supplied*, and Tables 10, 11, 12, and 14 for *Prices*. These tables offer a deeper, more detailed perspective on the numbers presented in the summary.

Refinery Activity (Thousand Barrels per Day)

	Four Weeks Ending		
	7/21/17	7/14/17	7/22/16
Crude Oil Input to Refineries	17,197	17,099	16,670
Refinery Capacity Utilization (Percent)	94.1	93.6	92.6
Motor Gasoline Production	10,331	10,316	10,089
Distillate Fuel Oil Production	5,131	5,160	4,977

See Table 2.

Stocks (Million Barrels)

	7/21/17	7/14/17	7/22/16[1]
Crude Oil (Excluding SPR)[2]	483.4	490.6	490.5
Motor Gasoline[3]	230.2	231.2	241.5
Distillate Fuel Oil[3]	149.6	151.4	152.0
All Other Oils	452.1	451.5	473.0
Crude Oil in SPR	678.9	678.9	695.1
Total	1,994.2	2,003.6	2,052.1

See Table 1.

Net Imports (Thousand Barrels per Day)

	Four Weeks Ending		
	7/21/17	7/14/17	7/22/16
Crude Oil	6,987	7,106	7,576
Petroleum Products	-2,552	-2,759	-1,575
Total	4,435	4,347	6,001

See Table 1.

Products Supplied (Thousand Barrels per Day)

	Four Weeks Ending		
	7/21/17	7/14/17	7/22/16
Motor Gasoline	9,726	9,655	9,752
Distillate Fuel Oil	4,223	4,136	3,729
All Other Products	7,214	6,961	6,757
Total	21,163	20,752	20,238

See Table 1.

Prices (Dollars per Gallon except as noted)

	7/21/17	7/14/17	7/22/16
World Crude Oil (Dollars per Barrel)	–	–	–
Spot Prices			
WTI Crude Oil - Cushing (Dollars per Barrel)	45.78	46.53	43.41
Conv. Regular Gasoline - NYH	1.569	1.565	1.331
No. 2 Heating Oil - NYH	1.411	1.417	1.231
Ultra-Low Sulfur Diesel Fuel - NYH	1.516	1.514	1.331
Propane - Mont Belvieu	0.659	0.643	0.473

	Retail Prices		
	7/24/17	7/17/17	7/25/16
Motor Gasoline - Regular	2.312	2.278	2.182
Motor Gasoline - Midgrade	2.582	2.551	2.434
Motor Gasoline - Premium	2.816	2.781	2.656
On-Highway Diesel Fuel	2.507	2.491	2.379

See Table 10,11,12,14.

Figure 62 - Tables from Highlights report (www.eia.gov)

You can download every complete table from the report page on the EIA website, for more analysis and comparison with the previous periods. You can see an example of this in table 2 regarding *U.S. Inputs and Production* (Figure 63).

The table below is more comprehensive with the additional possibility of comparing the current data with that of the last two years, but it also contains many items that you do not care about. Personally, unlike what I do with WASDE where I always take a look at the tables, here, however, I just read the highlights that give me a clear and immediate assessment of what happened in the last week.

Table 2. U.S. Inputs and Production by PAD District
(Thousand Barrels per Day, Except Where Noted)

Product / Region	Current Week 7/21/17	Last Week 7/14/17	Difference	Year Ago 7/22/16	Percent Change	2 Years Ago 7/24/15	Percent Change	Four-Week Averages 7/21/17	7/22/16	Percent Change
Refiner Inputs and Utilization										
Crude Oil Inputs	17,285	17,119	166	16,586	4.2	16,762	3.1	17,197	16,670	3.2
East Coast (PADD 1)	1,063	1,045	17	1,019	4.3	1,158	-8.2	1,083	1,084	-0.1
Midwest (PADD 2)	3,851	3,907	-57	3,713	3.7	3,782	1.8	3,881	3,717	4.4
Gulf Coast (PADD 3)	9,185	9,144	41	8,788	4.5	8,601	6.8	9,171	8,747	4.8
Rocky Mountain (PADD 4)	647	626	21	616	5.1	617	4.9	638	626	1.9
West Coast (PADD 5)	2,539	2,396	142	2,450	3.6	2,603	-2.5	2,424	2,496	-2.9
Gross Inputs	17,556	17,500	56	16,924	3.7	17,084	2.8	17,520	16,957	3.3
East Coast (PADD 1)	1,065	1,046	18	1,085	-1.9	1,200	-11.3	1,084	1,112	-2.5
Midwest (PADD 2)	3,853	3,909	-56	3,719	3.6	3,790	1.6	3,883	3,719	4.4
Gulf Coast (PADD 3)	9,297	9,353	-56	8,889	4.6	8,779	5.9	9,334	8,842	5.6
Rocky Mountain (PADD 4)	646	628	18	617	4.7	614	5.2	637	628	1.5
West Coast (PADD 5)	2,695	2,564	131	2,614	3.1	2,700	-0.2	2,582	2,656	-2.8
Operable Capacity[1]	18,621	18,621	0	18,320	1.6	17,962	3.7	18,621	18,317	1.7
East Coast (PADD 1)	1,256	1,256	0	1,278	-1.7	1,269	-1.0	1,256	1,278	-1.7
Midwest (PADD 2)	3,999	3,999	0	3,924	1.9	3,842	4.1	3,999	3,924	1.9
Gulf Coast (PADD 3)	9,742	9,742	0	9,515	2.4	9,271	5.1	9,742	9,514	2.4
Rocky Mountain (PADD 4)	692	692	0	680	1.8	647	7.0	692	678	2.1
West Coast (PADD 5)	2,933	2,933	0	2,924	0.3	2,933	0.0	2,933	2,924	0.3
Percent Utilization[2]	94.3	94.0	0.3	92.4	--	95.1	--	94.1	92.6	--
East Coast (PADD 1)	84.8	83.3	1.4	84.9	--	94.6	--	86.3	87.0	--
Midwest (PADD 2)	96.3	97.7	-1.4	94.8	--	98.7	--	97.1	94.8	--
Gulf Coast (PADD 3)	95.4	96.0	-0.6	93.4	--	94.7	--	95.8	92.9	--
Rocky Mountain (PADD 4)	93.4	90.8	2.6	90.8	--	95.0	--	92.1	92.6	--
West Coast (PADD 5)	91.9	87.4	4.5	89.4	--	92.1	--	88.0	90.8	--

Figure 63 - EIA report Table 2, U.S. Inputs and Production (www.eia.gov)

Reports such as the WASDE and the Weekly Petroleum Status Report play a crucial role because they offer a detailed and reliable overview of supply and demand, key elements for the functioning of any commodity market. In a market often influenced by unpredictable events such as weather, geopolitical, or economic conditions, these reports provide traders with essential data to interpret price movements.

But why are these reports so influential?

a) They provide up-to-date and comprehensive data: reports like the WASDE offer accurate projections on production, stocks, and consumption of major crops and agricultural products globally. The commodity market is particularly sensitive to even minor changes in these numbers, as a reduction in supply or an increase in demand can cause sharp price fluctuations. On the other hand, the Weekly Petroleum Status Report monitors weekly oil and derivative stocks in the United States, a crucial figure for predicting the price trend of crude oil, one of the most traded commodities in the world.

b) Transparency and reliability: since these reports are issued by government agencies like the USDA and the EIA, they are considered reliable and impartial sources. Markets react quickly to the data contained in these reports because they are seen as the most accurate available picture of the current and future market conditions.

c) Future insights: these reports do not only describe the current state of the market but also provide forecasts based on historical data and advanced economic models. This makes them particularly useful for traders, who can base their strategies not only on what is happening now but also on projections of how supply and demand will evolve in the coming months.

Now that you have understood the importance of these reports, how should you use them?

1. Interpretation of supply and demand: for every trader, understanding the balance between supply and demand is essential for predicting price movements. For example, an increase in oil inventories may indicate an oversupply, leading to a price drop. Conversely, a decrease in inventories may signal an imminent shortage and push prices higher. Traders use these signals to decide whether to enter or exit the market.

2. Reacting to real-time data: since these reports are released at specific and predictable times, professional traders are often ready to react immediately to the published data. An unexpected change in numbers can cause significant short-term price movements, creating trading opportunities for those who are prepared.

3. Historical analysis and comparison: these reports not only provide current data but also allow for comparisons with historical data to identify market trends and cycles. Traders can, for instance, compare this week's Weekly Petroleum Status Report with those of previous weeks to see if a bearish or bullish trend in oil inventories is developing.

In recent years, the evolution of economic, climatic, and geopolitical conditions has made the interpretation of these reports even more complex and important. Events such as the COVID-19 pandemic or the conflict in Ukraine have had drastic effects on commodity markets. During the pandemic, for example, global demand for oil plummeted, driving inventories to unprecedented levels.

Traders who closely monitored the weekly reports on inventory trends were able to quickly adjust their positions accordingly. WASDE wheat data has become particularly relevant during geopolitical crises that have affected agricultural exports. In times of uncertainty over trade routes in key regions, traders consult these reports not only to monitor production but also to understand the geopolitical implications and their impact on prices.

These two reports you have just seen are among the most important in the commodity world, and each time they are published, they have a strong impact on market prices. In the next chapter, you will delve into another fundamental report, the C.O.T., which provides valuable information on the sentiment of major traders and speculators in the commodity market.

THE C.O.T. REPORT

CHAPTER 11

One of the most important aspects concerning commodities is to see and know how the positions held by financial institutions (those who speculate in the market) and operators (those who work with a commodity and access the market for hedging purposes) are divided.

This is made possible by the Commodity Futures Trading Commission (CFTC) which every week (usually Friday) releases a report, the Commitments of Traders (COT). The report shows market data for the previous Tuesday, so it is slightly delayed, but this is not a big problem. The report shows, for each commodity, the long and short positions held by each market participant, as shown below:

- Producer/Merchant/Processor/User: an entity that predominantly engages in the production, processing, packing, or handling of a physical commodity and uses the futures markets to manage or hedge risks associated with those activities.

- Swap dealer: an entity that deals primarily in swaps for a commodity and uses the futures markets to manage or hedge the risk associated with those swaps transactions.

  The swap dealer's counterparties may be speculative traders, like hedge funds, or traditional commercial clients that are managing risk arising from their dealings in the physical commodity.

- Money manager: a registered commodity trading advisor (CTA); a registered commodity pool operator (CPO); or an unregistered fund identified by CFTC. These traders are engaged in managing and conducting organised futures trading on behalf of clients.

- Other reportables: every other reportable trader that is not placed into one of the other three above categories.

In the Figure 64, you can see the corn C.O.T. taken on 7 December 2021 for futures only in the short format. The CFTC also releases a long format and a version where it aggregates futures positions with options positions.

```
-----------------------------------------------------------------------------
Disaggregated Commitments of Traders- Options and Futures Combined Positions as of December 7, 2021
:                         Reportable Positions                    :
:---------------------------------------------------------------------------:
: Producer/Merchant :        :            :                       :
: Processor/User    : Swap Dealers :  Managed Money  : Other Reportables  :
: Long : Short : Long : Short :Spreading: Long : Short :Spreading: Long : Short :Spreading:
-----------------------------------------------------------------------------
CORN - CHICAGO BOARD OF TRADE  (CONTRACTS OF 5,000 BUSHELS)             :
CFTC Code #002602             Open Interest is 1,724,182            :
: Positions                                 :
: 413,381 1,048,382 294,322  26,227  27,272  358,318  25,817 138,307 107,335 39,757 215,155 :
:                                           :
: Changes from:   November 30, 2021                              :
: 17,163  45,989  -3,389  -987  2,143  6,726 -10,506  3,135  3,493  2,328  6,877 :
:                                           :
: Percent of Open Interest Represented by Each Category of Trader      :
:  24.0   60.8   17.1   1.5   1.6   20.8   1.5   8.0   6.2   2.3   12.5 :
:                                           :
: Number of Traders in Each Category        Total Traders: 829       :
:   323    417    29    8    24    112    20   72   80   90   102 :
-----------------------------------------------------------------------------
```

Figure 64 - Corn C.O.T. disaggregates report (cftc.gov)

Commodity	Number of contracts
Agricultural:	
Wheat	100
Corn	150
Oats	60
Soybeans	100
Soybean Oil	200
Soybean Meal	200
Cotton	50
Frozen Concentrated Orange Juice	50
Rough Rice	50
Live Cattle	100
Feeder Cattle	50
Lean Hogs	100
Sugar No. 11	400
Sugar No. 14	100
Cocoa	100
Coffee	50
Natural Resources:	
Copper	100
Gold	200
Silver Bullion	150
Platinum	50
No. 2 Heating Oil	250
Crude Oil, Sweet	350
Unleaded Gasoline	150
Natural Gas	175

Figure 65 - Reporting levels (cftc.gov)

All entities in the C.O.T., therefore, are required to report their positions if they exceed a certain number of contracts called the Reporting level (Figure 65 above). The Reporting level is set by the CFTC and is updated over time.

Small traders and investors do not have to declare their positions as they are very unlikely to exceed the Reporting levels.

Now, the breakdown of subjects that you have seen is what is known as disaggregated. There is also a 'version' that aggregates the four subjects into just two as follows:

Commercial = Producer/Merchant/Processor/User + Swap dealer

Non-Commercial = Money manager + Other reportables

- Commercial are the real experts. They know the real value (price) of raw material, the actual supply and demand, and any problems. They move against the trend, buying on the lows and selling on the highs.
- Non-Commercial or Large traders (banks, hedge funds, Commodity Trading Advisors, etc.); trend followers who use futures as speculative instruments for pure profit.
- Nonreportable Positions. They are small speculators who do not hold a position large enough to be reported to the CFTC. They tend to follow the Non-Commercial.

Below in Figure 66, you can see the same corn C.O.T. taken on 7 December 2021 seen above, but in the Legacy (aggregate) version.

```
CORN - CHICAGO BOARD OF TRADE              Code-002602
FUTURES ONLY POSITIONS AS OF 12/07/21        |
--------------------------------------------------| NONREPORTABLE
    NON-COMMERCIAL    |   COMMERCIAL   |  TOTAL   | POSITIONS
-------------------------|----------------|----------------|----------------
LONG | SHORT |SPREADS| LONG | SHORT | LONG | SHORT | LONG | SHORT
----------------------------------------------------------------------
(CONTRACTS OF 5,000 BUSHELS)           OPEN INTEREST:  1,430,401
COMMITMENTS
482,428  71,614  157,271  663,484  1031357  1303183  1260242  127,218  170,159

CHANGES FROM 11/30/21 (CHANGE IN OPEN INTEREST:   25,296)
 8,074  -7,828  -2,656  15,864  42,643  21,282  32,159  4,014  -6,863

PERCENT OF OPEN INTEREST FOR EACH CATEGORY OF TRADERS
  33.7   5.0   11.0   46.4   72.1   91.1   88.1   8.9   11.9

NUMBER OF TRADERS IN EACH CATEGORY (TOTAL TRADERS:   778)
   175    93   127   265   395   505   568
```

Figure 66 - Corn C.O.T. Legacy report (cftc.gov)

Let me now show you how to read and use the C.O.T.

- Regardless of the type of report used, the number of long and short contracts is shown for each category. In this way, you can immediately see whether operators tend to be bullish or bearish.

- **Spreading and Spreads** reports the number of contracts held in a spread. That is those positions balanced created with the purchase of a futures contract of a commodity and the associate sale of another futures contract on the same commodity but with different delivery (expiration). Therefore, it is easy to realise that the figure only reports Intramarket spreads (for those not familiar with spread trading, an Intramarket spread is created by buying and selling futures contracts of the same commodity, but with different deliveries).
- **Changes from** shows the change from the previous week's report.
- **Percent of Open Interest Represented by (FOR) Each Category of Trader** reports the percentage of open interest held by each category.
- **Number of Traders in Each Category** shows the number of traders in each category. A point of clarification is in order. Also, as reported by the CFTC, the number of traders in each category generally exceeds the actual number of traders in each category since spread traders may also be present in long and short positions.

The total open interest reported, since each long position corresponds to a short position, is obtained by adding up the long or short positions in each category, as you can see in the example above with the corn:

Open Interest Long = 482.428 + 157.271 + 663.484 + 127.218 = 1.430.401

Open Interest Short = 71.614 + 157.271 + 1.031.357 + 170.159 = 1.430.401

The same information can be found in the long format of the report, both Legacy and disaggregated.

As it stands, this information tells you little, it does not allow you to understand the real behaviour of the various market players. What you need to do is put the data on a chart and compare it with its price chart.

Fortunately, you do not have to do this yourself, there are sites and software that offer these charts for free. Personally, I use the SpreadCharts app which, apart from being free, I think is the best for analysing a spread.

To put things in perspective, how do we use this information in our trading? contrary to what people think, the C.O.T. is not something that gives signals to buy or sell, but only gives indications of the sentiment of the main market players, often anticipating trend reversals. Therefore, the C.O.T. must be interpreted and evaluated together with price trends and other important data.

Another important aspect, from my experience, is that C.O.T. is not of the same importance for all commodities. I only use it for grains and softs. I also use it for copper, as it is one of the non-ferrous metals that the investment company, I work with invests in it a lot, but for the other commodities, I tend to ignore it. It is useful to use it as confirmation with technical and fundamental analysis regardless of which C.O.T. group you trade whether gold or natural gas.

The best thing, as aforementioned, is to create a chart with the net positions of the two entities (Commercial and Non-Commercial). In Figure 67, you can see an example of the net positions on the daily chart of soybeans.

Figure 67 - Soybean daily chart with C.O.T. (Finviz.com)

The coloured lines below the chart are the net positions of each of the three categories in the market, and they are obtained simply by subtracting the short positions from the long ones.

Figure 68 - Corn daily chart with C.O.T. (Finviz.com)

As I said before, the change in net position over time is the real information you are looking for. It tells you how the funds and large investors are positioned. In fact, in Figure 68, most of the time an increase in the net position of Non-Commercial is matched by an increase in the price of the underlying asset.

In contrast, even though not highlighted, because of an increase in short positions by the Commercial, you can see how the price of the underlying rises and vice versa, as long positions increase, the price falls. This occurs because Commercial, who are typically hedging, often take positions opposite to market trends, influencing price movements indirectly. As their short positions increase, it reflects confidence in higher prices, and when their long positions grow, it signals an expectation of lower prices.

To complete this chapter, let me show you a couple of ways in which the C.O.T. gives me likely trend reversals.

Excessive buying/selling. In the commodity market, there are certain net position levels that, when exceeded, indicate an excess of long or short positions. These extreme levels reflect situations where speculators have pushed beyond normal values, creating a significant imbalance in the market. It is important to note that such excesses can persist for several months, continuing to drive the market in one direction without providing immediate signals of a reversal. Therefore, the fact that the net position is above or below certain levels does not necessarily mean that a reversal is imminent, but rather indicates that the market is in a condition of strong overbought or oversold territory.

In these situations, the crucial aspect to monitor is the return of the net position to more normal levels. Only when this occurs can there be a more concrete signal of a possible end to the trend. In other words, an excessive trend, whether it has moved too far up or down, requires a phase of consolidation before it is possible to consider opening new positions with a more manageable risk.

For further clarity, let me show you a practical example. In Figure 69, you can see the chart of the last 20 years of the coffee market. At the top of the chart, the C.O.T. (Commitments of Traders) is displayed, which highlights the net position of Speculators (also known as Non-Commercials and Large Traders), while at the bottom, you can see the continuous chart of coffee prices. I have drawn two horizontal lines: a blue one representing a support level (-20K) and a red one representing a resistance level (40K). From time to time, the net position falls below the support level or rises above the resistance level, indicating that speculators are strongly bearish or bullish.

In these circumstances, it is not advisable to open positions in an attempt to anticipate a trend reversal. Such an approach would be akin to trying to catch a moving train, exposing you to significant risk, as the market may continue in its current direction without showing signs of slowing down. The safest strategy is to wait for the net position to decrease and return to more normal levels, such as a value of -15K after falling below the support or 30K after rising above the resistance, before considering opening a trade. This cautious approach helps to mitigate risk and ensures that you are not caught in a prolonged trend before it begins to correct itself.

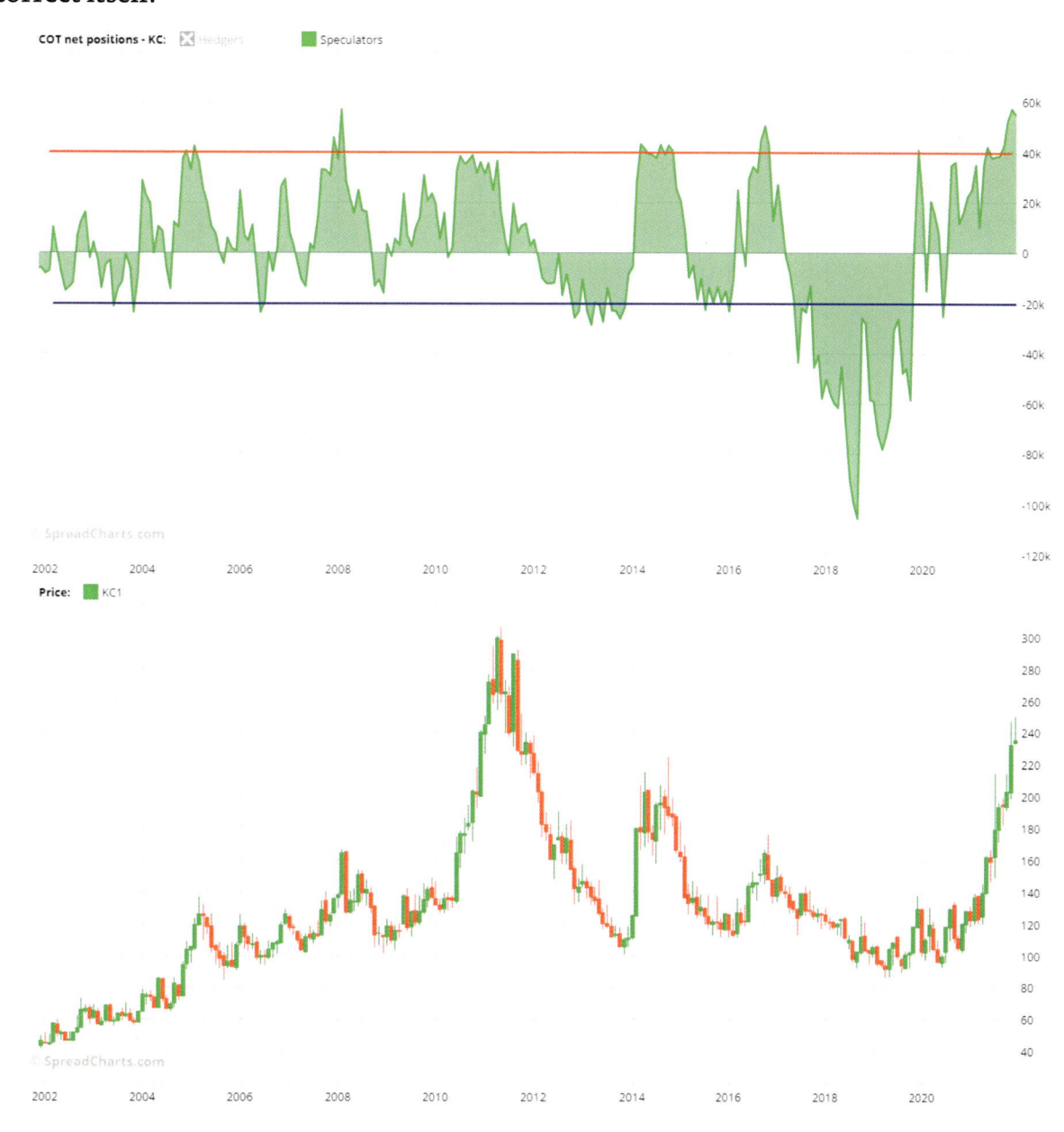

Figure 69 - Coffee chart with net position (SpreadCharts.com)

Looking at the chart, you can notice that every time the net position reaches or exceeds the upper line, the price hits a peak and then begins to decline. Similarly, when the net position falls below the support line, the price forms a bottom and follows an upward movement. This behaviour occurs in most cases, providing valuable signals about market sentiment.

However, it is crucial to remember that these levels vary depending on the commodity in question. For this reason, a key part of your analysis should focus on identifying the overbought or oversold levels specific to each commodity, so that you can quickly recognise phases of strong speculation. By doing so, you will always be able to monitor the situation and make decisions based on the sentiment of the Speculators.

Divergence. Another aspect that gives me a proof is the divergence between price and net position. It means that the strong hands are losing interest and that it is very likely that you will see a reversal of the price.

You can see an example below with soybeans (Figure 70).

Figure 70 - Soybeans chart with net position (SpreadCharts.com)

The price of soybeans in the bottom chart (green shaded area) continued to rise sharply while on the top chart (pink shaded area) the Speculators' net position decreased, this makes it very difficult to know when the trend started to reverse. In these cases, it is not possible to set rules, often, experience and knowledge of the commodity also the general market condition count for a lot.

84

The Commitments of Traders (C.O.T.) is, therefore, an important tool, but as you have seen, it should not be considered in isolation. I will tell you now that in my analysis, the C.O.T. is one of five key elements: neither more nor less important than the other four.

Its usefulness lies in interpreting net position data relative to the behaviour of Speculators and Commercials, with a focus on overbought or oversold levels, which signal speculative imbalances.

However, the C.O.T. does not provide direct trading signals, and its real strength emerges when it is integrated into the broader context of your analysis. For example, understanding the dynamics of supply and demand or the impact of macroeconomic events on commodity markets can either confirm or contradict the indications derived from the C.O.T. You are monitoring not only the sentiment of Speculators but also how they are positioning themselves in relation to general economic conditions and specific market circumstances.

The C.O.T. offers valuable insights into market sentiment, but it performs best when integrated into a comprehensive analysis that considers both the fundamentals of the commodity and macroeconomic factors. The most robust trading decisions are based on the ability to combine C.O.T. data with other variables, such as commodity fundamentals and global events that may influence its price.

FPD, FND and LTD

CHAPTER 12

FPD, FND, and LTD are three crucial acronyms that anyone working in the commodities market, not just traders, is well-acquainted with. Let's take a detailed look at what they signify:

- FPD, First Position Day, is the first day on which an investor holding a short position in a commodity futures contract can notify the clearinghouse of their intent to deliver the commodity. This day also serves as the final opportunity for trading that futures contract. After this date, all traders must close their positions, otherwise, their broker will do so on their behalf, which is generally advised against.
- FND, First Notice Day, is the first day the clearinghouse may notify an investor who is set to take physical delivery of a commodity purchased via futures. This step signals the approach of the contract's expiry and the delivery process.
- LTD, Last Trading Day, is the final day on which a futures contract can be traded or closed. After this date, the contract proceeds to physical delivery, or alternatively, cash settlement.

To make this clearer, let's use a practical example with the soybeans futures contract. The next expiry (as of today, 6 February 2017) is in March. The *First Position Day*, i.e., the last day to close a position in the March contract, is 27 February. The *First Notice Day* will fall on 28 February, while the *Last Trading Day*, marking the definitive expiration for all Commercials, is set for 15 March.

But what does all this mean in practice? Let's stick with the soybeans contract as our example. After the First Position Day, while speculative funds and smaller traders will likely have already shifted their attention to the next delivery (May), the Commercials, who have a direct relationship with the commodity, continue operating on the March contract, where physical delivery is still possible. Only after the Last Trading Day, i.e., from 15 March, will they also transition to the next delivery.

If you closely observe the various spreads, you will notice that historically, prices have often begun to make significant movements (both upwards and downwards) right around the Last Trading Day, typically around the middle of the month. To illustrate this, I will show you a few examples, starting with the ZSN7-ZSX7 soybean futures spread, as shown in Figure

71.

Soybean futures have expiration months in January (F), March (H), May (K), July (N), August (Q), September (U), and November (X). Look at what happens when the previous delivery concludes for Commercials, and they gradually shift towards the next expiry, significantly influencing the market's behaviour.

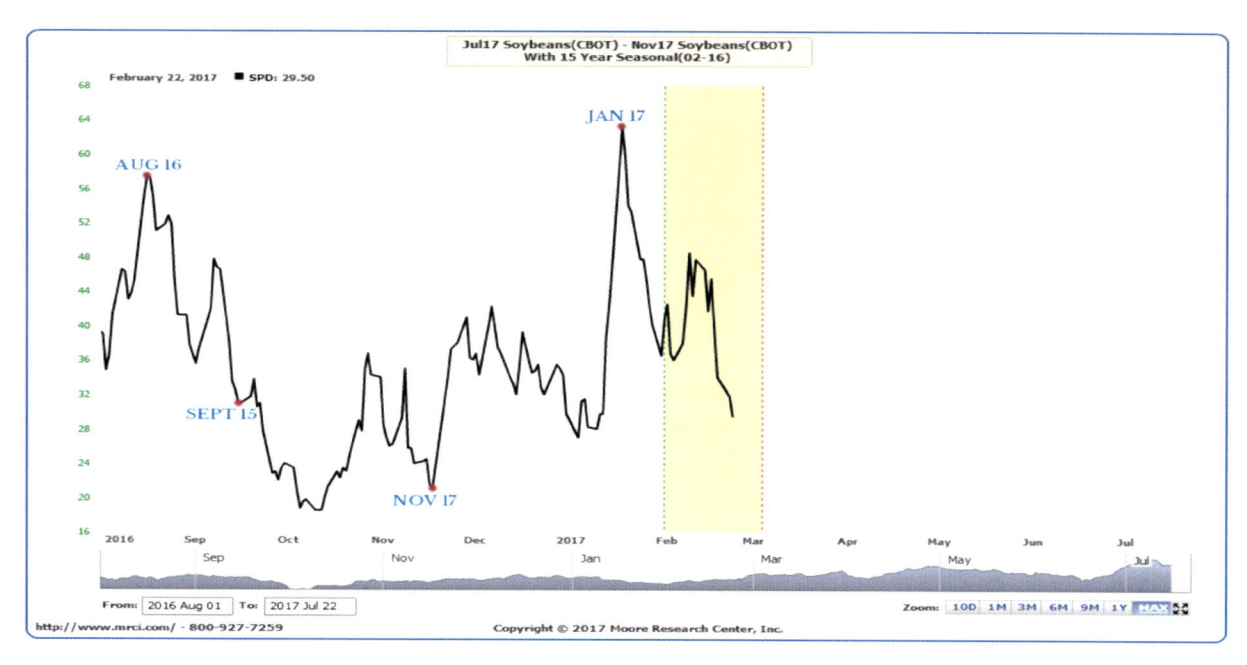

Figure 71 - ZSN7-ZSX7 chart (www.mrci.com)

The second example involves wheat, and here you can observe how, between the FND and LTD, the price tends to move in the opposite direction to that which it follows after the delivery period ends (Figure 72). This is primarily due to the Commercials, who begin gradually reducing their positions in preparation for the shift to the next delivery, while the Non-Commercials and Small Traders continue to trade actively, thereby creating temporary imbalances in the market. These movements, although temporary, can be significant and may mislead those unaware of the underlying dynamics at play during this period.

During this transitional phase, it is generally advisable not to open new positions in the two weeks between the FND and LTD. This is the time when Commercials begin to close or gradually roll their positions to the next delivery, which can result in unpredictable and often volatile movements in the spread. Rather than attempting to outguess the market during such an uncertain phase, it is far more prudent to wait until this process is completed, thereby minimising the risk of suffering unnecessary losses due to the heightened volatility that typically characterises this period.

Once the Commercials have completed their transition to the new delivery, the market usually stabilises, providing a more predictable and steadier environment for trading. By waiting for this moment, you are able to avoid sudden and erratic price swings, allowing you to operate with greater confidence, taking advantage of more stable and favourable market conditions.

Figure 72 - Wheat Future delivery March (www.mrci.com)

When will the Commercials shift to the next delivery? This transition will occur once the physical delivery is complete, and once again, the shift is clearly visible on the chart. This concept is not limited to soybeans; it applies universally to all commodities. Here are three additional examples you can observe below: lean hogs (Figure 73), coffee (Figure 74), and copper (Figure 75).

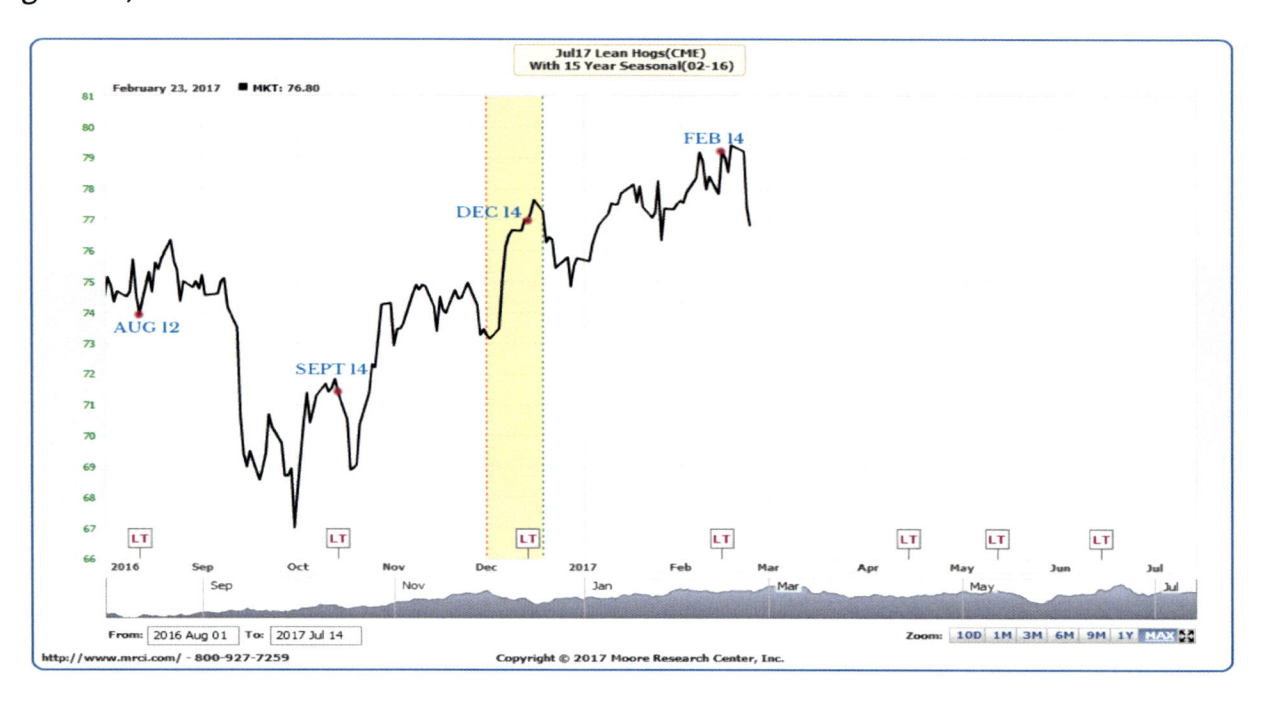

Figure 73 - Lean hogs delivery July 2017 (www.mrci.com)

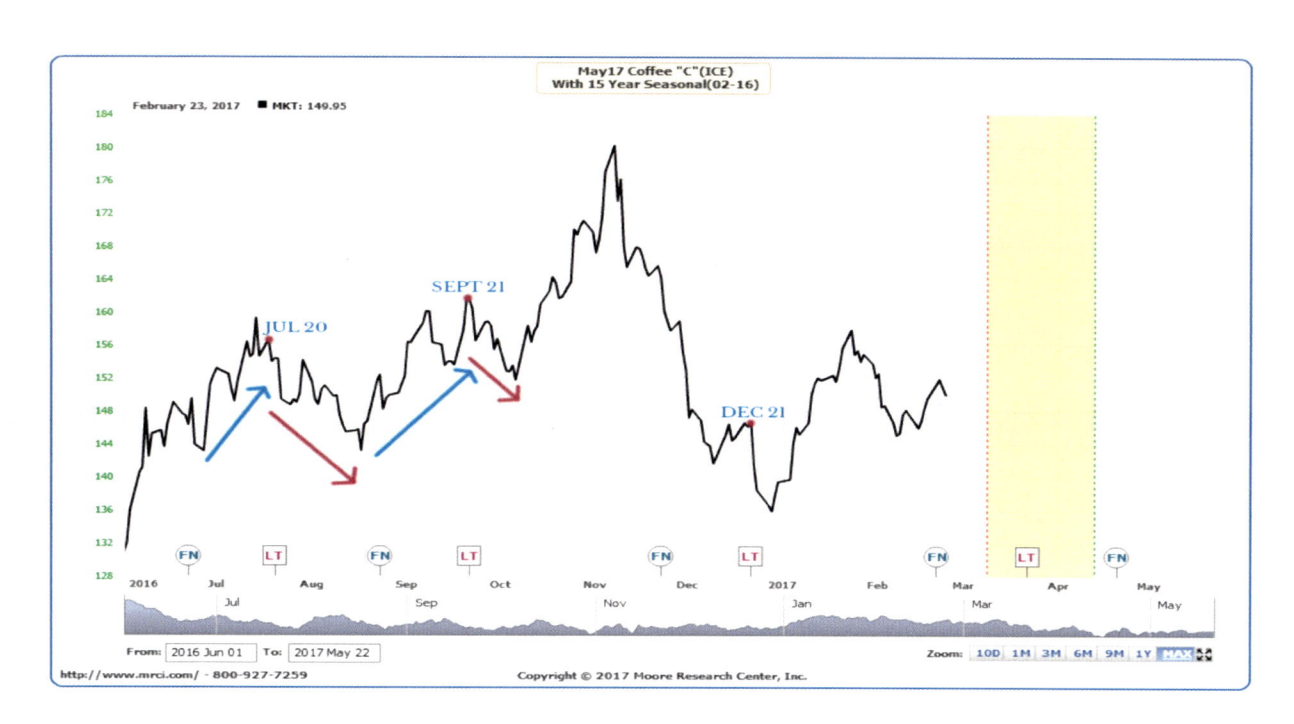

Figure 74 - Coffee delivery May 2017 (www.mrci.com)

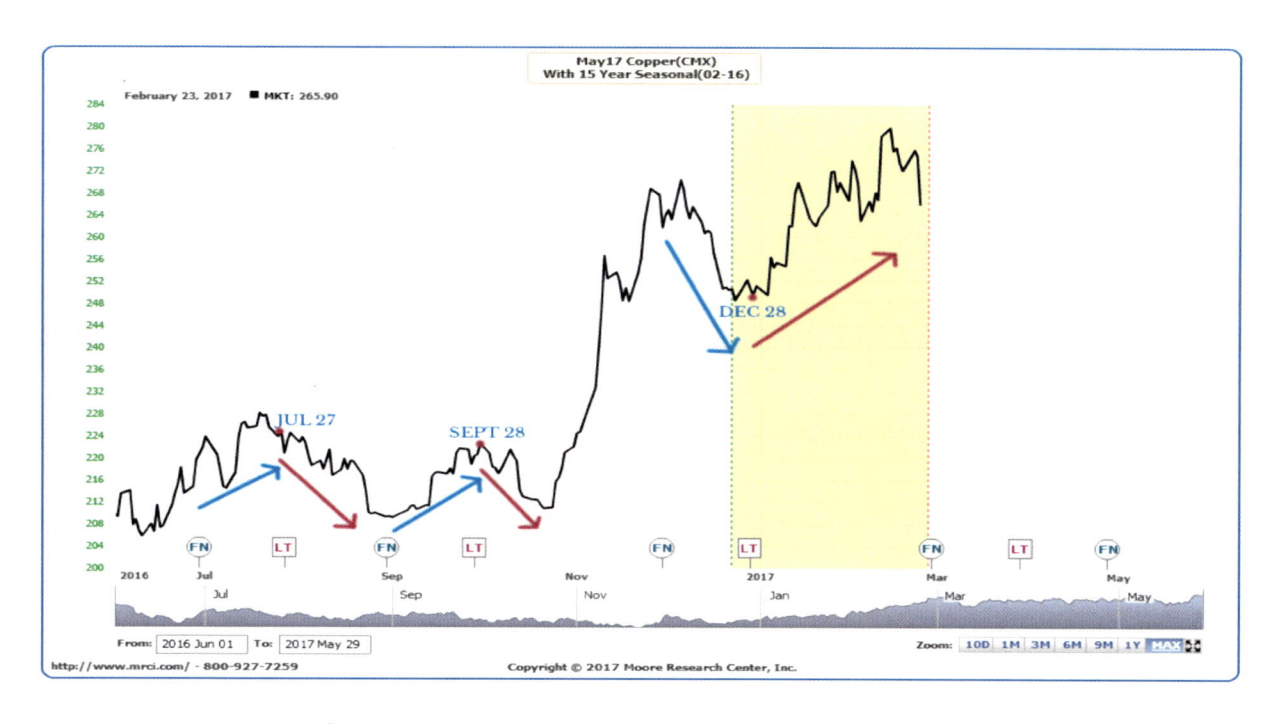

Figure 75 - Copper delivery May 2017 (www.mrci.com)

You can find the FND and LTD for all commodities in Appendix C at the end of the book.

When I discussed spread trading in the earlier chapters, listing its advantages, I added: "*Do not even think for a moment that spread trading is easy; there are several aspects you need to consider*". In the commodity market, numerous factors influence the price of an asset. It is essential to understand them thoroughly, especially since these dynamics are unique compared to other markets.

FPD, FND, and LTD are not just technical deadlines; they represent key moments that offer strategic opportunities. Around these dates, volatility often increases, as the Commercials close or shift their positions, causing significant price movements. An astute trader can take advantage of these movements by entering the market when changes in volume or price begin to emerge.

As these deadlines approach, spreads can also present opportunities. The fluctuations between the different expiration dates of futures contracts can create favourable moments to open positions on spreads. For example, after the Last Trading Day, when the Commercials complete their transition to the next expiration, the spread can stabilise, making market movements more predictable.

It is also essential to pay attention to volumes and market dynamics during these phases. If you notice an increase in volumes before these dates, it could indicate that the Commercials are starting to move, and this could be a useful signal to adjust your trading strategies.

If all of this has piqued your interest, the next chapter will tackle a less exciting but no less crucial topic: money management. For traders, money management is akin to mathematics for students: frequently underestimated, but absolutely fundamental to achieving success in trading.

Money Management

CHAPTER 13

~

Money management is the cornerstone of your investments and the focal point of all your trading activities. Despite its importance, few traders apply proper money management principles, which is why approximately 85% of traders end up losing their money.

Money management consists of two key aspects: *Position Size*, which determines the portion of your capital to allocate to each trade and how to distribute capital across various assets in your portfolio, and *Risk Management*, which deals with the risk associated with the positions you decide to take in the market.

First of all, you need to determine the percentage of your capital to use for each trade. For instance, if you have $10,000 in your account, you might decide to allocate 5%, or $500, to each trade. If a trade requires more than that amount (in percentage terms), simply do not take that trade, and instead, allocate your capital to something more suitable and in line with your money management rules.

Every trader who consistently makes profits over time adheres strictly to the rules of money management. It is crucial to decide from the outset how much of your capital to allocate to each trade, as your primary goal should always be the protection and preservation of your capital, maximising profits comes second.

POSITION SIZE	
$30,000 or less	5% equity
Between $30,000 and $50,000	4% equity
Between $50,000 and $100,000	3% equity
More than $100,000	1.5-2% equity

Table 1 - Position size

A famous Wall Street adage says: "*Cut your losses short and let your profits run*". What strikes me about this saying is that it first emphasises keeping losses small and only then reminds traders to let profits grow. Protecting your capital must always come first because losses are an inevitable part of trading. Anyone who claims never to have experienced a loss either has never traded or is not telling the truth.

If you can limit your losses and allow your profits to grow, you will almost certainly be profitable in the long term. To achieve this, you need a strategy, a solid plan of action. Even before opening a trade, you must know how much you are willing to lose so that you are not caught off guard by an adverse situation. The more aware you are of your potential losses, the more calmly and stress-free you can trade.

Trading should be treated as a business, something that can provide an income, but it should never become a burden or negatively impact your quality of life.

The most critical aspect of trading is risk control. To do this, you need a well-defined trading plan, and it is essential to always stick to it.

The first method to place a stop-loss. The best way to control risk is by using a proper stop-loss. However, stop-loss levels are not the same for every spread, as different spreads can vary greatly in margin requirements and volatility. A simple rule to calculate a proper stop-loss is as follows:

> Stop-loss = half of the margin, with a minimum of $200 and never exceeding 2.5% of the equity

This simple rule uses the margin as a measure because it already accounts for the risks involved in the trade. The higher the perceived risk by the broker, the larger the margin will be.

If 50% of the margin exceeds 2% of your capital, then you should avoid taking that trade. One of the fundamental principles of money management is to *never engage in trades you cannot afford*.

However, beyond the margin that is required by the broker, you can always decide what your risk is, which is also the maximum loss that you can accept. That is what most interests you relative to the margin of the entire operation.

Setting rules and limits is essential to ensure the long-term survival of your account and the potential to generate consistent income.

Especially if you are a beginner in spread trading, or you have limited funds in your trading account, this is the method that I recommend you use to establish stop-loss.

The second method to place stop-loss. A very important aspect to take into account when you decide where to put the stop-loss is the volatility of the spread. Volatility is a measurement of the change in the price of a market over time. The more a market is volatile, the more prices will change rapidly. Volatility is, therefore, more difficult to manage and control.

In spread trading, volatility is not always the same. In Intramarket spreads, volatility is usually lower than in Intermarket spreads. The same commodities have different volatility; some are more aggressive and volatile than others. Not only that but also the same commodity has greater or lesser volatility depending on the time of year.

Therefore, you should always consider volatility when you place a stop-loss which you can see in the last column in the table of a spread by Moore Research (*Worst Equity Amount*) or, also the last column in the table in the Backtest by SeasonAlgo (*Drawdown*).

For example, Moore recommends a protective stop for each futures contract and spread. A stop-loss based on the momentary losses of previous years. This may be a good level to put the stop-loss, but it is not always in line with your money management rules and, above all, with your trading capital.

The same reasoning can be applied to SeasonAlgo. You can decide the stop-loss based on past drawdowns. As mentioned above, this methodology is a good way to establish the stop-loss. However, it involves a big trading account (that not all traders have), that allows you to bear greater losses than the first method.

If the potential losses that occurred in the past are too high, it means that the spread has high intrinsic volatility. For example, if spread in the past, often incurred losses during the seasonal window (drawdown) of $ 800 or more, to use a stop-loss of $ 200 would make no sense. Rather, if it is not in line with your trading guidelines, or with your money management rules, you mustn't open that trade.

The third method to decide on the stop-loss. This last method is the one used by fund managers and investment banks. It has the advantage of cancelling your emotions (not a small thing), but it is not suitable for small accounts. This is the Value-at-Risk (VaR).

You will see it in detail in the next chapter.

In conclusion, the advantage of using stop loss is risk reduction. It is preferable to take a little loss and to close the trade when it goes against you. It is also important to be flexible with your trade ideas. If you make a mistake, and the market has not moved as you had analysed, you simply close the trade: end of the story.

I have seen people who refused to close a trade in the loss, sitting in front of a monitor hoping and praying, but this is not what trading is about. I did the same initially; it is part of the human character to reject losing.

Ideally, you should always define the maximum loss that you can afford. If the loss gets to that level and is no longer tolerable, or the risk becomes too high, you close the trade and accept the loss. This is probably the most difficult thing in trading, at least for me this has been the case.

Another aspect that is misunderstood by traders is when the stop-loss has not been hit and it's in positive territory, they don't take partial profit but rather wait. The price reverses and they've missed an opportunity. You should always make sure that the risk/reward ratio (R/R) is at least 1:1. That means if you place the stop-loss at $ 200 from your market entry, the take profit should be at least $ 200.

To establish the target profit, you have to use subjective probability (Chapter 22), just like with market entry.

It is always better to open a trade with more than one contract if your capital allows you to, even for better management of the position. This will enable you, for example, to close one or more contracts to the first target, and to move the stop to breakeven for the other contracts, with a second target.

To better manage risk, it is advisable not to open multiple correlated positions. Instead, you should opt for uncorrelated spreads, ideally across different sectors. For example, if you are long with a spread on corn, it would be better for you to avoid spread trading with corn (different deliveries) or wheat but, instead, you should trade with crude oil or gold (investment diversification).

If, however, you want to open more correlated trades, you need add up the respective risks. What does this mean? For example, if you decide to open two Intermarket trades, selling soybean meal futures and buying soybean oil futures but with different deliveries, the sum of the two stop-loss should not exceed 2% of your account. However, as mentioned, it would be preferable to avoid multiple correlated trades, especially within the same commodity sector.

To conclude this chapter, one of the questions that people ask me is: "*What is the minimum capital to trade spreads?*"

The answer is always the same: it depends. It depends on what kind of trades you want to open. With an account of lower than $ 10,000, you can make only those trades that require a low margin, in the order of $ 300-400. So generally, Intramarket spreads with grains and little more.

If you want to work with all the commodities, including metals, energy, and to do all the Intermarket spreads that the commodities market offers, this requires an account of at least $ 40,000-50,000.

Value-at-Risk (VaR)

CHAPTER 14

Value-at-Risk (VaR) is a statistical measure used to quantify the potential loss in value of an asset or portfolio over a specified period and within a given confidence interval. In simple terms, VaR tells you what the maximum expected loss on an asset might be over a given time horizon, with a certain level of probability.

For example, if the VaR on wheat is 8.30% over one week at a 95% confidence level, there is only a 5% chance that the value of wheat will fall by more than 8.30% in a given week. This does not mean that losses will be capped at that level, but rather that it is unlikely the losses will exceed this threshold within the specified time frame, barring extreme events.

Value-at-Risk is a fundamental tool used by commercial banks and investment banks to assess the potential loss in value of their portfolios due to adverse market movements. This measure enables financial institutions to compare the potential loss with available capital and liquidity reserves, helping them evaluate whether such losses can be absorbed without jeopardising the stability of the firm.

In my case, however, I use Value-at-Risk in a slightly different way: to determine more precisely where to set stop-loss levels in trading operations. This approach helps remove much of the uncertainty and emotional bias that often accompany the decision of where to place a stop-loss.

Suppose you decide to purchase a wheat futures contract at a price of $780.50. By applying an 8.30% stop-loss on the entry price (which would be set at $715.75), you are establishing that there is only a 5% chance that the price will fall to that level or beyond within a week. This data-driven method is far more reliable and less prone to error than a decision made 'on a hunch' or based solely on technical analysis. It allows you to manage risk in a more structured and rational way, removing much of the emotion from the decision-making process and ensuring greater consistency in trading.

There are three key elements of VaR:

1. a specified level of loss in value
2. a fixed time period over which risk is assessed (1 day, 1 week, etc.)
3. a confidence interval (usually 95% or 99%)

The VaR can be specified for an individual asset, a portfolio of assets or an entire firm, and the idea behind it is volatility, as you have seen previously.

Three basic approaches are used to compute Value-at-Risk, though there are numerous variations within each approach:

- Historical method: it represents the simplest way of estimating the Value-at-Risk for many assets and portfolios. In this approach, the VaR for a portfolio is estimated by creating a hypothetical time series of returns on that portfolio, obtained by running the portfolio through actual historical data and computing the changes that would have occurred in each period.
- Variance-Covariance method: it assumes that the daily price returns for a given position follow a normal distribution. From the distribution of daily returns calculated from daily price series, you estimate the standard deviation. The daily Value-at-Risk is simply a function of the standard deviation and the desired confidence level.
- Monte Carlo simulation: this approach is similar to the Historical method except for one big difference. The hypothetical data set used is generated by a statistical distribution rather than historical price levels. The assumption is that the selected distribution captures or reasonably approximates price behaviour of the assets or portfolios.

Which method should you use? The most stable results likely come from the historical method. This is because the approach is not constrained by the normal distribution assumption. The Variance-Covariance method is the most popular approach. However, it also faces the most criticism, given its assumption of normality.

Monte Carlo simulation may seem quite appealing, but in most simulators, the default distribution used is also normal. This essentially places the results in the same category and range as the Variance-Covariance method.

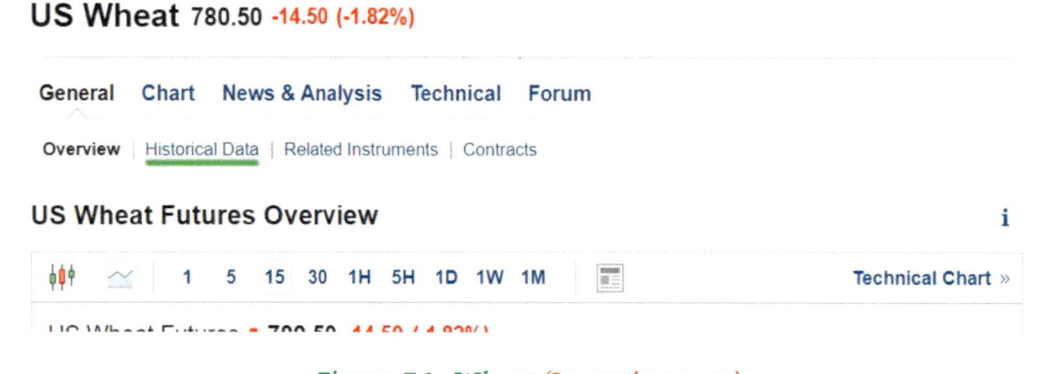

Figure 76 - Wheat (Investing.com)

All methods share a common foundation in the concept of assessing risk, but they differ significantly in how they actually calculate Value-at-Risk. Each approach uses different techniques and assumptions to estimate potential losses, reflecting the complexity of financial markets. However, there is a common issue across all these methods: they assume that past market behaviour is a reliable indicator of future performance. This assumption can be limiting, especially in highly volatile scenarios or during unexpected events.

Now it's time to see how to practically calculate Value-at-Risk and use it to set the stop-loss level. To simplify the process, I will use the historical method. First, I go to the Investing.com website and search for the commodity I am interested in. In this example, I will use wheat (Figure 76).

After opening the page dedicated to the chosen commodity, in this case wheat, I need to click on the Historical Data section. This will take me to a new page displaying the historical data for wheat, as shown in Figure 77.

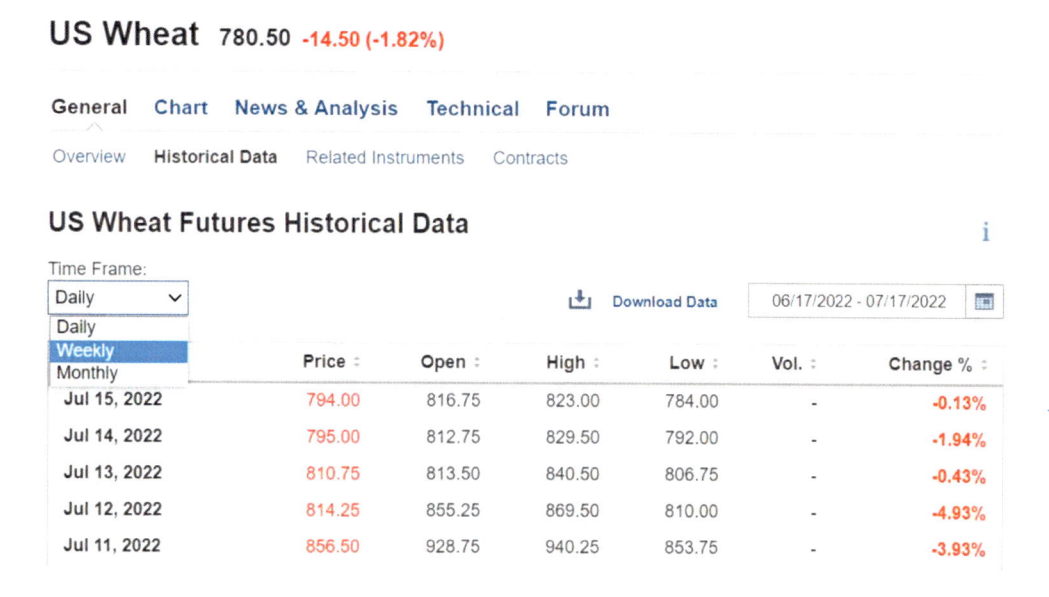

Figure 77 - Wheat Historical Data (Investing.com)

On the next page, on the left I select Time Frame, Weekly, and on the right, I choose the period of time, which must cover at least the last five years. Then, you click on Download Data.

Now I need to open the .csv file with Excel. The only data I need is the Close, so I can delete everything else (Figure 78).

The first thing I do is calculate the absolute value of the Performance for each week. The formula is simple: I need to subtract each closing price from the one immediately below it and divide the result by the second of the two values. For the spreadsheet above, the formula for the first Performance is as follows:

$$=ABS((B3-B4)/B4)$$

In reality, the absolute performance should not be calculated, this is my modification, but rather, depending on the type of trade, you should select the negative values (for a long position) or the positive ones (for a short position).

	A	B
1	Date	Close
2		
3	Jul 10, 2022	794.00
4	Jul 03, 2022	891.50
5	Jun 26, 2022	846.00
6	Jun 19, 2022	923.75
7	Jun 12, 2022	1,034.25
8	Jun 05, 2022	1,070.75
9	May 29, 2022	1,040.00
10	May 22, 2022	1,157.50
11	May 15, 2022	1,168.75
12	May 08, 2022	1,177.50
13	May 01, 2022	1,109.50
14	Apr 24, 2022	1,055.25
15	Apr 17, 2022	1,065.50
16	Apr 10, 2022	1,096.50
17	Apr 03, 2022	1,051.50

Figure 78 - Wheat weekly Close

I need to calculate the return for each close. Therefore, it is enough to copy and paste the first formula into all the other cells, as shown in Figure 79.

	A	B	C
1	Date	Close	Performance
2			
3	Jul 10, 2022	794.00	0,109366237
4	Jul 03, 2022	891.50	0,053782506
5	Jun 26, 2022	846.00	0,084167794
6	Jun 19, 2022	923.75	0,106840706
7	Jun 12, 2022	1,034.25	0,034088256
8	Jun 05, 2022	1,070.75	0,029567308
9	May 29, 2022	1,040.00	0,101511879
10	May 22, 2022	1,157.50	0,009625668
11	May 15, 2022	1,168.75	0,007430998
12	May 08, 2022	1,177.50	0,061288869
13	May 01, 2022	1,109.50	0,051409619
14	Apr 24, 2022	1,055.25	0,009619897
15	Apr 17, 2022	1,065.50	0,028271774
16	Apr 10, 2022	1,096.50	0,042796006
17	Apr 03, 2022	1,051.50	0,068054850

Figure 79 - Wheat weekly Performance

Now, I need to arrange the 'Performance' column in descending order. However, this is not possible since the column consists of numbers resulting from a formula. So, I must copy the 'Performance' column, and after right-clicking in the next column, under Paste Special, I choose Values. Now, I can sort it from the largest value (first) to the smallest value (last). In column D, you can see the Descending Performance.

Additionally, in the adjacent column E (No.), I number the Descending Performance starting from 1 (1, 2, 3, 4, etc.) up to the second-to-last value (the last one, being '#DIV/0!', is not valid data). You can see the result of these two steps in Figure 80.

	A	B	C	D	E
1	Date	Close	Performance	Perf. Descending	No.
2					
3	Jul 10, 2022	794.00	0,109366237	0,599051008	1
4	Jul 03, 2022	891.50	0,053782506	0,191394659	2
5	Jun 26, 2022	846.00	0,084167794	0,12921074	3
6	Jun 19, 2022	923.75	0,106840706	0,109366237	4
7	Jun 12, 2022	1,034.25	0,034088256	0,106840706	5
8	Jun 05, 2022	1,070.75	0,029567308	0,106826945	6
9	May 29, 2022	1,040.00	0,101511879	0,103982301	7
10	May 22, 2022	1,157.50	0,009625668	0,101511879	8
11	May 15, 2022	1,168.75	0,007430998	0,099445015	9
12	May 08, 2022	1,177.50	0,061288869	0,091911765	10
13	May 01, 2022	1,109.50	0,051409619	0,091286112	11
14	Apr 24, 2022	1,055.25	0,009619897	0,084167794	12
15	Apr 17, 2022	1,065.50	0,028271774	0,083035714	13
16	Apr 10, 2022	1,096.50	0,042796006	0,072214941	14
17	Apr 03, 2022	1,051.50	0,068054850	0,072031793	15

Figure 80 - Wheat Performance Descending and Position

At this point, I have all the data to calculate the Value-at-Risk. I leave a blank column to create some space. At the top, I enter the total number of data points, which is the last number in column E (Figure 81).

258	Aug 20, 2017	410.00	0,015015015	0,000681849	256
259	Aug 13, 2017	416.25	0,052361981	0,000478011	257
260	Aug 06, 2017	439.25	0,034615385	0	258
261	Jul 30, 2017	455.00	0,054545455	0	259
262	Jul 23, 2017	481.25	#DIV/0!		

Figure 81 - Wheat last position number

Now I calculate the VaR (95%). First, I need to use the following formula to find the VaR position (95%):

$$= (1-95\%)*G3$$

Where G3 is the cell number where I entered the total number of data points (you will use the cell you've chosen). You can see the result in Figure 82.

D	E	F	G	H	I
Perf. Descending	No.				
0,599051008	1		259		
0,191394659	2				
0,12921074	3		VaR(95%)		13
0,109366237	4				
0,106840706	5				
0,106826945	6				
0,103982301	7				
0,101511879	8				
0,099445015	9				
0,091911765	10				
0,091286112	11				
0,084167794	12				
0,083035714	13				
0,072214941	14				
0,072031793	15				

Figure 82 - Wheat VaR(95%)

The one-week VaR (95%) for wheat is found at position number 13 in the Descending Performance column, which is 0.083035714, or 8.30% in percentage terms.

To conclude, I will also mention that besides VaR, there is also CVaR. The Conditional Value at Risk (CVaR) is an extended measure of risk (from the Value at Risk) and quantifies the average loss over a given time period from unlikely scenarios that exceed the confidence level.

In this example, the one-week CVaR (95%) for wheat is 14.66%, meaning the expected loss from the worst-case scenarios (the remaining 5%) over the course of one week is 14.66%. This is a very high percentage because, with the outbreak of the war in Ukraine, wheat exports were halted, causing the price to rise by nearly 50% in just one week, which affected the calculation of the CVaR (and the VaR as well). The Conditional Value at Risk is also known as Expected Shortfall.

VaR provides a range of potential losses, while CVaR gives an average of those losses. CVaR is generally considered a better approximation of potential losses.

The calculation is very simple. I need to divide 1 by the position number I found in the VaR calculation (in the example above, '13') and then multiply the result by the sum of the first 13 returns (again, based on the example) in the Descending Performance column.

The formula for the Excel sheet shown above is as follows:

=(1/I5) *SUM(D3:D15)

Below, you can see the result (Figure 83).

	A	B	C	D	E	F	G	H	I
1	Date	Close	Performance	Perf. Descending	No.				
2									
3	Jul 10, 2022	794.00	0,109366237	0,599051008	1		259		
4	Jul 03, 2022	891.50	0,053782506	0,191394659	2				
5	Jun 26, 2022	846.00	0,084167794	0,12921074	3		VaR(95%)	8,30%	13
6	Jun 19, 2022	923.75	0,106840706	0,109366237	4		CVaR(95%)	14,66%	
7	Jun 12, 2022	1,034.25	0,034088256	0,106840706	5				

Figure 83 - Wheat, VaR and CVaR

You have now seen how to calculate and use VaR or CVaR to set a stop-loss in a clearer and more precise way. By applying these tools, not only will you have a stop-loss level with a low probability of being reached, but you will also have eliminated much of the doubt and emotions that often negatively influence trading decisions. This approach allows you to operate with the same rigorous methodology as investment bank fund managers.

This applies to any futures. As for spreads, the mechanism is the same; however, you cannot download historical data from the internet (at least, I do not know of any sites that allow it). You have to do it manually. It requires a bit more work, but it is worth the effort.

In conclusion, using Value-at-Risk (VaR) and Conditional Value-at-Risk (CVaR) as risk management tools is essential for any trader who wants to operate in a structured and strategic way. These tools offer a quantitative and rational approach to risk assessment, allowing for precise identification of potential loss levels and setting stop-losses in a scientific, rather than emotional, manner.

By adopting VaR and CVaR in your trading, you can reduce the influence of emotions, often responsible for impulsive and harmful decisions, and build a solid and replicable risk management strategy. This approach improves the consistency of operations and increases the likelihood of long-term success, ensuring that your capital is protected even in times of high volatility or adverse market scenarios. Ultimately, VaR and CVaR are not just mathematical tools but true allies in successfully navigating the complex world of trading.

THE TERM STRUCTURE

CHAPTER 15

∼

You have already seen that one of the most fascinating and intriguing aspects of commodities is their seasonality, which offers recurring cycles on which many strategies can be based. These cycles often provide a reliable foundation for traders to predict price movements and structure their trades. However, there may be periods, sometimes even prolonged ones, during which the trend of a commodity undergoes unexpected and significant changes. During these times, the usual seasonal cycles that typically influence prices are ignored, causing a disruption in the traditional seasonal patterns, making it harder for traders to rely on past trends.

The reasons behind these scenarios can be varied and complex. For example, an excessive strengthening of the US dollar, particularly adverse weather conditions, or sudden imbalances between supply and demand can all play a role in distorting the usual market behaviour.

Even commodities with a strongly marked seasonality, such as grains, can be negatively affected, meaning you may find yourself in situations where it is difficult to open trades for an extended period. When a market moves counter to its seasonality, it is common for correlated markets to follow this same anomalous trend, further complicating the trading landscape.

In the financial world, however, crises or difficulties can often turn into opportunities. Even when a spread seems less attractive or profitable due to these disruptions, there may be moments when interesting opportunities arise, especially for those who know where to look and can identify emerging patterns.

Before delving into trading strategies, particularly those involving multi-leg spreads (which will be covered in Chapter 16), it is important to take the time to thoroughly understand the term structure of futures. This deeper understanding will provide you with the analytical tools to evaluate not only a specific spread but also the broader commodity sector, allowing you to better navigate its seasonal factors and other key dynamics.

The term structure refers to the yield curve of contracts with different delivery dates. Futures are available with different maturities for each underlying asset, and each contract is traded at a distinct price, reflecting varying expectations regarding the future price of the underlying asset. This structure can reveal important insights into market expectations and help traders refine their strategies.

To better clarify the concept, you can see a practical example with the term structure chart of corn shown in Figure 84.

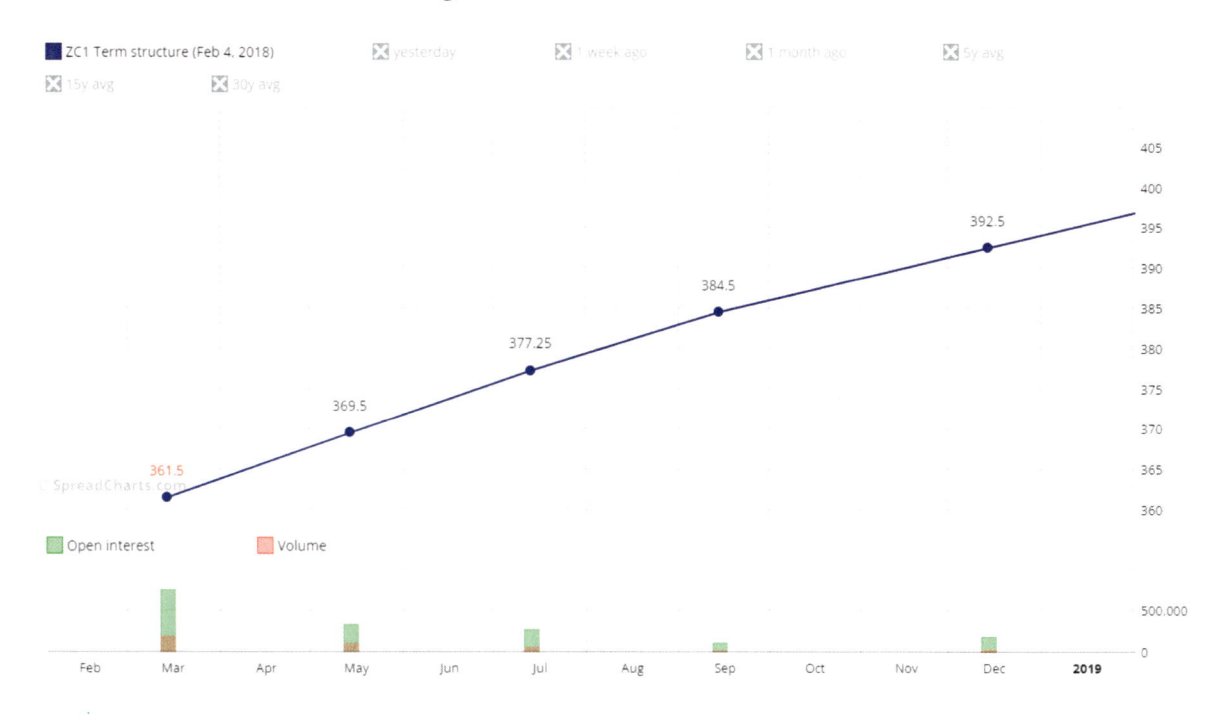

Figure 84 - Corn futures term structure (SpreadCharts.com)

Overall, the returns form what is commonly referred to as the 'term structure'. This yield curve often reveals crucial information that can significantly influence a trader's decisions. By analysing the shape of the curve, important insights can be gained regarding the future dynamics of the market.

The curve generated by the term structure of a commodity can take on various shapes. Since futures returns reflect expectations about the future prices of the underlying asset, the shape of the curve provides useful information about the supply and demand for the commodity and helps you assess whether investing in that particular commodity is advantageous.

When the term structure shows an increase in prices as the more distant deliveries approach, an upward-sloping curve is formed, known as 'Contango'. This is the most common configuration for the term structure, as returns tend to rise in line with the increasing prices of the commodity when looking towards future deliveries.

In the chart in Figure 85, you can observe an example of a contango term structure for the coffee futures contract. A structure of this type suggests to investors a generally positive outlook for the market. There are no significant signs of imbalance between supply and demand for the traded commodity, and it often reflects expectations of inflation in the coming months. This context can encourage investors and traders to maintain an optimistic view of the market's long-term trajectory.

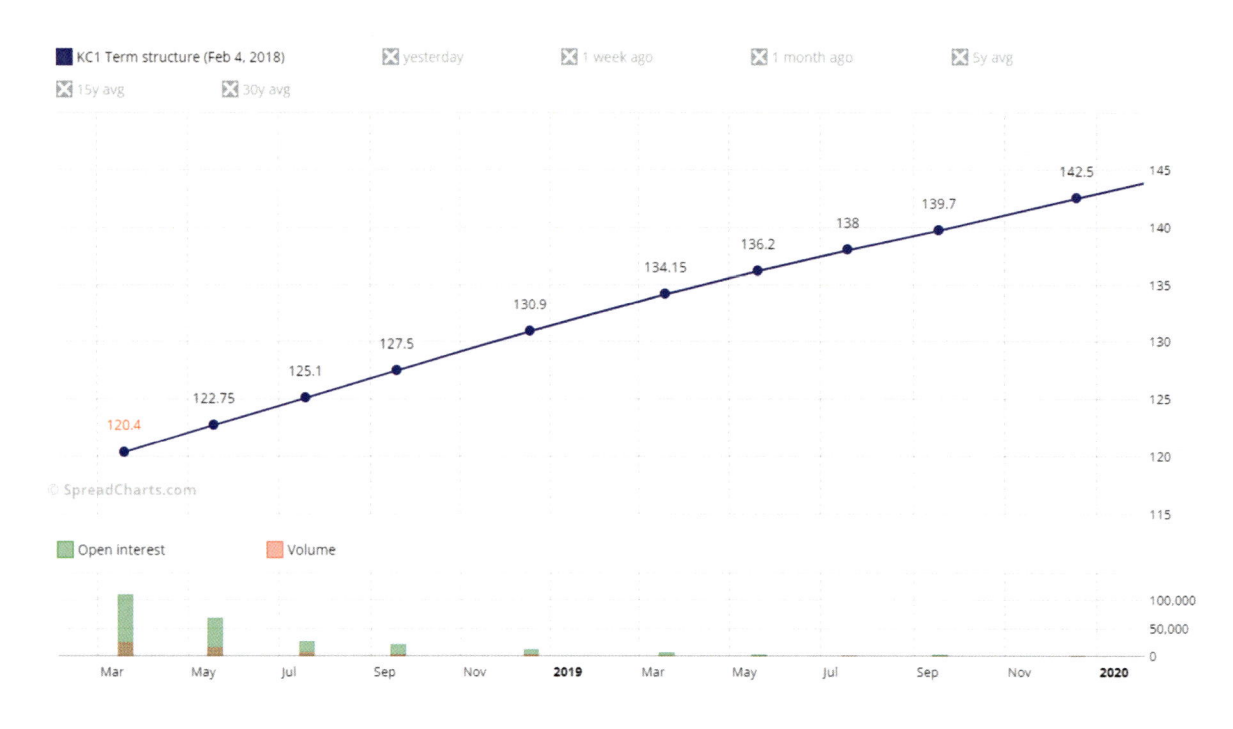

Figure 85 - Coffee futures term structure in Contango (SpreadCharts.com)

The futures term structure that sees the price drop concurrently with a longer delivery generates a negative curve known as 'Backwardation'.

Most of the time, Backwardation is linked to financial futures such as the index S&P500 because these contracts are not based on physical commodities, whereby stored, and delivered later. You can see an example in Figure 86 above with the T-Note 10-year futures term structure chart.

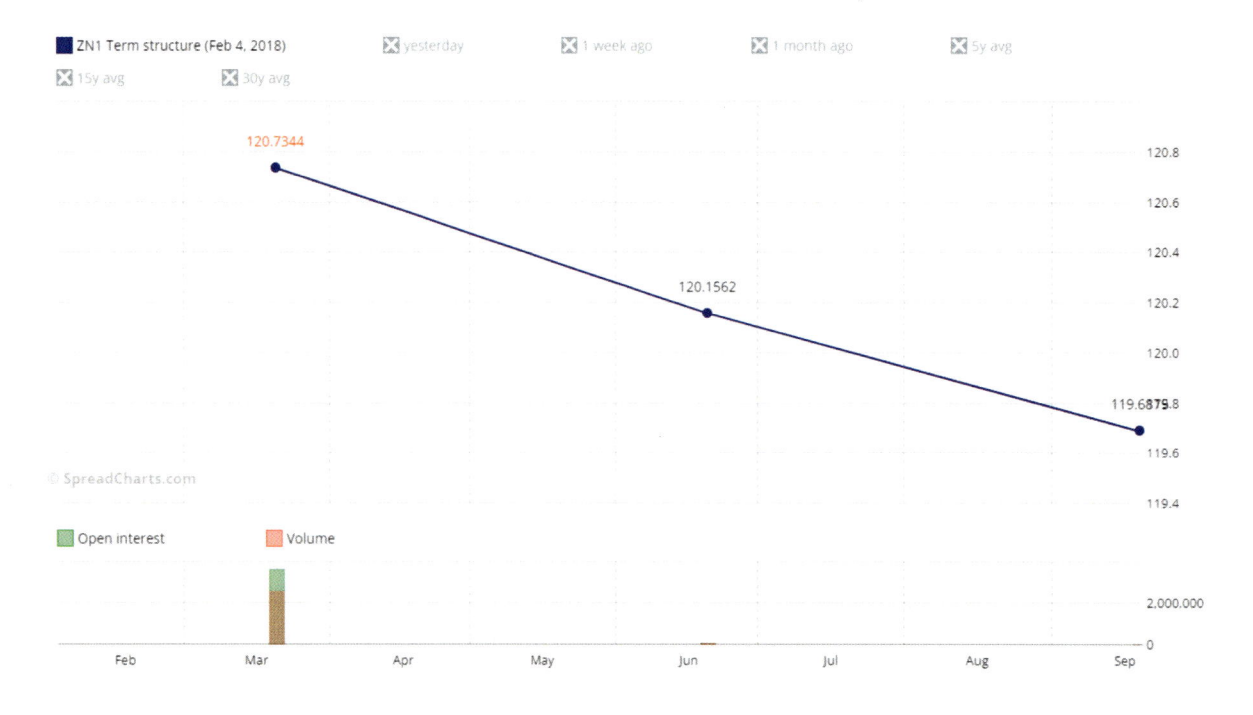

Figure 86 - T-Note 10-year futures term structure in Backwardation (SpreadCharts.com)

The angle of curvature of the term structure gives the investor an indication concerning the moments in which violent swings in prices of the underlying are foreseen. In general, the steeper the trend of the curve, regardless of which market is being analysed, the more volatility is anticipated in the following months. Sometimes these curves, both steep and flat, are influenced by seasonality.

Not only this, but futures close to delivery also have higher oscillations than those further away. Consequently, the trend of the curve seems to be determined by their residual life, as it generates these variations of yield.

Going back to Backwardation, it can also occur for futures in commodities for short periods of strong imbalance between supply and demand. In fact, some commodities seasonally fluctuate between Contango and Backwardation.

After figuring out how the futures term structure works, especially of the commodities, let's understand how to transform this knowledge into practice and how to gain a profit.

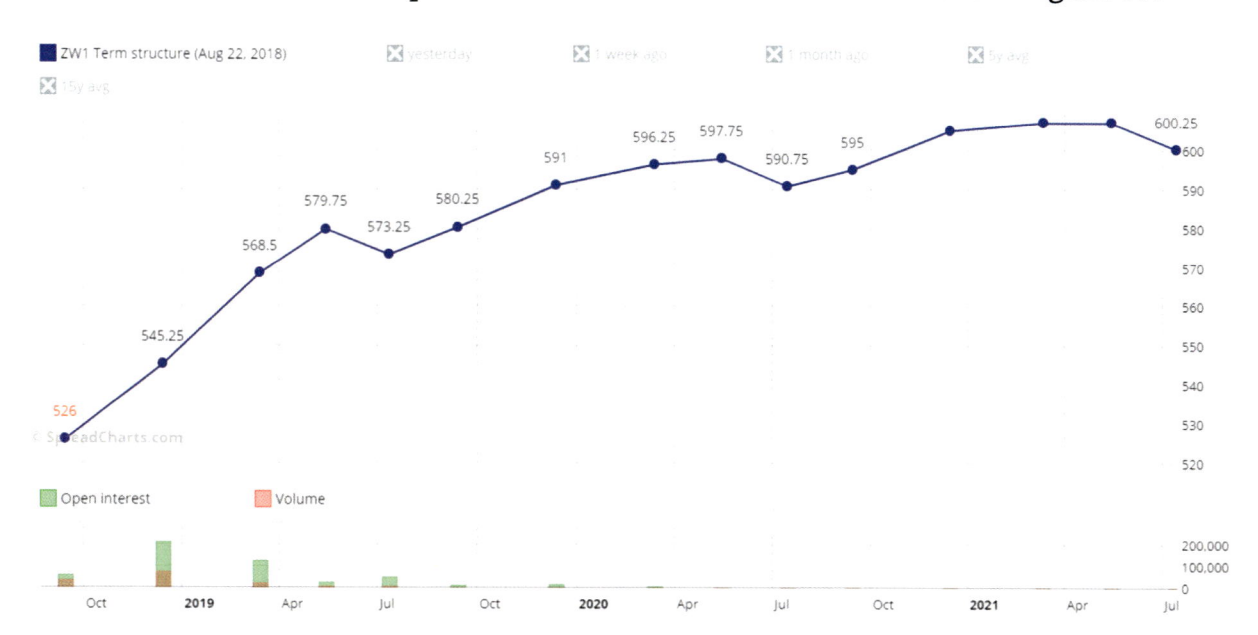

Let's see an example with the wheat futures term structure in Figure 87.

Figure 87 - Wheat futures term structure (SpreadCharts.com)

What immediately stands out is that every year the July delivery is in backwardation compared to the May delivery, meaning that the price of the futures expiring in July is lower than those expiring in May. This phenomenon is linked to supply dynamics, which reach their lowest point before the harvest. In May, when stocks are low, prices tend to be higher. As the harvest approaches, beginning in late June and continuing through July, prices decrease in anticipation of the new crop entering the market, as occurs each year, significantly increasing supply.

This behaviour is not limited to agricultural commodities. In other sectors of the commodity market, the term structure follows similar patterns. Production cycles, seasonal factors, or supply and demand dynamics can influence the futures curve, causing price movements across different expiries. The backwardation observed in these markets often reflects a response to seasonal or cyclical variations that impact the balance between supply and demand.

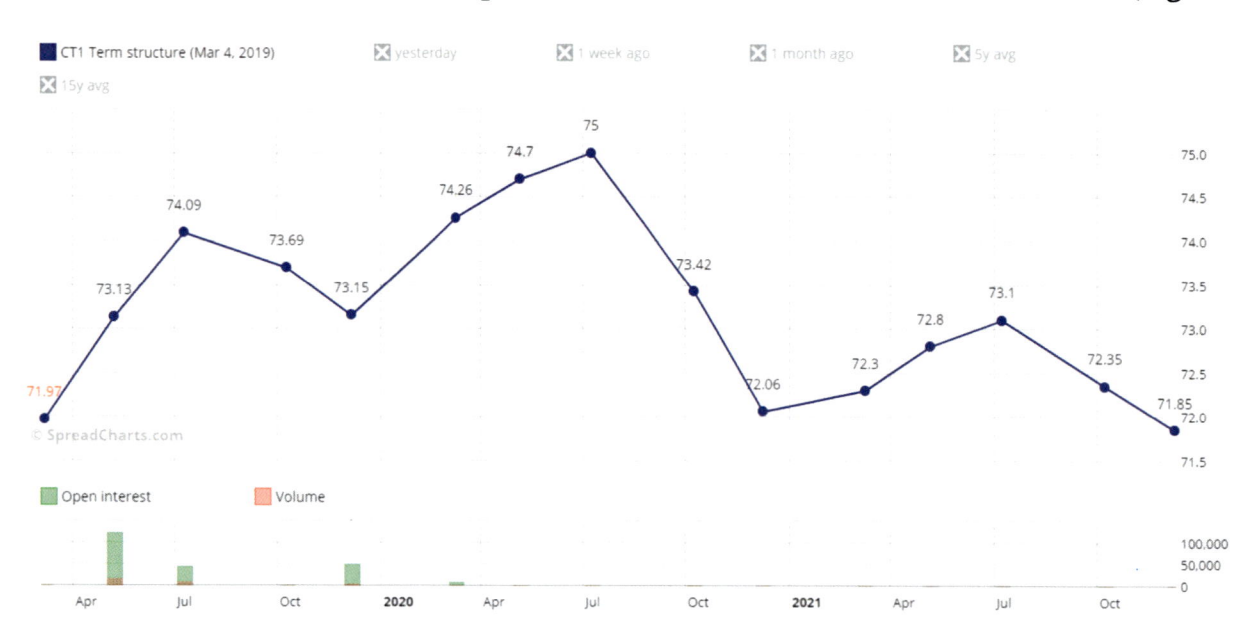

Let's see another example. Below, is the cotton futures term structure (Figure 88).

Figure 88 - Cotton futures term structure (SpreadCharts.com)

The reason for the recurring backwardation in the cotton market is due to the harvest taking place between September and December. During this period, supply increases significantly, causing the price of cotton to reach its annual low, as it does every year. (I am giving you a preview of what we will explore in more detail in Chapter 17). This price drop is a cyclical feature tied to the seasonal cycle of the crop, and it is consistently reflected in the term structure.

Studying the term structure gives you a clear and precise indication of the price trends of a commodity across its different maturities. It allows you to identify whether there are recurring anomalies that repeat year after year, or if you are observing temporary anomalies caused by specific factors such as weather events, economic conditions, or exceptional market dynamics.

When you encounter a backwardation in the term structure, the first step is to compare it with the historical averages of the curve to determine whether it is a recurring pattern or caused by particular circumstances, such as adverse weather or excessive speculation. Each backwardation can have different causes, and understanding the reason behind it is essential for interpreting it correctly.

What I am about to say may seem obvious, but it is important to emphasise that not all backwardations are the same; they depend on the causes that generated them. For example, you cannot equate a backwardation in wheat, like the one seen earlier, to one caused by an extraordinary event such as a drought. To clarify this concept, below you can see an example of the term structure of sugar (Figure 89).

Figure 89 - Sugar futures term structure (SpreadCharts.com)

Figure 90 - Sugar futures term structure with 5-year average (SpreadCharts.com)

At first glance, it seems that backwardation is a recurring feature of the sugar market, with May and July deliveries in backwardation both in 2021 and 2022. However, if you compare it with the 5-year average (as shown in Figure 90 above), you will immediately notice a significant difference. In the 5-year average, backwardation had given way to a contango for the 2020 deliveries.

This indicates that the current backwardation in sugar has persisted longer than usual this year. But there is more. If you compare the current term structure with that of just one month earlier (Figure 91), you will notice that sugar had already returned to contango, following the usual market trend. However, some new factor must have intervened, causing May and July 2020 deliveries to shift back into backwardation.

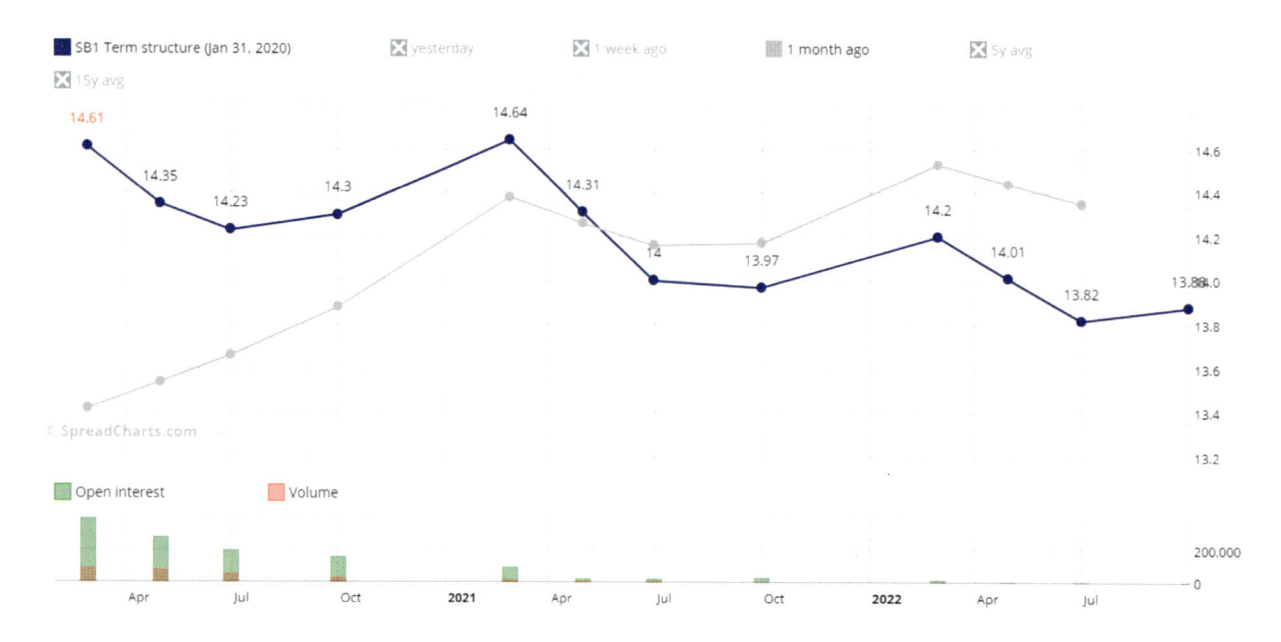

Figure 91 - Sugar futures term structure a month before (SpreadCharts.com)

Sugar had returned to contango, following the typical market pattern. However, a new factor intervened, causing the May and July 2020 deliveries to shift back into backwardation. Good data (November) pushed the price of sugar too far. So, you can say that the sugar backwardation is due to too much 'speculation' (an anomaly that is not overly uncommon to see).

In conclusion, whether you directly trade a futures contract or use spread trading, it is always important to check the term structure of a commodity as it tells you its current 'health condition'.

Multi-Leg Spreads

CHAPTER 16

Two-leg spreads are the initial step for traders looking to exploit price differences between two deliveries or markets. However, with time and experience, you realise that profit opportunities often lie beyond the simple comparison of two delivery dates or markets, hidden among multiple factors.

This is where multi-leg spreads come into play, meaning spreads with more than two legs. These instruments offer traders the ability to further reduce risk compared to two-leg spreads, as they allow for better compensation of counter-seasonal fluctuations and the exploitation of more complex anomalies that occur within the term structure. Multi-leg spreads enable speculation not only on the price of the underlying asset but also on the internal configuration of the various contracts that form the yield curve.

The main strategic advantage of multi-leg spreads lies in their ability to balance risk more effectively. By adding more legs, traders can distribute their exposure across different maturities, reducing their vulnerability to sudden events or drastic market changes. Furthermore, since many brokers recognise these spreads as reduced-margin positions, they also offer a potentially higher ROI (Return on Investment), making them attractive tools for experienced traders.

Let me begin by illustrating two multi-leg strategies: the Butterfly Spread and the Condor Spread.

Butterfly Spread

Even for multi-leg spreads, you should use *Intramarket* and *Intermarket* typologies. Usually, multi-leg Intramarket spreads are used precisely for speculating on changes in the futures' term structure.

The Butterfly is a complex spread, built on three different deliveries/legs. These three legs form the Butterfly's body and wings.

The Butterfly Futures Spread combines a near-term bull spread and a longer-term bear spread (or vice versa if bearish). This means that you buy two different months and then sell one month twice. The month you sell twice is referred to as the 'whipping post'. For example:

Bull Spread = Corn July '19 - Corn September '19

Bear Spread = - Corn September '19 + Corn December '19

The Butterfly is

Corn July '19 – 2*Corn September '19 + Corn December '19

You use a Butterfly Spread because you believe that mid-term futures prices are going down and you expect an increase or, at the very least, certain stability in short- and long-term futures yields. These oscillations in the term structure fall into the normal seasonal behaviour of some commodities and can occur both in a Contango market and in Backwardation.

With a Butterfly, you create a differential between two correlated spreads, removing individual outright direction from the trade. So, you speculate about the changes in the contracts' term structure, rather than on the underlying movements.

This type of spread is popular because it reduces margins, and many traders perceive it as less risky since it involves being both long and short on the same commodity.

In a market like corn (and all the grains in general), term structure offers many opportunities to get profits from price changes over the months. Due to the basics of the grain markets, and the fact that new supply will be on the market only a few times a year, the term structure may change dramatically depending on the demand/supply ratio and the Hedge Funds.

Obviously, depending on the situation, a Butterfly Spread can be purchased or sold. In a scenario where you decided to sell the same spread seen above with corn, you would have to build it as follows:

Bear Spread = - Corn July '19 + Corn September '19

Bull Spread = Corn September '19 - Corn December '19

The Butterfly is

- Corn July '19 + 2*Corn September '19 - Corn December '19

As mentioned, a Butterfly Spread can be either Intramarket or Intermarket. The most popular Intermarket commodity spreads involve the simultaneous execution of multiple futures positions designed to replicate the inputs and outputs of several real-world product transformations or to hedge that production process by putting on the opposite spread. Examples of these are Crush and Crack spreads.

Soybean Crush Spread. The term 'crush' comes from the processing of soybeans: you buy soybeans and 'crush' them to obtain soybean meal and soybean oil to sell. The Soybean Crush Spread represents the difference between the combined value of *soybean meal* (ZM) and *soybean oil* (ZO), and the value of *soybeans* (ZS).

In a Crush Spread, the trader takes a long position on soybean futures and short positions on soybean meal and soybean oil futures. The value of the spread reflects the [Gross Processing Margin](#), which is the potential profit derived from transforming soybeans.

I will spare you from having to read all the calculations concerning the quotas of each commodity; they are not necessary as you do not have to know them. Software like SeasonAlgo and SpreadCharts are already programmed to create all these types of spreads accurately. The gross processing margin (GPM) allows producers to compare the input cost of beans with the output revenues of bean products. It is built as follows:

Soybean Crush = -Soybean + 2.2*Soybean Meal + 11*Soybean Oil

A more accurate estimate of the crush margin would be if the trader used 2 contracts of soybean, 5 contracts of soybean meal and 22 contracts of soybean oil as shown below:

Soybean Crush = -2*Soybean + 5*Soybean Meal + 22*Soybean Oil

Of the two, the second version more accurately reflects the actual crush ratio. However, trading a spread of this size requires more margin than most traders are willing to risk, as the total dollar exposure could be substantial. Larger trades can be useful for well-funded traders (institutional, investors), whilst less funded traders (retail traders) will probably find smaller versions to be more suited to their needs.

In futures trading, you can use Board Crush, which is a GPM calculation when applied to the soybean futures product complex traded on the CME. Board Crush can be traded as 'mini-size' in 1:1:1 ratio or, more precisely:

Soybean Crush = -10* Soybean + 11* Soybean Meal + 9* Soybean Oil

When you build a Soybean Crush Spread, you should consider the delivery of soybean meal and soybean oil futures two months later than the one for soybean. This allows approximately one month for shipping and one month for crushing. Here is an example:

-10*ZSU19 + 11*ZMX19 + 9*ZLX19

A soybean producer concerned with rising production costs can buy soybean and sell soybean meal and soybean oil. If soybean price rises, the higher purchasing costs are compensated by a profit on the soybean futures. On the other hand, a fall in the price of soybean meal or soybean oil, which reduces producer's revenues, is compensated by gains in the short futures positions.

When you trade using the Soybean Crush Spread, you should look at the divergence between the products. If the spread is narrow, the potential profit will incline in the direction of soybean meal and oil contracts (the cost to process the soybean is too high to produce a reasonable profit). If the spread is wide, producers will sell soybean meal and soybean oil in order to realise their profits.

<u>Cattle Crush Spread</u>. A process similar to the 'Crush' also exists in livestock farming, but with the difference that various inputs are transformed into a single final product. Operators buy feeder cattle, feed them for a period, and then sell live cattle ready for slaughter.

The <u>Cattle Crush</u>, or Cattle Feeding Spread, involves purchasing futures on *feeder cattle* (GF) and *corn* (ZC) and selling the futures contract on *live cattle* (LE). This spread reflects the economics of livestock farming, allowing traders to estimate the profitability of the operation and manage the risks associated with margins. Additionally, it offers profit opportunities for traders.

The difference between the cost of the purchased inputs and the value of the sold cattle is called the <u>Gross Feeding Margin</u>, which represents the return per hundredweight of cattle after deducting the costs of feeder cattle and corn. Since the feeding margin can vary significantly, farmers seek solutions to protect themselves from financial risks. The Cattle Crush is a useful tool for managing price-related risks.

Avoiding long explanations on the calculations of quantities of the various commodities for a balanced spread, here is how the Cattle Crush is built:

Cattle Crush = 2*Live Cattle – Feeder Cattle - Corn

However, the construction of Cattle Crush depends on the production parameters of a given cattle feeding operation, a 2-1-1 (live cattle-feeder cattle-corn) Cattle Crush may over- and under-hedge each of the commodities. Commercial cattle feeders can compensate for this by using different hedge ratios which may closely follow specific production parameters (for example, 4-2-1).

Besides the number of contracts, the arrangement of contract months is equally important. The feeder cattle contract should be four to six months earlier than the live cattle contract. This represents the amount of time required to feed an animal until it reaches slaughter weight. The contract month for corn usually falls between the feeder cattle and live cattle contract months. This is done to represent the average cost of corn for the duration of the feeding period.

Below, in Figure 92, you can see a table with possible contract months for a Cattle Crush Spread.

Feeder Cattle	Corn	Live Cattle	Feeder Cattle	Corn	Live Cattle
January	March	June	August	December	December
March	May	August	September	December	February
April	May	August	October	December	February
May	May	October	November	December	April

Figure 92 - Possible contract months for Cattle Crush Spread

So, for example, a Cattle Crush is:

Cattle Crush = 2*LEU18 - GFG19 - ZCZ18

Taking the example above, you assume that in May a feedlot operator plans for cattle to begin feeding in September. If the prices noted earlier are trading in May, the spread would be profitable. To hedge the risk that the margin may turn unfavourable by September, a Cattle Crush Spread is put on.

In September, the operator will purchase feeder cattle in the cash market. As that process unfolds, the feeder side of the hedge will be offset and, as the corn component is purchased, so will the corn hedge. If by September feeder prices have risen, the operator will realise a gain in the value of the long futures position.

Similarly, if corn prices rise, this will result in a profit for the long futures position. The gains from the futures positions for the inputs will be used to offset the increased cost in the cash market. If the short position in live cattle futures is kept in place until February, it will protect the operator from any decline in prices for finished cattle.

Crack spread. In the petroleum industry, refineries are most concerned about hedging the difference between their input costs and output prices. Their profits are tied directly to the spread between the price of crude oil and the prices of refined products, gasoline and distillates. This spread is called the Crack spread. The term 'crack' derives from the refining process that 'cracks' crude oil into its constituent products.

In a typical refinery, gasoline output is approximately double the distillate fuel oil. This refining ratio translates as a 3:2:1 Crack spread; it means three *crude oil (CL)* contracts versus two *gasoline (RB)* contracts and one *heating oil (HO)* contract. So:

Crack spread = -3*CL + 2*RB + HO

The rationale behind the speculation on the Crack spread is again very similar to that on the other processing margin spreads. When purchasing a Crack spread, a refiner expects the crude oil price to fall more than its products.

On the other hand, if a refiner expects the crude oil price to hold steady, or rise somewhat, while its by-products fall (a declining Crack spread), the refiner would need to 'sell the crack'; that is, he will have to buy crude oil futures and sell gasoline and heating oil futures.

The combined value of gasoline and heating oil must cover the price of crude oil and refining production costs. The Crack spread can be affected by seasons. For example, during the summer months, gasoline is in greater demand than heating oil. During the winter months, the demand will shift to heating oil.

If the spread is too narrow to make a refining profit, you can expect that product prices will rise to meet crude oil prices; thus, you should favour heating oil and gasoline contracts over crude oil ones.

On the other hand, if the spread between product and crude oil prices is large, you should expect refineries will push production and selling of unleaded gasoline and heating oil to take advantage of the profit. This sell off should push product prices lower, which can favour crude oil over gasoline and heating oil.

Condor Spread

Another kind of multi-leg spread is the Condor Spread, which is very similar to the Butterfly Spread, with the crucial difference being that the body of a Condor has two legs rather than one. In this way, it covers a wider range of expiries.

The Condor Spread, in fact, consist of 4 legs within the same product group and with consecutive quarterly expiration months (i.e., Z18-H19-M19-U19). By buying a Condor, this spread involves the purchase of 1 of the closer month leg, the sale of 1 of the next expiration leg, the sale of 1 of the following expiration leg, and the purchase of 1 of the furthest expiration leg.

Condors are mainly made on crude oil and Eurodollar with expiries depending on the distance between the first and the last contract; usually, they are at 3, 6, 9 and 12 months.

You can see an example of Condor Spread with the Eurodollar futures:

Condor Spread = EDZ18 - EDH19 - EDM19 + EDU19

Condor, like Butterfly, can range pretty well, and is also the best way to play different parts of the term structure. You should always take the Eurodollar if, for example, you think that the curve will become steeper in the near-term rather than the long-term of the curve. You can take advantage of this by buying a Condor Spread.

If instead you think that the curve will be flatter in the near-term than in the long-term of the curve, then you should consider selling the Condor Spread in order to get a profit.

Multi-leg strategies are more complex than simple spreads with two legs. They require greater knowledge about the term structure and the seasonality of individual commodities. Let us now take a look at what the pros and cons of multi-leg spreads are.

PROS:

- Many more opportunities for profit than the outright futures position. Intramarket commodity spreads allow you to speculate on mean reverting tendencies or enable you to take a directional approach. Intermarket commodity spreads allow you to profit on commercial hedgers strategies.
- Seasonality is driven by strong fundamentals.
- Multi-leg spreads recognised by Exchange enjoy lower margin requirements and therefore increase your ROI.

CONS:

- More legs take up more commission, making the bid/ask wider.
- Some brokers may not support complex spreads, meaning you have to leg in and out of spreads.
- Spreads with longer-term contracts can have a small volume and low liquidity.

- Analysis of term structure changes or processing margin calculations can be more complicated than analysis of price changes of the outright trades.

Now it is time to see two graphical examples. The first (Figure 93) is a Soybean Crush, more precisely, the spread ZSU18-ZLV18-ZMV18 constructed by buying the September 2018 soybean futures contract, selling the October 2018 soybean oil futures contract, and selling the October 2018 soybean meal futures contract.

Figure 93 - Soybean Crush ZSU18-ZLV18-ZMV18 (SeasonAlgo.com)

This spread had already been in a downtrend well before the start of the seasonal window proposed by SeasonAlgo. From a technical analysis point of view, the fall was stronger than a bullish divergence that formed just before the entry date. It produced only a couple of short rebounds, proving that technical analysis gives clear signals, but unfortunately, it often leads to losses.

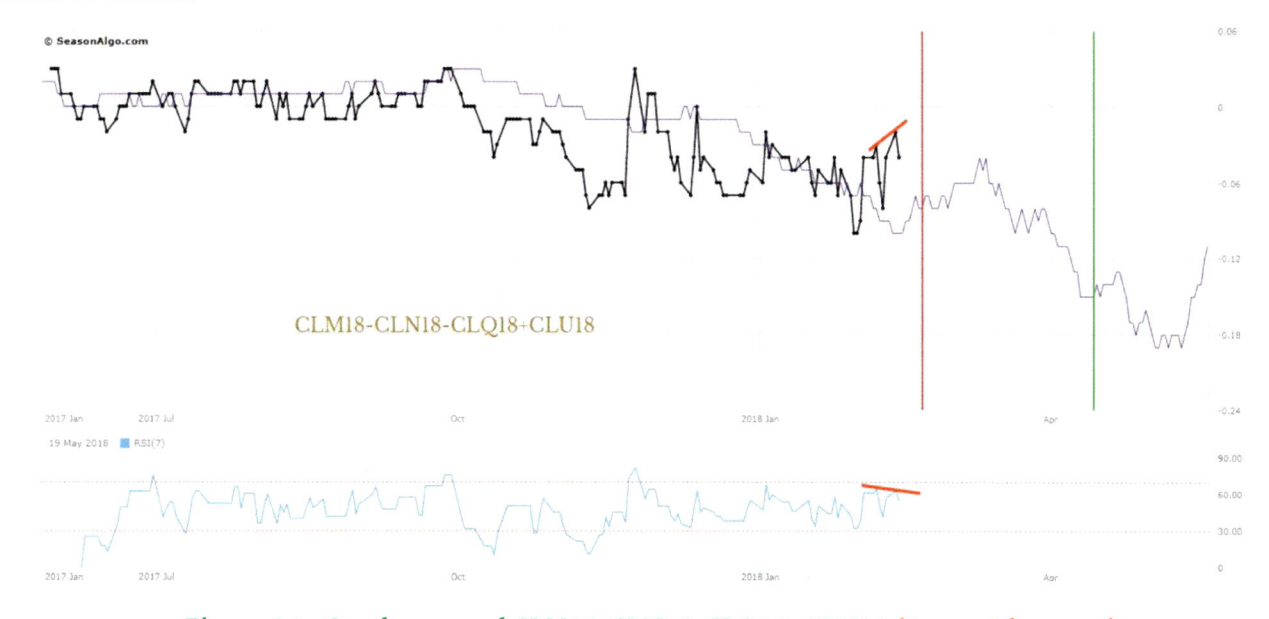

Figure 94 - Condor spread CLM18-CLN18-CLQ18+CLU18 (SeasonAlgo.com)

The second example concerns a Condor Spread on crude oil, also recommended by SeasonAlgo, CLM18-CLN18-CLQ18+CLU18, constructed by buying the June 2018 crude oil futures contract, selling the July 2018 contract, selling the August 2018 contract, and buying the September 2018 contract, which you can see in the chart in Figure 94.

As I have said, deliveries depend on the distance between the first and last contract; usually, they are at 3, 6, 9 and 12 months, in this case, they are 1, 2, 3 and 4 months.

Seasonality has not started yet, but here again, for all those who use technical analysis, on this chart there is a bearish divergence (perhaps it will turn out better than in the previous example).

This particular spread relies on the fact that in the summer, crude oil will fall in price and July and August deliveries will be more penalised than the other two (May and September).

I know I have covered a rather complex topic, which requires time and practice to fully grasp the concepts discussed, such as the term structure. Multi-leg spreads, in particular, are advanced tools that you should not use from the outset, but rather as a resource to integrate once you have mastered two-leg spreads. They should be seen as another arrow in your quiver to better take advantage of market opportunities. Once you understand the basic mechanisms, multi-leg spreads will offer you new horizons and greater risk control.

Contango & Backwardation

CHAPTER 17

Understanding contango and backwardation in depth is crucial for every spread trader. These two terms not only define the current state of the market but also offer valuable insights into future price expectations and can open up excellent profit opportunities. A clear grasp of these concepts allows traders to better navigate market fluctuations, positioning themselves strategically to take advantage of shifts in supply, demand, and market sentiment.

Contango and backwardation are terms used to define the structure of the forward curve. When a market is in contango, the futures price of a commodity is higher than the spot price, and more distant deliveries trade at a premium compared to closer ones. This typically occurs when the market expects prices to rise over time, whether due to inflationary expectations, storage costs, or simply an abundant supply relative to current demand (Figure 95).

In such a scenario, traders might perceive less urgency to buy immediately, driving up the prices of later deliveries. While contango is considered the normal market condition for many commodities, especially those with high storage costs, it also indicates that there are no significant concerns about near-term shortages.

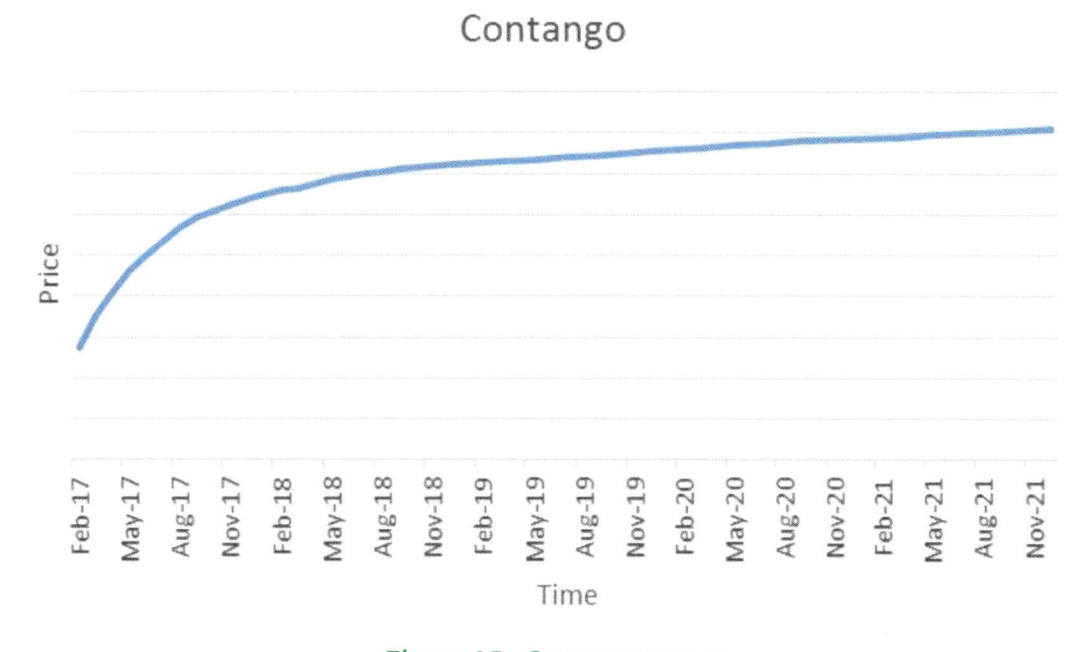

Figure 95 - Contango curve

The deliveries of the futures are in contango because of three factors:

1. costs of storage
2. financing (the cost to carry)
3. insurance costs

When a market is in backwardation, the futures price of a commodity is lower than the spot price, closer deliveries have a higher price than more distant ones (Figure 96).

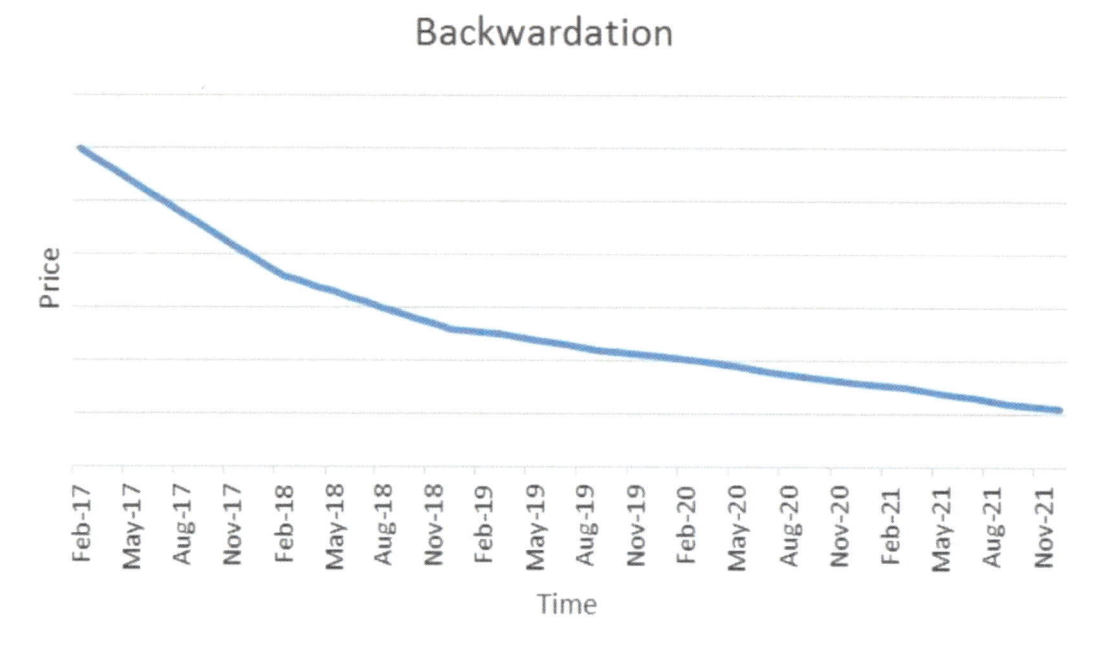

Figure 96 - Backwardation

Over time, as a futures contract approaches maturity, the futures price will converge with the spot price. Otherwise, an arbitrage opportunity would exist.

Therefore, the significant of market situations are:

- when demand and supply are balanced, markets are normal (contango)
- when demand is weak and supply is excessive, markets tend to amplify contango
- in a situation of excess demand, the markets tend to reduce the contango to the point of reversing the curve, turning it into backwardation

Questa This is the textbook definition. Certainly interesting, but on its own, it does not offer much practical value. To fully understand the dynamics of backwardation or strong contango, you need to go beyond the theory and analyse the underlying reasons behind these phenomena. Only then can you gain genuinely useful insights to improve your trading decisions.

When there is a bearish trend in the medium or long term, the forward curve is in contango. In this scenario, producers tend to sell further out contracts at higher prices because they expect the price of the commodity to rise over time. This reflects the market's expectations of abundant supply and stable or decreasing demand.

However, if something unexpected happens in the short term, raising concerns about a potential sudden price increase, operators who have sold medium- or long-term contracts find themselves in a position where they must keep their short positions open, but at the same time, they buy short-term contracts to hedge against immediate uncertainty. This action generates a significant increase in prices for near-term maturities, creating a short-term backwardation, where the price of near-term futures exceeds the spot price.

If this situation persists and the pressure on short-term prices extends to the medium and long term, you will see buying progressively shift to later maturities. At this point, the forward curve starts to show backwardation not only on the near-term maturities but also on future deliveries. The curve can progressively flatten until even the furthest maturities enter backwardation, while the most distant contracts might still remain in contango for a period.

On the other hand, if contango increases, it means that the market sees no signs of a supply shortage for that commodity, which generally represents a bearish signal. In practice, if a commodity is in contango and the price starts to rise, the forward curve tends to flatten as demand grows. If, conversely, the price decreases, contango increases, signalling low demand pressure and excessive supply.

You can see a concrete example of how a trend is reflected in the forward curve by observing WTI crude oil. Figure 97 shows a daily chart that clearly illustrates this dynamic.

Figure 97 - WTI Crude oil daily chart (TradingView.com)

Below, you can see the forward curve of WTI Crude oil. The current forward curve is in blue, and the one from a month earlier is in grey (Figure 98).

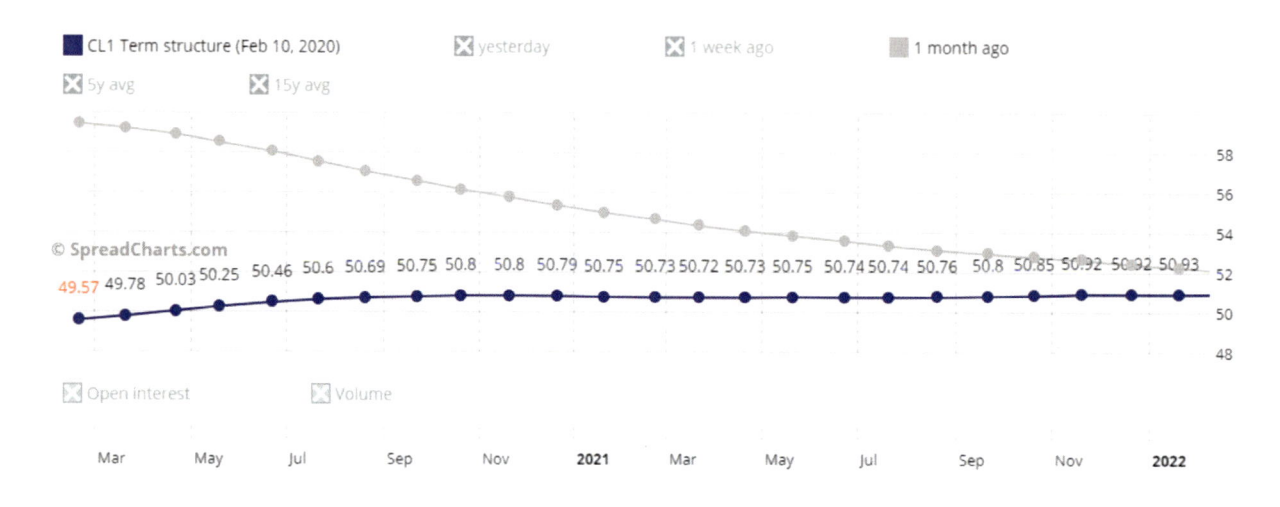

Figure 98 - WTI Crude oil term structure (SpreadCharts.com)

Above in Figure 98, the WTI Crude oil term structure. The blue line represents the current term structure, while the grey line shows the structure from a month ago.

One month earlier, during the bullish phase, despite the trend having ended a few days prior, the forward curve remained in backwardation. Later, during the bearish phase, prices shifted from backwardation to contango.

When trading, a key word to always keep in mind is FOCUS. Diversifying your trades is undoubtedly beneficial, but you must avoid operating in too many markets simultaneously. Focus only on the ones you know well and resist the temptation to multiply your trades to increase the number of transactions. In trading, doing more trades does not equate to making more profits; in fact, often the opposite happens.

And that is exactly what I do. I do not trade all commodities, but rather limit myself to the ones I know thoroughly, which are about a dozen.

Becoming an expert in a narrow group of commodities will allow you to develop a deep and informed understanding of the markets you trade. Specialising not only enables you to better capture the opportunities offered by each market but also helps you manage risks more effectively. In trading, the key is not to operate on too many fronts but to have a clear focus on what you know best, turning this knowledge into a competitive advantage.

Below, you will find some important characteristics regarding the seasonality, as well as contango and backwardation, of some of the commodities I follow.

Grains

Around the time of harvest deliveries, prices are usually low and in backwardation.

Corn: the harvest takes place between August and September, so the September delivery usually has a lower price than the July one.

Wheat: in the milder regions, the harvest takes place in May, in those with the coldest winters, in late July. Hence, the May and July deliveries are usually in backwardation (Figure 99).

Figure 99 - Wheat term structure (SpreadCharts.com)

Soybeans: the harvest takes place about a month after that of corn. Regarding the term structure, the trend follows the same pattern, with the September delivery priced lower than the August one, and sometimes even lower than July.

After the harvest, prices return to contango. Backwardation is due to a lack of raw materials, just before the arrival of the subsequent harvest.

Soft

Cotton: just like with grains, from July to December there is backwardation, and after the harvest, the prices return to contango (Figure 100).

Figure 100 - Cotton term structure (SpreadCharts.com)

Figure 101 - Sugar term structure (SpreadCharts.com)

Sugar: the bullish seasonal window is located between autumn and winter (deliveries in October and March), a critical period for the Brazilian harvest, while between spring and summer (deliveries in May and July), operators usually tend to liquidate some of the bullish positions on the old crop, in favour of the new crop for the following season. This usually leads to a backwardation (Figure 101).

Coffee: backwardation occurs only due to tensions (geopolitical events, droughts, etc.). Unlike with grains, there is no question of harvests here. At the time of writing this chapter, coffee was in strong contango because there was no tension with the quantities produced by Robusta (India) and Arabica (Brazil).

Energy

Natural Gas: it is a commodity that I do not follow. However, I have a friend in New York who trades it professionally. In February/April there is a strong backwardation, of about 10/15% due to sudden cold waves. If the cold goes on, backwardation will continue, otherwise, contango will return (Figure 102).

Figure 102 - Natural Gas term structure (SpreadCharts.com)

In such cases, you need to quickly determine whether the backwardation is due to inherent market characteristics (as explained earlier) or unrelated factors like drought, frost, geopolitical events, or strong speculation.

This could save you from making a bad trade due to wrong analysis and assessments of that raw material.

In conclusion, doing this will ensure you become an expert in the commodity market, and as a result, a good spread trader.

THE STARTING DATE

CHAPTER 18

∽

The entry date is one of the most delicate aspects of seasonal spread trading. Many traders rely on the dates suggested by platforms such as SeasonAlgo and Moore Research without questioning them. However, blindly following these dates can expose traders to hidden risks, such as market manipulation, which can challenge even the most experienced. As I've already mentioned, manipulation is far less common in spread trading than in individual futures, but it's not entirely absent.

If you observe the trading volumes, you will notice they tend to rise as the seasonal window's start date approaches, followed by a drop and a return to average levels. This makes the start date fertile ground for those looking to manipulate a spread and put traders in a disadvantageous position, taking advantage of the increase in volumes.

Those who purchased my book on the best seasonal spreads know that I don't provide precise dates for the start and end of a seasonal window, but rather indicate a month when these movements occur. In contrast, SeasonAlgo and Moore provide specific dates, which many traders follow closely.

Many traders, in fact, buy or sell a spread on the start date of a seasonal window simply because a statistical database suggests that a favourable seasonality begins. This is precisely what occurred with an orange juice spread I was following: the OJU18-OJX18 spread. You can see the chart in Figure 103.

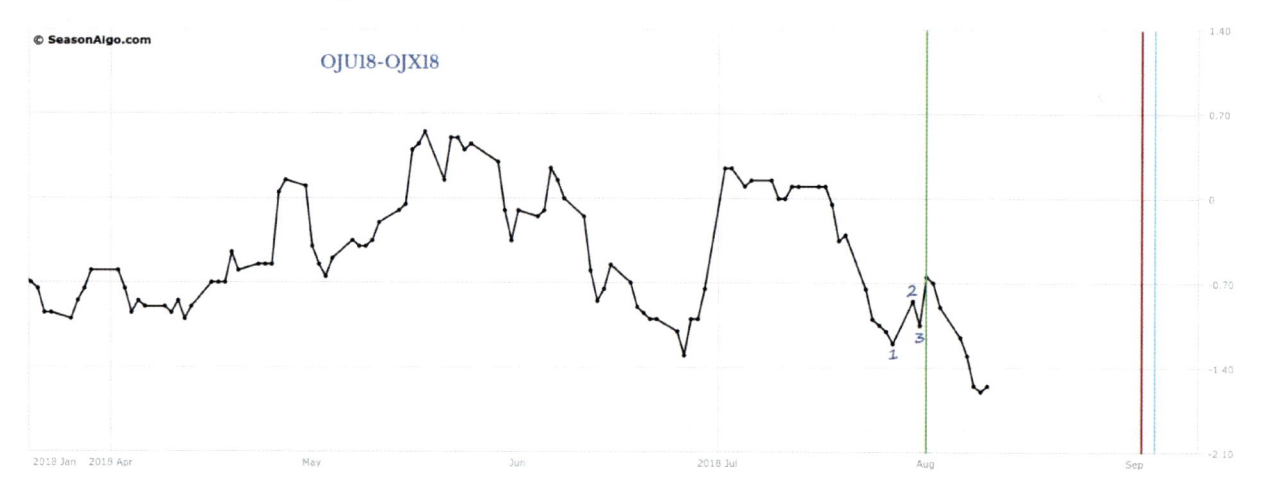

Figure 103 - Spread OJU18-OJX18 (SeasonAlgo.com)

The seasonality is bullish, even though it ends just two days before the First Notice Day, a moment that often brings an increase in volatility. From a technical analysis standpoint, the spread has formed a classic Ross 1-2-3 low pattern, which is highly regarded among analysts. On the very first day of the seasonal window, the price rose above point 2, a perfect signal according to the textbook. However, starting the next day, the spread began to decline, leading many traders to close their positions with a stop loss a few days later, those who had followed the technical pattern.

Of course, this does not always happen, but such situations do arise from time to time. When a technical signal is too perfect, it should raise a red flag and make you suspect that there is a manoeuvre aimed at putting traders in a difficult position.

Let me show you another couple of examples. In Figure 104, you can see the daily chart of the NGZ18-NGG19 spread.

Figure 104 - Spread NGZ18-NGG19 (SeasonAlgo.com)

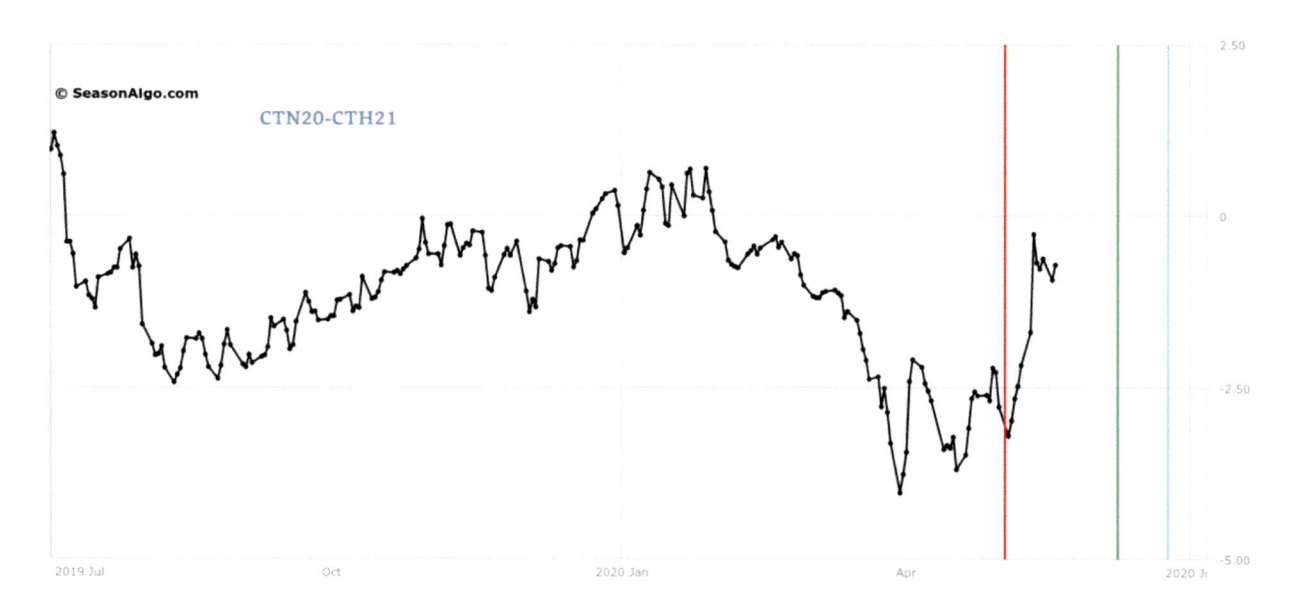

Figure 105 - Spread CTN20-CTH21 (SeasonAlgo.com)

The first vertical line (red) indicates a bearish seasonality, with the spread, on the start date (or more precisely the following day, as the date fell on a Sunday), hitting a low before reversing the trend. From that point onward, the price never dropped below that low.

In Figure 105 above, you can observe the chart of the CTN20-CTH21 spread. The seasonality of this spread is bearish, but surprisingly, the day after the start of the seasonal window, the price began a strong upward movement, putting all the traders who had sold the spread on the same day or in the days before in a difficult position, having followed the indicated seasonality.

As previously mentioned, these kinds of situations do not always occur. In most cases, at the start date of the seasonal window, the spread follows the expected movement without particular manipulations. Furthermore, the highs or lows reached by a spread on a specific day cannot always be attributed to market manipulation. Other factors may be at play, such as unexpected market news or simple coincidences (although I do not believe in coincidences).

It is still wise to pay special attention to the start of a seasonality and the optimised dates provided by platforms like SeasonAlgo and Moore Research. When you encounter a flawless technical pattern that aligns perfectly with the start date of the seasonality and provides a clear buy or sell signal, you should be aware that this may hide pitfalls. It is important not to be misled by signals that seem too perfect.

Despite these pitfalls, not all surprises are necessarily negative. Even when faced with perfect signals that raise suspicions of manipulation, they may still conceal advantageous opportunities. In the next chapter, you will explore how to turn these moments of uncertainty to your advantage and leverage market anomalies to gain a competitive edge in trading.

Exploit The Manipulation

CHAPTER 19

In recent years, spread trading has attracted an increasing number of traders, thanks to its unique characteristics that make it particularly appealing. This type of trading has not only drawn small traders but also some institutional investors, known as the so-called 'strong hands', the real players and dominators of the market.

You should not think that this market is free from speculation, manipulation, or forms of price control. Although spread trading offers superior protection compared to other assets, such as stocks or currencies, no market is entirely immune to these kinds of phenomena. This means that, from time to time, 'traps' for traders can appear in the form of false signals.

Speculation and manipulation may seem like obstacles, but with the right approach and a bit of patience, they can be turned into opportunities. In this chapter, you will see how events that at first glance seem unfavourable can, with a well-planned strategy, be exploited to gain an advantage.

For example, take cotton. As you can see from the chart in Figure 106, SeasonAlgo suggests a bearish seasonal window for the CTN17-CTZ17 spread, with an entry date of May 4th and an exit date of May 29th.

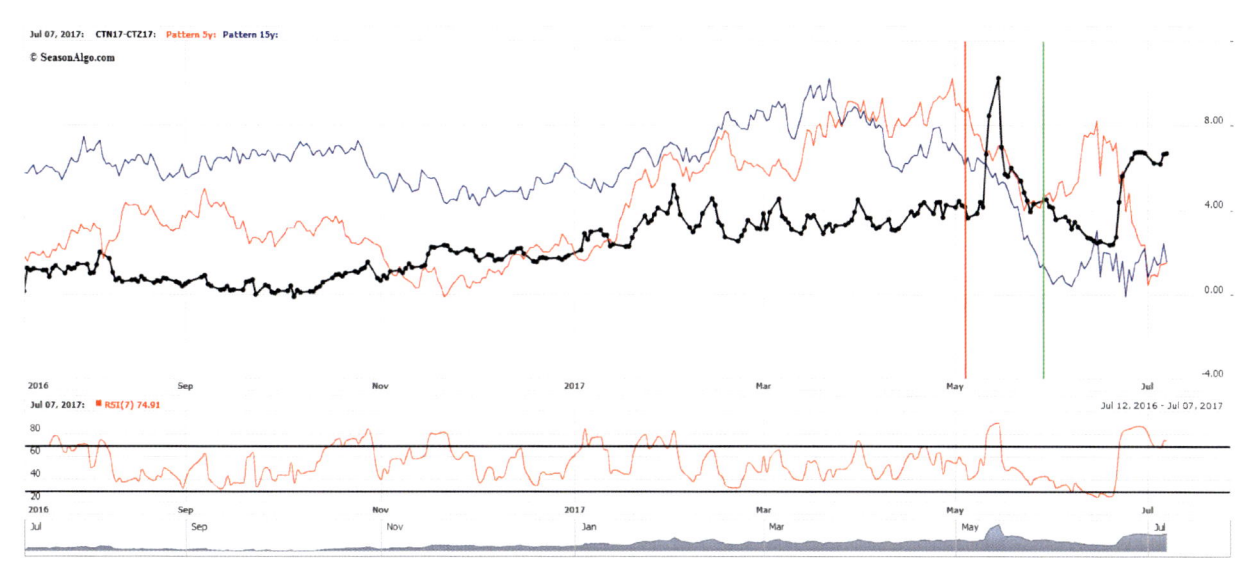

Figure 106 - Spread CTN17-CTZ17 daily chart (SeasonAlgo.com)

This kind of information can help you plan your trades, but it is always essential to analyse the market clearly and comprehensively and interpret the signals with caution.

Ultimately, while spread trading is not free from speculation and manipulation, it offers greater stability and fewer risks of distortion compared to other markets. With a well-structured strategy and careful market analysis, you can not only protect yourself from these events but also exploit them to your advantage to improve your long-term results.

Returning to the cotton example, immediately after the start of the seasonality, the spread moved differently from what you would have expected, and the price surged upwards. You can see that the same situation occurred, although in the opposite direction, with the HGM20-HGN20 spread (Figure 107).

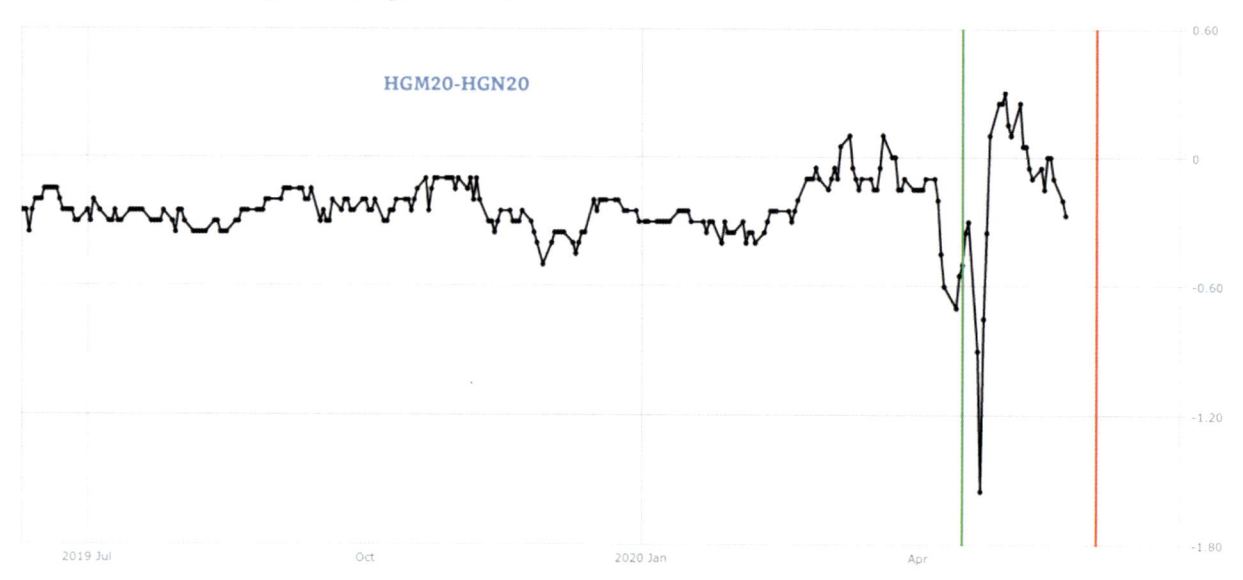

Figure 107 - Spread HGM20-HGN20 daily chart (SeasonAlgo.com)

In these circumstances, you cannot expect to beat the 'big players'; they have resources, capital, and information far beyond what is accessible to a small trader. Trying to compete directly with them is pointless and, frankly, impossible. Institutional investors and large operators have the ability to influence markets, move large amounts of capital, and are often able to dictate the market's direction.

However, your goal should not be to try to defeat these large operators, but rather to carefully observe their movements and use them to your advantage. It is not about winning against investment banks or hedge funds, but about leveraging their strength to your benefit, much like a sailor using the wind to sail faster in the desired direction.

Below is a chart of Live Cattle that you have already seen, the spread LEQ18-HEQ18 (Figure 108).

As you can see from the chart, right after the start of the seasonal window, with bearish seasonal patterns, the spread moved upward. The end of the seasonal window is still far off, leaving room for a potential bearish trade.

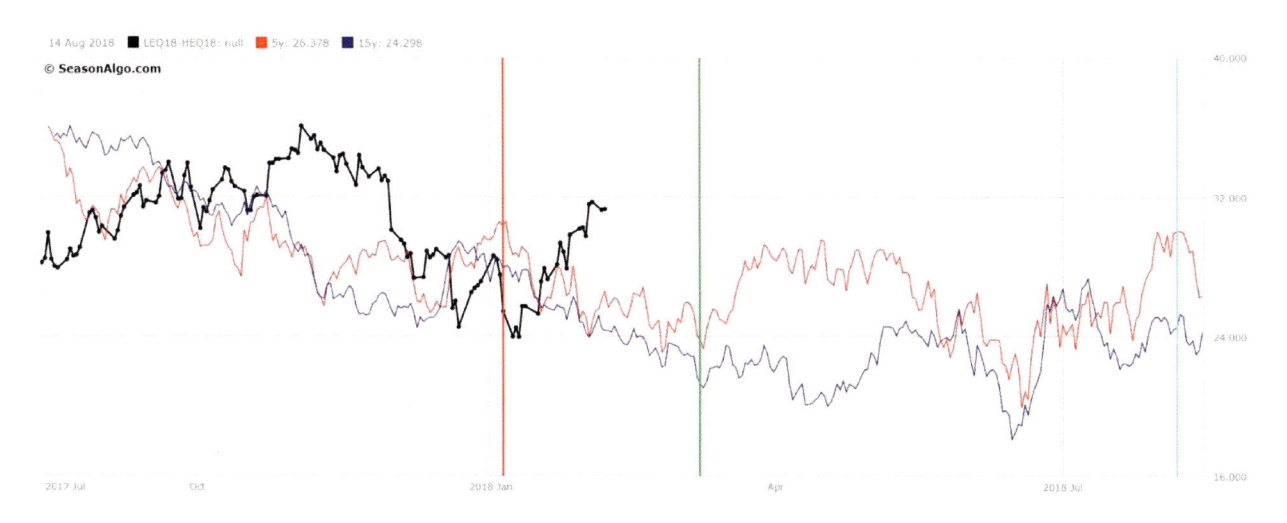

Figure 108 - Spread LEQ18-HEQ18 daily chart (SeasonAlgo.com)

Now, I do not know whether the spread will realign with seasonality in the near future or continue to rise, as much depends on the reason for the increase. However, by letting the speculators (or an external factor causing a price anomaly) exhaust themselves, you will have the opportunity to enter a trade under much more favourable conditions and with lower risk.

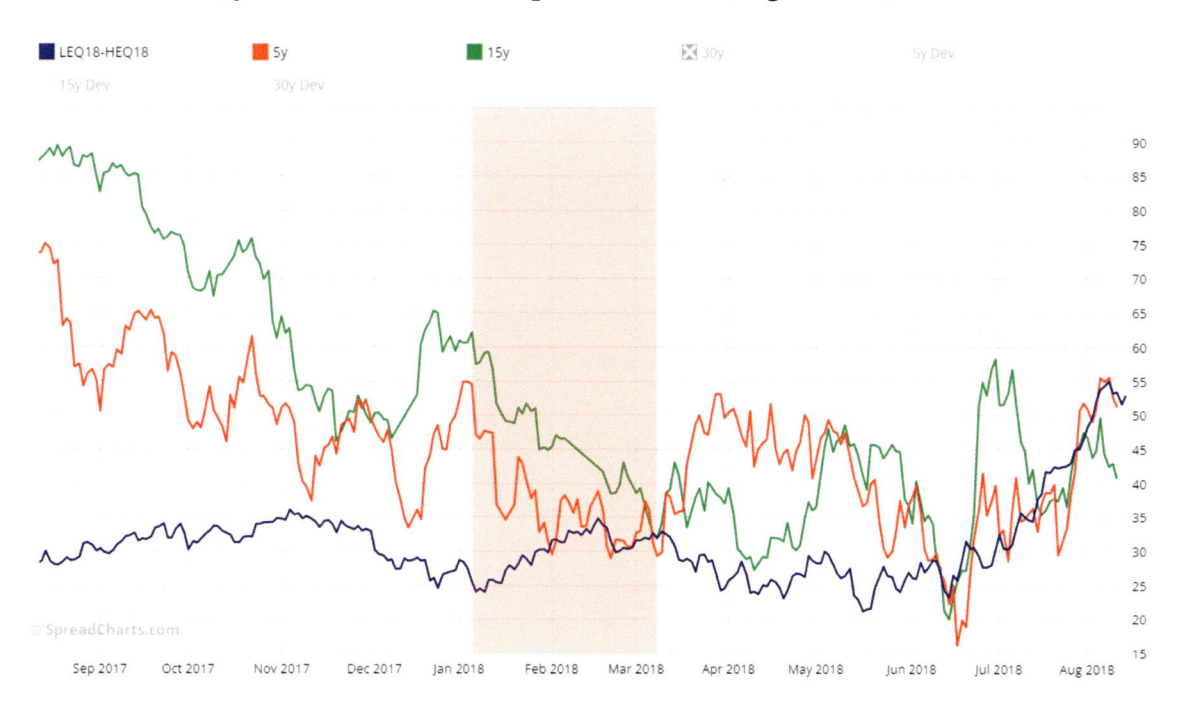

Below, you can see how the spread evolved (Figure 109).

Figure 109 - Spread LEQ18-HEQ18 (SpreadCharts.com)

The spread continued to climb until mid-February and then began a descent which led it to hit a new low about a month and a half after the end of the seasonal window. This example also shows you that, when these situations occur, a seasonal window can go on for several weeks longer than in the past. So, more elasticity is needed.

In the last example I show you a spread on lean hogs which at the time of updating this chapter I am following closely. It is precisely the HEM22-HEQ22 spread built by buying the lean hogs futures contract with delivery in June 2022 and selling the one with delivery in August 2022.

In Figure 110 you can see its chart with the bearish seasonality starting in December and ending in April.

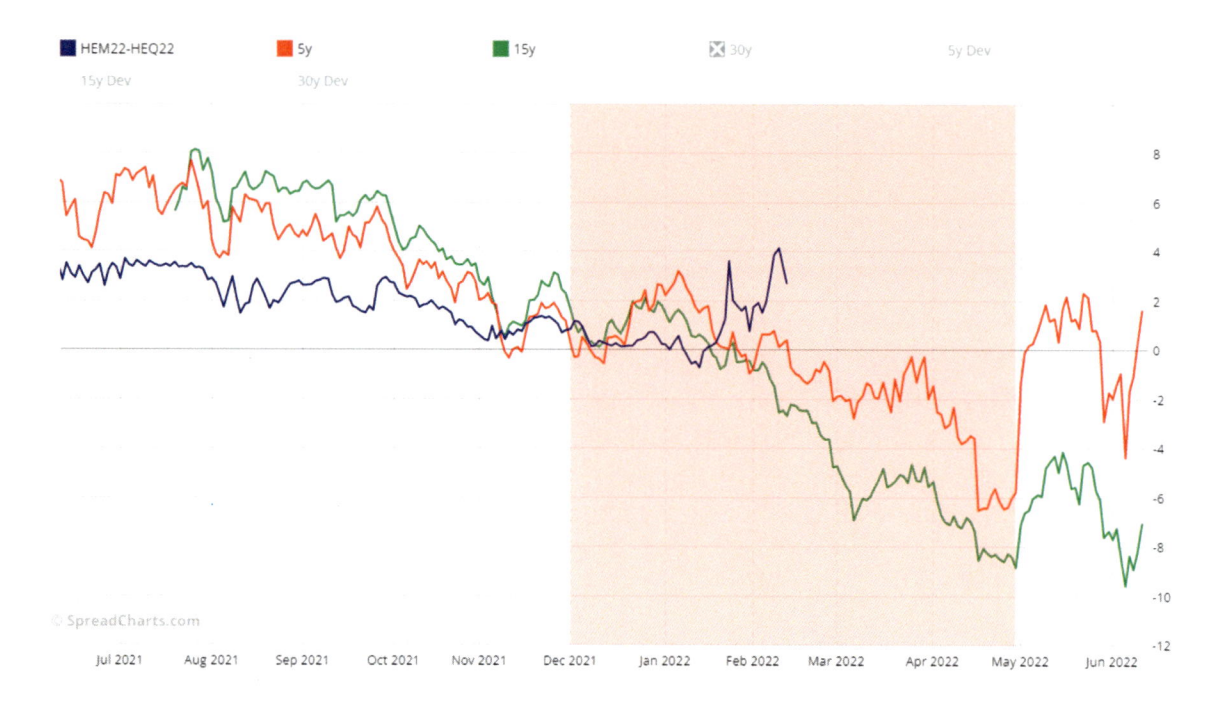

Figure 110 - Spread HEM22-HEQ22 (SpreadCharts.com)

After continuing the bearish trend that began in late September, the spread, well correlated with the two seasonal patterns, reversed course in mid-January, with a strong upward movement. From my analysis, I expect the spread to return to following the seasonality, and by selling it at $4, I was able to enter at a much better price compared to a few weeks earlier.

In conclusion, if you notice that a spread is moving against seasonality, it does not mean you should abandon the idea of trading it. First of all, you need to understand the reasons behind that movement and, if necessary, patiently wait for the right moment to enter the trade.

With the examples seen above, and other similar situations that those trading commodities regularly experience, you can realise how speculation, and in some cases manipulation, can influence a spread. When this happens, it is important not to intervene while all traders are focused on the spread, but to wait until institutional investors have made their moves. It is preferable to open a position when small traders have lost interest, and the 'strong hands' have finished their speculation.

Remember, even in spread trading, although to a lesser extent, you could fall into traps orchestrated by institutional investors. You need to carefully assess all aspects and keep in mind that, after a strong market movement, normalcy often follows.

These situations are not rare, but do not worry: with time and experience, you will learn to manage every aspect of spread trading better. Now, let's move on to something a bit more complex but equally useful.

RATIOS

CHAPTER 20

~

Ratios represent one of the most powerful tools in spread trading. These ratios between commodities not only reveal trading opportunities, but also provide a clear view of global economic dynamics. In this chapter, you will explore some of the most commonly used ratios and see how to exploit their fluctuations to gain a competitive advantage.

Ratio charts can reveal many interesting aspects. For example, they often indicate support and resistance levels where there is a high probability of reversal.

One of the ratios most commonly used by traders is the gold/silver ratio, which indicates the number of ounces of silver required to purchase one ounce of gold. The higher the gold/silver ratio rises, the greater the number of ounces of silver needed to purchase the same amount of gold. A decline in the gold/silver ratio tends to indicate a strengthening of silver relative to gold.

Below, in Figure 111, you can see the chart of the gold/silver ratio from 1980 to 2022.

Figure 111 - Gold/silver ratio (SpreadCharts.com)

With a few exceptions, the ratio generally ranges between 40 (support) and 80 (resistance). A value outside this range signals an excess of buying pressure on one metal or the other, presenting a potential trading and investment opportunity (as you will see in Chapter 14 of the second volume).

Therefore, for example, if, as happened in the spring of 2020, the ratio is higher and you believe it will soon decrease, you can choose to buy silver and short the same amount of gold. In simple terms, you can sell the GC-SI spread. This way, you can make a profit regardless of whether the price of the two metals rises or falls.

The gold/silver ratio is an index of the relative strength of the two metals, and it can indicate periods of [stress or euphoria in the financial markets](#). As such, it is also important for investors and traders to guide their decisions.

The use of silver in the world is significantly greater than that of gold. A decrease in the ratio indicates an appreciation of silver relative to gold, primarily due to higher demand for the metal in the market. This is a sign of a growing global economy.

On the other hand, if the gold/silver ratio rises, it is gold that increases its value relative to silver, and since gold is the ultimate safe-haven asset purchased during periods of economic difficulty, it indicates a crisis or at least financial market problems.

In Figure 112, you can see the chart of the S&P500 (in blue) and the gold/silver ratio (in black).

Figure 112 - S&P500 and gold/silver ratio (TradingView)

The chart clearly shows how, in March 2020, during the sharp fall in US equities, the gold/silver ratio shot up to around 125, meaning it took 125 ounces of silver to buy 1 ounce of gold.

Whereas the gold/silver ratio is useful for gauging the general health of financial markets, the gold/copper ratio offers valuable insights into the demand for industrial metals and the condition of the real economy. This ratio is particularly interesting when analysing correlations with the bond market and other asset classes. In Figure 113, you can see the chart of the gold/copper ratio (in red) with the US 10-year T-Note (in black).

Figure 113 - T-Note 10-year and gold/copper ratio (TradingView)

The chart clearly shows a correlation between the two markets, gold and copper, and, at the moment, the ratio between these two metals is at minimal levels. This can be interpreted as a sign of weakness in the U.S. bond market, suggesting that we might witness a further decline in bond prices in the coming weeks.

Since the bond market tends to have a positive correlation with the dollar, a drop in bonds could also lead to a devaluation of the greenback. A decline in the dollar, in turn, would be a positive factor for commodities, as a weaker dollar makes dollar-denominated commodities more affordable for international buyers, thereby boosting demand and encouraging higher levels of market activity.

In trading, it is crucial to understand that correlations between different markets play a key role in anticipating future movements. Even elements that at first glance may seem distant or irrelevant to the commodities market can, upon closer analysis, turn out to be key indicators of imminent changes. Macroeconomic dynamics and the relationships between assets, such as the bond market and the dollar, can deeply influence the commodities market, opening up trading opportunities that might otherwise be missed.

It is not just metals that offer interesting insights for spread trading. Many other ratios can be used to identify favourable situations. One of these is the ratio between coffee and sugar (Figure 114), which is currently showing significant signals for traders seeking strategic entry points.

Figure 114 - Coffee/sugar ratio (SpreadCharts.com)

    The chart clearly shows that the value of the ratio has once again reached the blue resistance line. Historically, every time the coffee/sugar ratio has touched or exceeded the threshold of 14, it has then started a downward phase. This recurring behaviour provides a valuable indication, signalling that the ratio has reached an extreme level and suggesting a fair probability of a future reversal.

    So, how can you effectively take advantage of this situation? You can take advantage of the fact that the ratio's peaks tend to coincide with those of the Intermarket spread between coffee (KC) and sugar (SB). Consequently, it is likely that, once these levels are reached, the spread will begin to decline, offering a selling opportunity with the expectation that the value will return to more appropriate levels.

    Now, let me present a specific example: the KCN22-SBN22 spread, which is constructed by buying the coffee futures contract with delivery in July 2022 and selling the sugar futures contract with the same delivery. You can see the chart in Figure 115 along with the two seasonal models for 5 and 15 years.

    Since November, seasonality has indicated a bearish trend, as shown by the two seasonal models. However, the spread did not immediately follow this trend and instead moved in the opposite direction, as can also be seen from the ratio chart, which reached its highest level in the last twelve years.

    This divergence between seasonality and the actual behaviour of the spread can be interpreted as confirmation that the spread is currently in a strong upward phase. When these divergences occur, as mentioned earlier, it is essential to closely monitor the market's performance, as compelling trading opportunities may arise, as is the case here. However, what these situations do not provide is the exact moment to enter a position, namely when to sell the spread.

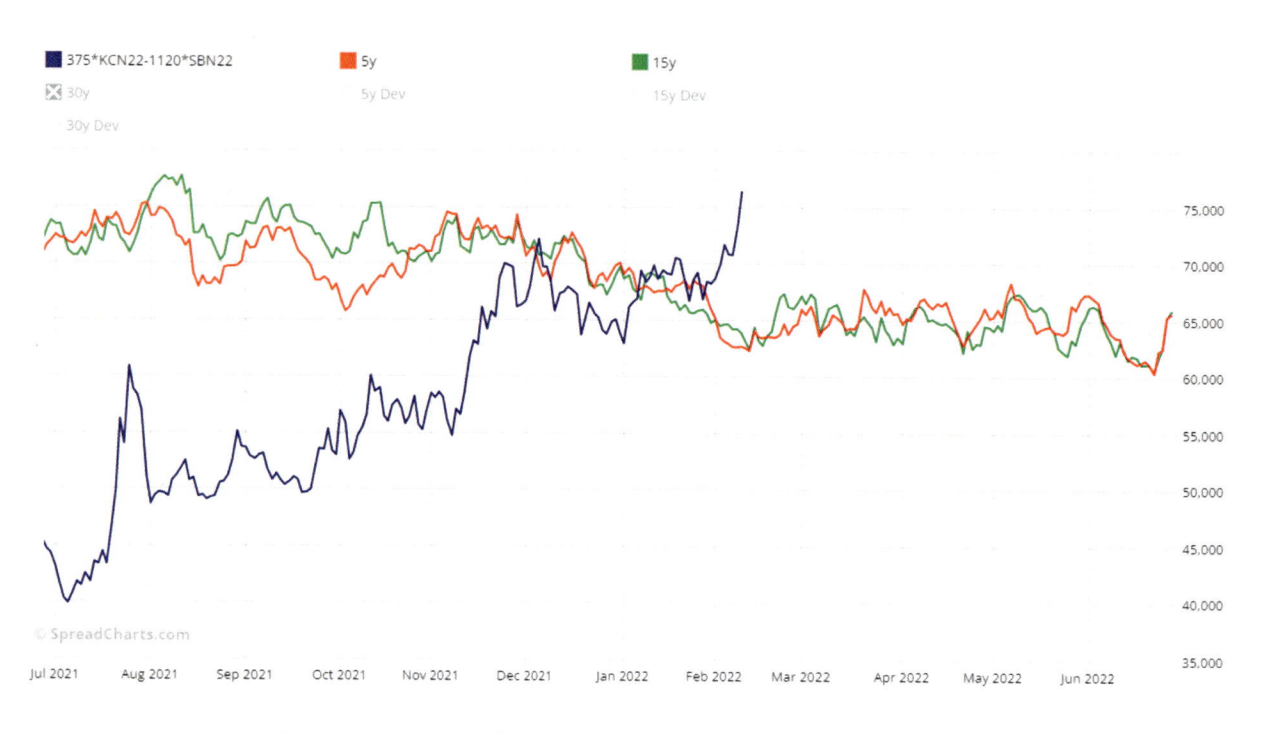

Figure 115 - Spread KCN22-SBN22 chart (SpreadCharts.com)

In Figure 116, you can see the Continuous histogram.

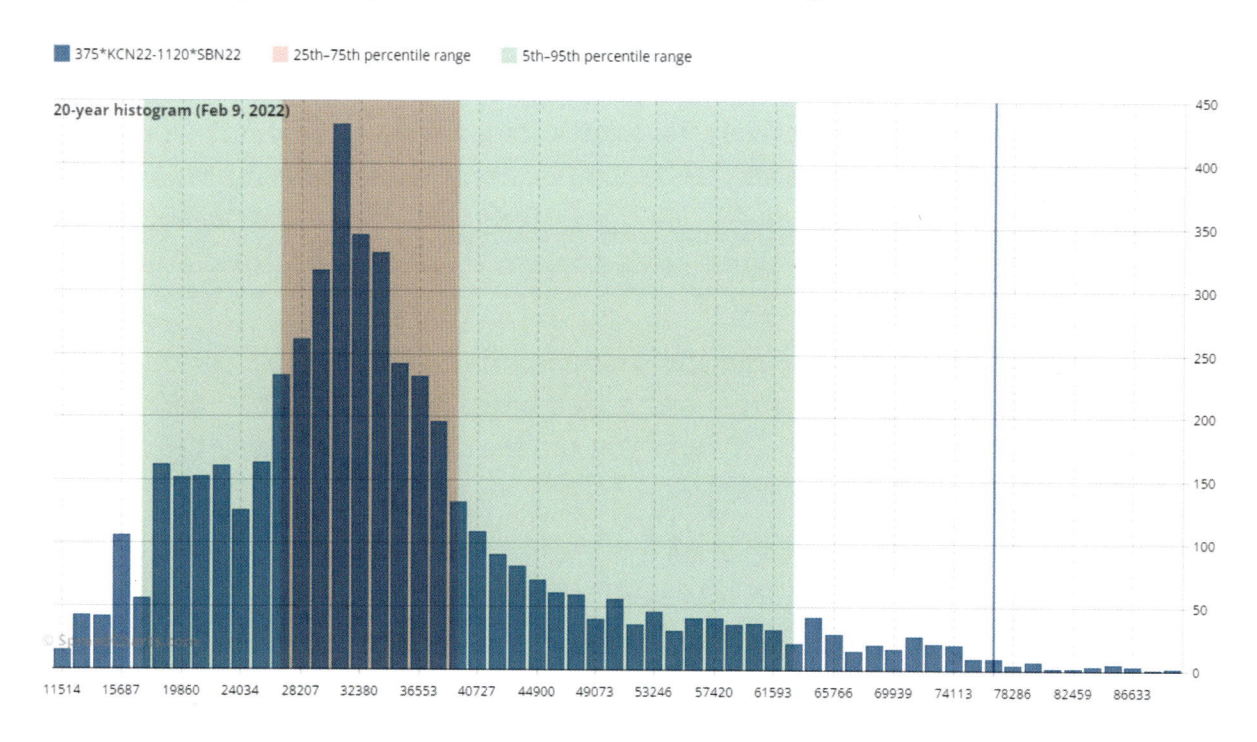

Figure 116 - KCN22-SBN22 Continuous histogram (SpreadCharts.com)

The price of the KCN22-SBN22 spread is at an extreme contango level. It is therefore likely that the price will return within the red area in the coming weeks/months, the one with the higher bars that acts as a 'magnet' for the price. The spread presents a compelling opportunity from a bearish perspective.

Another ratio I suggest is feeder cattle/live cattle (Figure 117).

Figure 117 - Feeder cattle/live cattle ratio (SpreadCharts.com)

For good reason and which you will see in Appendix A of the second volume, the ratio moves within the 1.10/1.40 range most of the time. A deviation out of this range represents an anomaly with one of the two futures heavily speculated. An anomaly, which, however, may not last long.

Again, an appropriate trading strategy can be studied whenever the ratio is outside the range.

Figure 118 - Corn/live cattle ratio (SpreadCharts.com)

There are numerous other examples, including combinations of grains, WTI crude oil with Brent or its derivatives, live cattle/lean hogs which behaves similarly to feeder cattle/live cattle, and so on. You can experiment by creating various combinations, like corn/live cattle, which you can see above (Figure 118).

In conclusion, what you have seen is probably the best investment strategy for experienced spread traders. You take a simple mathematical equation (in this case a ratio between two commodities) and plot the historical price behaviour. When you see values reaching extreme levels and then returning to historical values over and over again, you try to buy/sell into these temporary price anomalies and then wait for the value, much like the pendulum swing, to inevitably move in the opposite direction.

Do you now see why relying solely on seasonality fails to provide a full picture of the spread? It also prevents you from capturing many excellent trading opportunities.

Open Interest

CHAPTER 21

When trading commodities, whether through futures or spreads, it is crucial to seek as many confirmations as possible when making decisions. Market analysis requires discipline and hard work. However, this hard work can be incredibly rewarding when it enables you to piece together the fragments of a complex puzzle.

You have already encountered two important tools, volume and open interest, which I use in my analysis of a commodity or spread. These are essential technical indicators for understanding price direction. Let's first take a closer look at the difference between volume and open interest.

Volume

In trading, volume refers to the total number of contracts, shares, or units of a particular security, futures, ETF, etc., traded over a given period of time. It is a crucial aspect of market analysis and provides valuable insights into the strength and liquidity of that market.

The primary reasons volume is significant include:

a) Market activity: Volume reflects the degree of market activity and the strength of buying and selling pressure. Higher volume in a security indicates stronger market interest and suggests that a larger number of participants are actively trading the security.

b) Liquidity: Volume is closely linked to liquidity, which refers to how easily an underlying asset can be bought or sold without causing significant price movements. Higher volume generally indicates greater liquidity, making it easier for traders to execute their orders without significantly affecting the price of the security.

c) Trend confirmation: Analysing volume can help confirm the validity of price trends. In an uptrend, rising volume during price increases and declining volume during price pullbacks confirms the strength of the trend. Conversely, in a downtrend, higher volume during price drops and lower volume during price rallies validates the bearish sentiment.

d) Reversal signals: Significant changes in volume can indicate potential trend reversals. For instance, a volume surge accompanied by a sharp price decline could signal a shift from a bullish to a bearish trend, or vice versa. Traders often look for divergences between price and volume to identify potential turning points in the market.

Analysing volume patterns in conjunction with price patterns can provide valuable insights into market dynamics. For example, sudden volume spikes often indicate significant market events or news releases that attract a large number of traders. Volume surges can offer clues about potential trend reversals, breakouts, or the start of new trends.

Additionally, divergences, where price and volume move in opposite directions, are highly significant. For example, if a security's price is rising but volume is falling, it could suggest a weakening trend or a lack of conviction from market participants.

Therefore, volume represents the real interaction between supply and demand. It identifies whether there is an increase or decrease in investor interest towards a particular market.

Open Interest

Open interest is the total number of open derivative contracts, futures or options, that are not yet closed. While volume counts every contract that trades, open interest only counts those contracts that still have open market risk.

The open interest provides a more accurate picture of the options trading activity, and whether the money flowing into the futures and options markets is increasing or decreasing.

Rising open interest indicates the strength behind a move. If a market is moving higher or lower, and increasing open interest accompanies that move, it often signals validation of the direction of the movement and that the price is likely to continue in that same direction.

Decreasing open interest can signify that a market is entering a period of less active trading because market participants are not taking new positions and are closing out existing ones.

With the C.O.T. report, you have seen how to use open interest data. However, in my analysis, I also look at the open interest in the options, even though it is not easy to interpret it.

First, let's see what an option is (just the basics).

An option is a contract which gives the buyer the right, but not the obligation, to buy or sell an underlying asset at a specified price (strike), prior to or on a specified date (expiry), depending on the form of the option, by paying an amount of money (premium).

Thus, the options are derivatives (that is, their value derives directly from the markets and not by reference companies) as futures, they have an expiry/delivery time, and an open interest.

There are two types of options:

1. CALL, the buyer has the right, but not the obligation, to buy an underlying asset at a specified price (strike), before or on a specified date (expiry), depending on the form of the option, by paying an amount of money (premium).

2. PUT, the buyer has the right, but not the obligation, to sell an underlying asset at a specified price (strike), before or on a specified date (expiry), depending on the form of the option, by paying an amount of money (premium).

An option can be purchased but also sold. When you sell options, everything you have seen when buying is reversed.

So, an option is a contract which gives the seller the obligation to buy or sell an underlying asset at a fixed price (strike), before or on a specified date (expiry), depending on the form of the option, by cashing an amount of money (premium).

Compared to futures, however, the open interest in options is more difficult to interpret. While, as you have seen with the C.O.T. report, the open interest in futures is divided into long (that is, contracts bought and still open) and short (contracts sold and still open), and therefore it is possible to understand which of the two parties prevails, in order to then make different considerations, something which is not possible with options.

In fact, in the options, it is possible to see the open interest for each strike of each expiry both for the call and the put. As well as the total (all strikes and expires) for the two types of options.

What cannot be determined is how many options have been bought and sold, how many are used to hedge purchases or sales of the underlying, how many are used in spread strategies, and how many large traders there are (if any). However, you can also extrapolate some interesting data and make considerations that can help you in your analysis.

Before seeing the first data that you can get from the open interest, I will explain another aspect about options.

Depending on the price of the underlying asset, the strike can be of three types:

a) ATM (At The Money): the market price of the underlying asset is approximately equal to the strike price.
b) ITM (In The Money): the market price of the underlying asset is above (CALL) or below (PUT) the strike price.
c) OTM (Out The Money): the market price of the underlying asset is below (CALL) or above (PUT) the strike price.

So, the first data you get from the options open interest is the following: the PUT OTM strike of the nearest expiry with the highest open interest is an important support; the CALL OTM strike of the closer expiry with the highest open interest is an important resistance.

I will demonstrate this using a couple of examples. In Figure 119, you can see in the two columns in violet, the open interest of wheat options, both CALLS (left) and PUT (right).

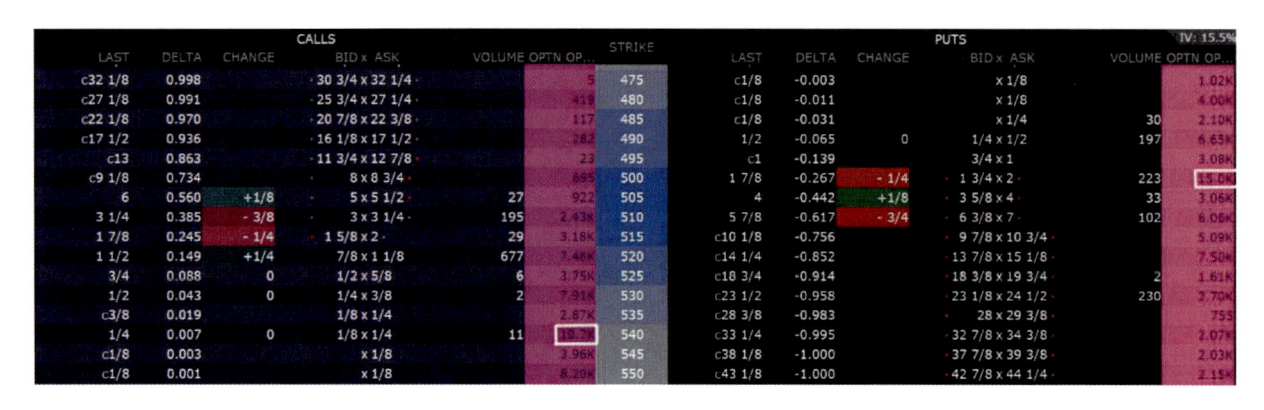

Figure 119 - Wheat options (Interactivebrokers.com)

First, the current price of the wheat futures is $ 508. Then, as you can see, for the CALL OTM options, the highest open interest is on strike 540 (10.4K), while for the PUT OTM options, the highest open interest is on strike 500 (15K).

Let's look at the Wheat futures chart with the two levels, $500 and $540 highlighted (Figure120).

You can visually see how the price of wheat has moved in the last few months between the two levels that you have identified with options open interest.

Figure 120 - Wheat daily futures chart (TradingView.com)

Let's see another example. In Figure 121, you can see the open interest of gold options, both CALLS (left) and PUTS (right).

142

Figure 121 - Gold options (Interactivebrokers.com)

The current price of gold futures is $ 1,322. The CALL OTM options strike with the highest open interest is $ 1,350 (6.23K), while the PUT OTM options strike with the highest open interest is $ 1,300 (5.31K).

In Figure 122 the gold chart with the two levels, $ 1,300 and $ 1,350, highlighted.

Figure 122 - Gold daily futures chart (TradingView.com)

Even in this case, the price is not insensitive to the two levels identified with the options.

Let's observe a final example before moving onto the reasons behind what you have seen. You can see in Figure 123 the open interest of natural gas options, both CALLS (left) and PUTS (right).

143

Figure 123 - Natural gas options (Interactivebrokers.com)

Using the same procedure as above, you have resistance at $ 2.75 (the CALL OTM options strike with the highest open interest) and support at $ 2.50 (the PUT OTM options strike with the highest open interest).

In Figure 124 you can see the natural gas chart with the two levels highlighted.

Figure 124 - Natural gas daily futures chart (TradingView.com)

The reasoning behind what you have seen above is very simple. When you sell options, you always try to do it at levels that you think the price cannot overcome. Very often you sell call options on a resistance (or above) and sell put options on a support (or below). On those levels, the contracts sold will be concentrated.

A second aspect you can get from the options open interest is the following.

The further a strike is from the At-The-Money price, the more the open interest will consist of contracts sold, and vice versa. The more a strike is close to the one At-The-Money the more its open interest will be made up of contracts bought. This includes both those that are directional on the market, and that buy options to hedge an opposite position on an underlying asset.

Now, I guess you are thinking, if you take the ATM strike and you subtract the PUT open interest from the one of the CALL, you will get a sort of net position of the C.O.T. Only in theory because the protagonists are different. In the C.O.T., you have seen they are the Non-Commercial, that is the hedge funds; the open interest in the options is mainly made up of retail traders. So, the forces on the ground are different.

But, why am I talking about this aspect? Precisely because the open interest of the options is mainly made up of small traders, it is visible to everybody, and therefore, the scene of manipulation precisely against the small traders.

I have had confirmation of this in the last two years (2018 and 2019), during my collaboration with a Swiss company that is involved in investments, especially in commodities. Working mainly with WTI crude oil, and also with EUR (the Euro futures), it was not uncommon to see on the day of the options expiry, the price close above a resistance or below a support. Actually, the whole week of the expiry of options is 'nervous' due to the consequent increase in volatility as well.

This is visible in commodities with liquid options, such as WTI crude oil or gold. In those with low open interest, like for example live cattle, it is practically absent. Therefore, when you work with certain commodities, pay attention to the expiration of the related options, there may be (for a few days at most) movements that do not reflect the fundamentals, particularly if the price is close to a support or resistance.

Nonetheless, you will understand this aspect better with experience and practice.

I conclude the part that concerns the open interest with a curiosity. Simply by reading the open interest of an underlying asset, you can understand if the price is in trend (bullish or bearish) or whether it is moving sideways (in a rectangular or triangular movement).

I am going to explain this better with a couple of examples. In both, I initially hide the column with the strike so as not to reveal the underlying asset. Below, you can see the open interest (Figure 125).

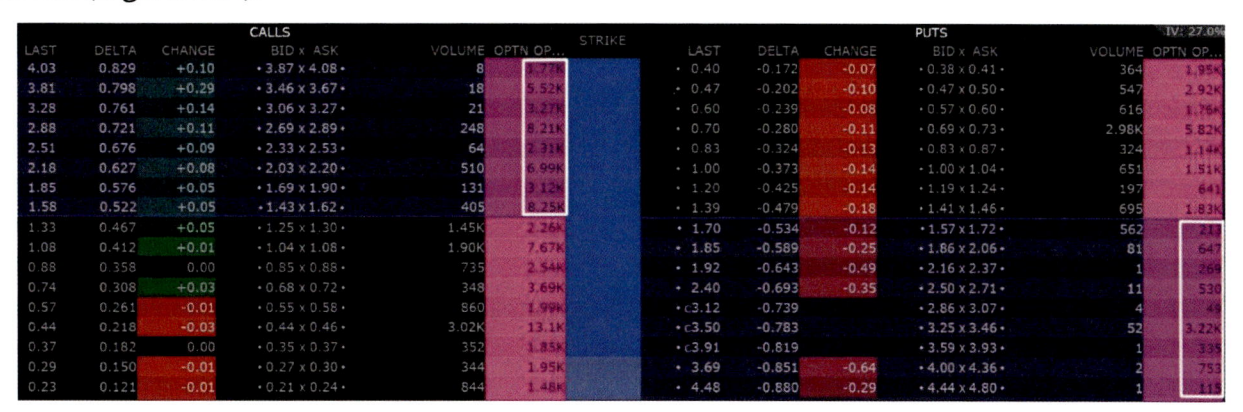

Figure 125 - Open Interest In-The-Money (www.interactivebrokers.com)

145

What you need to do is carefully examine the open interest of both In-The-Money (ITM) CALL and PUT options. As shown in the figure above, it is clear that the number of ITM CALL contracts significantly exceeds the number of PUT contracts. Furthermore, several CALL strike prices display a substantial open interest, indicating notable activity. So, what does this suggest?

It indicates that, in recent days or weeks, the price of the underlying asset has been rising, signalling an uptrend. Every time the At-The-Money strike price shifted upward, the volume of CALL options being purchased also increased. Meanwhile, those who had initially bought PUT options at those strike prices likely found themselves closing their positions at a loss, or in some cases, rolling their positions over to the next expiry in an attempt to recover.

Conversely, as the underlying asset's price climbed, those who had sold CALL options gradually began closing their contracts to limit exposure, reducing the overall supply of available CALL options. In simple terms, when you observe In-The-Money strike prices where CALL options have a high open interest and PUT options show relatively low open interest, it's a strong signal that the underlying asset is in a bullish trend. On the other hand, when PUT options dominate with a high open interest at ITM strikes and CALL open interest is significantly lower, this indicates a bearish trend in the underlying asset.

This information can provide valuable insights into market sentiment and positioning, as it reflects not only current market direction but also the behaviours and expectations of both buyers and sellers. Recognising this dynamic allows you to better anticipate potential moves in the underlying asset.

The open interest you saw above is that of the WTI crude oil, and you can see the chart in Figure 126.

Figure 126 - WTI Crude oil daily futures chart (TradingView.com)

The chart confirms what you read with the open interest, the uptrend of the underlying asset.

Let's see a second example, above in Figure 127 the open interest.

Figure 127 - Open Interest In-The-Money (www.interactivebrokers.com)

In this case, in regard to In-The-Money options, you have a low open interest for both, CALL and PUT options. This means that the underlying asset is moving sideways, as shown in the chart in Figure 128.

Figure 128 - Soybean daily futures chart (TradingView.com)

Soybean is the underlying asset, and the chart above demonstrates how prices move within an ascending triangle.

With that said, if you were to see a substantial increase in open interest in one of the two types of ITM options, it would mean that the price has at last broken out in either direction.

That concludes my discussion on options open interest. In addition to what has already been discussed, open interest can provide further insights and warning signals that may prove useful in your analysis. The best advice I can give you is to use it differently from how you saw it with the C.O.T. a few chapters ago. In other words, consider open interest as a tool that can be 'hunted' by the strong hands.

SUBJECTIVE PROBABILITY

CHAPTER 22

In the world of trading, making decisions solely based on chart patterns or technical signals can often lead to disappointing results. In this chapter, you will explore an alternative approach that relies on subjective probability, a concept that allows you to integrate personal experience and a deep understanding of the markets to improve your trading decisions.

Subjective probability is not just about numbers; it reflects the degree of conviction a trader has regarding a particular future event, based on careful analysis and detailed knowledge of market dynamics. Understanding how to apply this concept will enable you to more accurately pinpoint entry and exit points in your trades, bringing you closer to more professional trading.

Relying exclusively on a chart pattern to open a trade is a common mistake. Technical analysis, rather than being the solution, often represents an obstacle. It is essential to identify the key levels of a commodity where you should open a position, avoiding the sole reliance on chart patterns.

You need to use subjective probability, which is the numerical measure of probability reflecting the degree of personal conviction that a future event will occur.

Judgements in subjective probability are assessments of the likelihood of uncertain events or outcomes. It does not involve formal calculations and merely reflects the opinions and past experience of the subject.

It is widely believed that subjective probability is at the root of common mistakes and biases seen in the market. This does not surprise me, given the number of traders who lose money and the sheer amount of ignorance (understood as a lack of knowledge) that surrounds trading.

You know who Warren Buffett is. What you might not know is that Buffett's decision-making process is an exercise in subjective probability. Buffett uses 'risk arbitrage' ("*risk arbitrage is something I have been doing for forty years now*").

And if you dig deeper into your understanding of the Oracle of Omaha, you can clearly see that Buffett's risk arbitrage estimates are subjective probabilities. You can learn more about this in the book "*The Warren Buffett Portfolio – Mastering the Power of the Focus*

Investment Strategy".

Okay, now let's get practical. How can you use subjective probability to find an entry point in the market?

Let me start by saying that subjective probability differs from trader to trader. This is because everyone has different opinions and past experiences. It is precisely this experience, combined with your knowledge of commodities, that will be your best advisor. These factors will give you a level of sensitivity that will provide the greatest probability of success when entering the market.

Over time, you need to understand how a specific commodity or spread behaves, the movements it makes, and how it makes them. This will allow you to have a clearer view and identify the statistically most favourable levels for opening your trade.

Yes, I know, all this may seem complicated. But trading is not as easy as many people are led to believe, especially by certain advertisements and websites. Keep in mind that my results come from many years of study and practice. There was, and still is, a lot of work behind every decision I make.

You can achieve significant results in Spread Trading, even better than mine, but only if you follow what I explain in this book and, of course, if you work hard. You must change your mindset and become new people. You need to look at Spread Trading, and trading in general, with fresh eyes. A trader's mindset is the most important asset they have. A trader must have an entrepreneurial mindset and view trading as a business.

Let me give you an example. Below, you can see the daily chart of WTI crude oil (Figure 129)

Figure 129 - Crude oil daily chart (TradingView.com)

You will certainly have noticed how the $ XX.27 levels (i.e., $ 49.27, $ 50.27, $ 51.27, $ 52.27, etc.) for WTI crude oil are sensitive price levels.

This is just one aspect, one characteristic of WTI crude oil. Once you understand how a commodity moves, when you know it inside out, you will no longer need to open the chart to make your trading decisions.

And the world of commodities is full of these nuances; you need to thoroughly understand every commodity you trade. Below is another example. In Figure 130, you can see the daily chart of the wheat contract for delivery in July 2022.

Figure 130 - Wheat chart (TradingView.com)

I have highlighted the first three sensitive areas above the price level. Now, let us assume that after your analysis, you intend to sell the currency pair; at this point, you are only left with the decision of selecting the right level to open the trade.

One thing you must avoid at all costs is opening the trade at the current price, simply because your analysis has suggested that Wheat should rise or fall. This approach can lead to poor timing and suboptimal results.

Your analysis indicates where the commodity or the spread is likely to move in the medium to long term (assuming conditions remain stable), but in the short term, even in spread trading, which tends to be less manipulated, it is often speculation that drives price action.

If you look closely, you will notice that the three areas in the chart are marked with different colours. I have intentionally used these variations to help you better grasp the differing probabilities of the price reaching these levels and reversing its trend.

Assuming the conditions that led you to consider selling wheat have not changed, the first area (marked in orange) is the most likely to be reached by the price. However, it is also the area with the lowest probability of seeing the price stop and reverse into a renewed downward trend.

The second area (marked in yellow) has a lower probability of being reached by the price, but if the price does reach it, the likelihood of the currency pair resuming its downward movement increases. As for the third area (marked in green), it represents the zone with the highest probability of a trend reversal. However, there is a lower probability of the price reaching this level. If the price surpasses the green area, it is a clear signal to revisit your analysis as you may have misjudged the market conditions or overlooked a crucial factor.

There is no universal rule for determining the ideal level to place a sell order for wheat (or any other commodity or spread you may be trading). The decision hinges on your experience, intuition, and the probability you assign to the price reaching a particular level based on your analysis.

If your analysis proves to be accurate, there is a strong likelihood that the price will begin to move downwards in one of these three coloured areas. This is where you should aim to place your sell order. But which of the three levels is the best to choose?

Beyond your analysis, experience, and knowledge of the wheat market, it can be helpful to assess volatility as a determining factor. When volatility is high, the price will likely rise beyond the first level (orange) and may continue past the second level. On the other hand, in times of low volatility, the first level is often the most appropriate point at which to sell the currency pair.

So, wait for the price of wheat to reach the first area (orange). At that point, you should evaluate the strength of the trend, the volatility, and make an informed decision on whether to open a position or whether it might be wiser to continue waiting for better conditions.

Now, how do you set a profit target? The first and most important step is to determine your exit strategy in advance, before you even open the trade. This should be clearly laid out in your trading plan, which acts as your strategic guide. Your profit target needs to be both realistic and achievable, based on a solid statistical projection rather than arbitrary assumptions.

It is not just about setting any profit goal but applying the same rigorous analytical methods you used to determine your entry point. Use subjective probability to identify the optimal time and price level for closing the trade and securing a profit.

At this point, it is time to tell you that there is a method for identifying sensitive areas in a currency pair even though you lack significant experience. I will explain this technique using the daily chart of the SBN22-SBV22 spread. This spread is taken from my book, '*The Best Seasonal Spreads for 2022/2023*', and it was constructed by purchasing the sugar futures contract with delivery in July 2022 and selling the sugar futures contract with delivery in December 2022 (Figure 131).

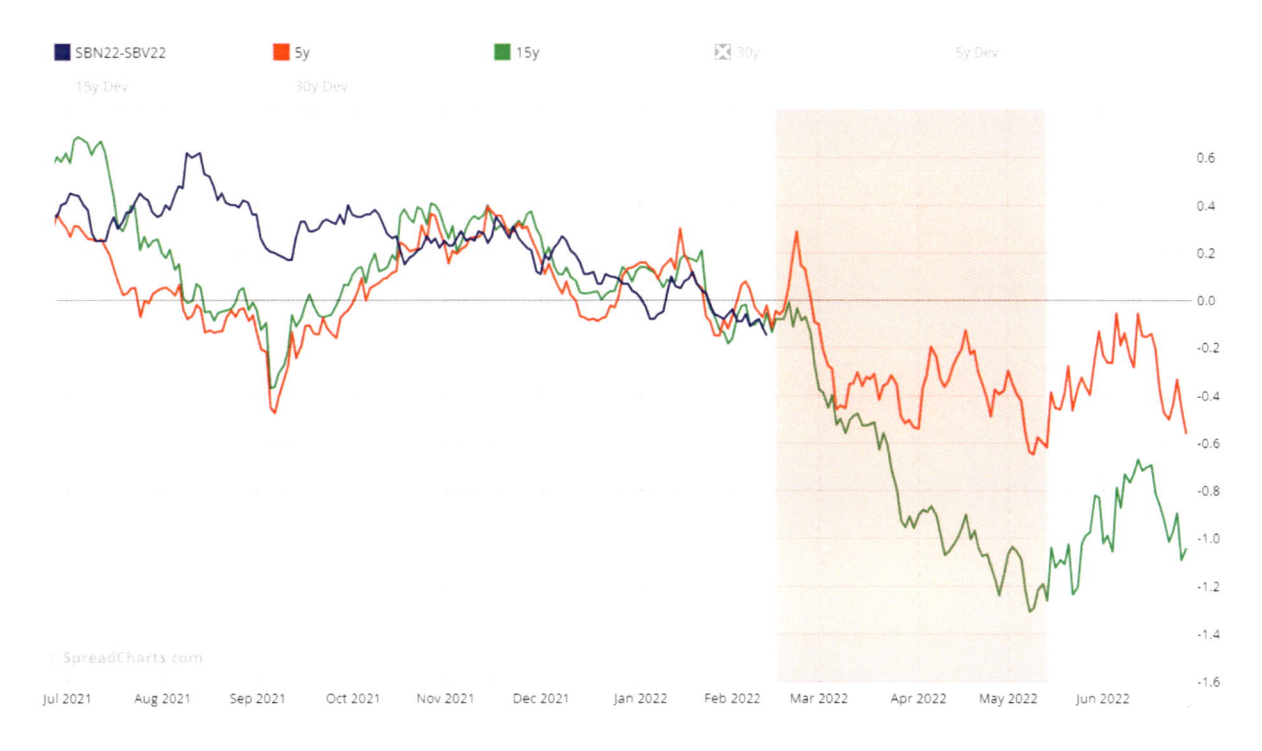

Figure 131 - SBN22-SBV22 chart (SpreadCharts.com)

Volume Profile is an advanced chart study that displays the amount of volume traded for an asset over a specific period and at specific price levels. You can see the first three sensitive areas of the sugar spread highlighted in Figure 132.

Figure 132 - SBN22-SBV22 chart with sensitive areas (TradingView)

Below, you can see the same TradingView chart, which, in addition to the same sensitive areas, also includes the Volume Profile (Figure 133).

Figure 133 - SBN22-SBV22 chart with Volume Profile (TradingView)

There are three different types of 'Volume Profile' that you can use in your trading. These types do not differ much in what they do; their difference lies in how they appear on the chart.

You should use the basic Volume Profile tool, VPVR (Volume Profile Visible Range), as it will help you visualise the amount of volume that forms at specific price levels. Volume Profile is essentially a volume study based on price; it differs slightly from the classic time-based volume that you typically see below the chart.

Let me briefly explain the main features using the SBN22-SBV22 spread chart shown earlier as an example. Volume Profile displays volume data as a histogram on the right side (although you can place it on the left side if you prefer) with different colours. The area marked in yellow and blue is called the Value Area (VA), and this is where 70% of the volumes are located.

The green line at the top (VAH or Value Area High) is the highest point of the Value Area, while the green line at the bottom (VAL or Value Area Low) is the lowest point of the Value Area. These are typically considered support and resistance levels.

Each individual bar in the Volume Profile histogram is called a 'Node'. The High Volume Nodes (HVN) are the points in the volume profile where there is significantly higher-than-average volume (blue lines), while the Low Volume Nodes (LVN) are points where the volume is significantly lower than average. The highest Volume Node in the volume profile (marked by the red line) is called the Point of Control (POC). It is the 'centre of gravity' on the chart, as it represents a significant retest point. The price tends to return to this level.

There is much more to say about the Volume Profile, but it would go beyond the scope of this book. If you have any doubts, curiosities, or questions, feel free to contact me via email, social media, or through my website.

What you have learned is how to find sensitive price areas through a strong increase in volume. Volume Profile helps traders identify where to enter and exit a trade. Over time, you will learn to recognise these areas even without the tool on your chart.

Two final things. First, if the time period on the chart increases, the Volume Profile changes (including the Value Area and most likely the POC). The same happens if the period decreases. This is because, naturally, with more or fewer trading days, there will be more or fewer volumes (which will be distributed differently). I typically use a chart covering the last 9-10 months.

Secondly, before you ask, here is the bad news. It is rare to find the Volume Profile for free on the various available platforms. To use it with TradingView, you need a pro account or a free trial (which is still limited to just one month).

In conclusion, no method in the world can guarantee 100% winning predictions; ultimately, it all comes down to a matter of probability. In subjective probability theory, it is up to you to analyse the assumptions and make the best decisions. This differs from technical analysis, which provides clear signals but often leads to losses.

Subjective probability is not just a matter of numbers and calculations; it is an art that improves with time and experience. Every trader develops their own sensitivity to market movements through constant observation and practice. This chapter has shown you how to use subjective probability to identify the best moments to enter or exit a trade, but remember, there are no foolproof methods.

The key to success in trading lies in your ability to adapt, learn from your mistakes, and continuously refine your techniques. Over time, you will learn to recognise the right signals and trust your judgement, making subjective probability a powerful and indispensable tool in your trading.

CROP YEAR

CHAPTER 23

In spread trading, the least risky and volatile spreads are generally Intramarket spreads, meaning those where you are simultaneously long and short on futures of the same commodity but with different delivery dates (also known as calendar spreads or intra-delivery spreads). These spreads tend to be considered safer because both legs of the trade respond to similar market dynamics, as they involve the same underlying asset. Most brokers recognise the relatively low risk associated with this type of spread and, consequently, apply a discount to the required margin. However, this does not hold true in all circumstances.

In particular, in agricultural markets, certain calendar spreads on the same commodity may require significantly different margins, and the reason behind these differences lies in a factor many traders overlook: the Crop Year.

The crop year is a fundamental concept that all traders should take into account when analysing an agricultural spread. But what exactly is the crop year?

The crop year is the period that runs from the harvest of one year to the harvest of the following year for a given crop. Each crop has a different crop year, and this annual cycle can significantly impact the price of a spread, influencing the margins required by the broker. For example, if you buy the ZCN21-ZCU21 and ZCN21-ZCH22 spreads, you will notice that the margin required by the broker is very different: $370 for the first and $600 for the second (margins at the time of writing this chapter).

Why this difference? In the case of the ZCN21-ZCU21 spread, both delivery dates refer to the same harvest, so the two contracts respond similarly to market news, fundamentals, and reports related to that specific harvest. Therefore, the perceived risk is lower.

In contrast, with the ZCN21-ZCH22 spread, you are long on a futures contract for the old crop and short on a contract for the new crop. In this case, the old crop contract will be more affected by immediate factors, such as weather conditions or production data, while the new crop contract will be more influenced by long-term forecasts, as the crop in question has not yet been planted.

This difference in risk exposure is the reason why ZCN21-ZCH22 is considered riskier than ZCN21-ZCU21, and consequently, the broker requires a higher margin for the second spread. A higher margin serves to cover the uncertainty related to the difference between the crops and the potential events that can have very different impacts on each leg of the spread.

Below, you can see the table with the crop year of all major agricultural commodities (Figure 134).

CBOT Wheat	July	May
CBOT Corn	December	September
CBOT Oats	July	May
CBOT Soybeans	September	August
CBOT Soybean Oil	October	September
CBOT Soybean Meal	October	September
KCBT Wheat	July	May
MGE Wheat	September	July
NYBT Cocoa	December	September
NYBT Coffee C	December	September
NYBT Cotton No.2	October	July
NYBT Frozen Concentrated Orange Juice	January	November
NYBT Sugar No.11	October	July

Figure 134 - Crop Year of the major markets

CBOT: Chicago Board of Trade; KCBT: Kansas City Board of Trade; MGE: Minneapolis Grain Exchange; NYBT: New York Board of Trade.

The table shows data for commodities traded on U.S. exchanges. The crop year, of course, varies depending on the country and the type of crop. One example is coffee, which is divided into two main qualities: Arabica and Robusta. The former is primarily grown in Brazil, with a crop year running from April 1st to March 31st; the latter, mainly grown in Vietnam, has a crop year from October 1st to September 30th.

In conclusion, when constructing a spread, it is essential to always keep in mind the delivery calendar of the futures involved. Ensuring you know the relevant crop year will help you avoid unpleasant surprises and better understand how specific events can affect contract prices.

INTERMARKET SPREADS

CHAPTER 24

~

This book on spread trading and commodity market has come to an end. I have tried to explain as simply, clearly and comprehensively as possible all aspects of this type of trading; I have put in all my knowledge and experience. In the second volume '*Commodity Spread Trading - The Correct Method of Analysis*' you will find, as much as possible, what you have learned in this book in practice.

But before the final conclusions I will deal with the last topic. Last not in importance but in complexity. In fact, what I am about to explain is ignored by almost all traders.

As you have seen, there are three types of spreads: Intramarket, Intermarket and Inter-Exchange. Intramarket spreads are the simplest because they involve only one commodity and are therefore the result of a subtraction of prices between two futures contracts. The same applies to Inter-Exchange spreads since, even though they are quoted on different exchanges, the commodity on which the spread is constructed is always the same (e.g., wheat).

Things get a bit more complicated with Intermarket spreads as they are constructed with two (or more for multi-leg spreads) commodities. Different commodities mean different prices and different dollar value of price movement.

Unit Move

I have already broadly explained the Unit Move in Chapter 6, now I will elaborate on it. The Unit Move indicates the amount of money you gain or lose, with the price movement of a dollar, in the corresponding market. When you construct an Intermarket spread, the commodities used will not always have the same Unit Move, and in order for the spread to be constructed correctly you will need to multiply each commodity by its Unit Move.

An example is the gold-silver spread. The futures of the two metals have a different Unit Move, that of gold is $100, that of silver is $5,000. So, if you have to construct the GCZ22-2*SIZ22 spread you have to multiply each of the legs by its Unit Move, so:

100*GCZ22-5000*2*SIZ22

However, some software such as SeasonAlgo and Moore Research already have this type of operation built in, so you do not have to do anything. SpreadCharts on the other hand, is not programmed to do this type of calculation automatically and so you are required to enter the Unit Move in the spread if you want to see the chart correctly.

So far it is quite simple; if you are subscribed to SeasonAlgo or Moore Research you do not have to do anything, but if you are using SpreadCharts like me you simply multiply each leg by its Unit Move. In Appendix B you will find the Unit Move of all major commodities.

But there is a slight problem. In fact, the price of a spread built with SeasonAlgo is not always the same as the price on the platform of brokers such as Interactive Brokers. This is because SeasonAlgo for some commodities uses a different Unit Move. Taking the example of GCZ22-SIZ22:

- Interactive Brokers: 100*GCZ22-5000*2*SIZ22
- SeasonAlgo: 100*GCZ22-50*2*SIZ22

The reason is that while with Interactive Brokers the Tick Move (i.e. the smallest movement the futures contract can make) is $0.005, with SeasonAlgo it is $0.5. The Tick Move value is $25 with both software; however, the price of the spread is different.

This difference also occurs in some Intramarket spreads. I remember a few months ago I received an email about this very issue from a trader who noticed a price difference between SeasonAlgo and Interactive Brokers in an Intramarket spread on copper. For Interactive Brokers the Unit Move of copper is $25,000 with a Tick Move of $0.0005 while for SeasonAlgo the Unit Move is $250 and the Tick Move is $0.05. For both, the Tick Move is $12.5.

The commodities that have a different Unit Move are:

- Coffee: $37.500 (IB) - $375 (SeasonAlgo)
- Copper: $25.000 (IB) - $250 (SeasonAlgo)
- Cotton: $50.000 (IB) - $500 (SeasonAlgo)
- Orange Juice: $15.000 (IB) - $150 (SeasonAlgo)
- Silver: $5.000 (IB) - $50 (SeasonAlgo)
- Sugar: $112.000 (IB) - $1.120 (SeasonAlgo)

As mentioned, you will find all the correct Unit Moves of the major commodities in Appendix B. To make sure you display the chart correctly, the best thing to do when building an Intermarket spread is to do as I do, build it on SpreadCharts using the correct Unit Move. This does nothing when you go to trade the spread on Interactive Brokers, the Tick Move will have equal value.

Now I will tell you about a variable that practically nobody considers when it comes to Intermarket spreads, that is volatility.

Volatility

Volatility, by definition, measures the price variation of an asset (such as a commodity) over a specific period of time. It is a fundamental parameter for determining the level of risk associated with a trading operation. The higher the volatility, the higher the perceived risk of the asset, and consequently, the trading operation will be considered more dangerous. This is a crucial aspect that you must always bear in mind when analysing a market, because volatility can influence not only the behaviour of the individual asset but also the spread you have chosen to trade.

When working with Intermarket spreads, you will find yourself comparing two (or more) commodities that will inevitably have different levels of volatility. In some cases, the difference will be minimal and therefore negligible, not significantly affecting the spread. However, there are situations where the commodities involved have very different volatilities, and this imbalance can greatly impact the movement of the spread and, consequently, your trading results.

One of the common mistakes traders make is underestimating this aspect. As I have already mentioned, most traders tend to focus solely on the opportunity offered by a statistical database, passively accepting the proposed spread. Their priority is not to complicate matters too much.

However, there are experienced traders who choose to adopt a more sophisticated approach by modifying an Intermarket spread to make it more balanced. Their goal is to prevent the higher volatility of one of the commodities from disproportionately influencing the price of the spread. This technique requires a deeper understanding of the behaviour of the individual assets and their relationship within the spread, but it can make a significant difference, especially in terms of trade stability and predictability.

How do these traders modify an Intermarket spread? The primary method involves increasing or decreasing the number of contracts on one of the commodities involved to balance the different volatilities. This allows you to have greater control over the movement of the spread, reducing the risk that the higher volatility of one asset might create undesirable imbalances.

Let's look at some examples to clarify this concept. One of the most common and well-known spreads is the gold-silver spread. In this case, all major databases construct the spread in the form GC-2SI, meaning one gold futures contract minus two silver futures contracts. This specific structure takes into account the fact that silver is generally more volatile than gold, and therefore, to compensate for this volatility, a ratio of two silver contracts for each gold contract is used.

The spread GCZ22-2SIZ22, constructed with SpreadCharts, can be represented as:

100GCZ22-5000 2SIZ22

Which, when simplified, becomes:

GCZ22-50 2*SIZ22

In this way, the spread, as shown in Figure 135, is balanced, taking into account the different volatilities of the two metals.

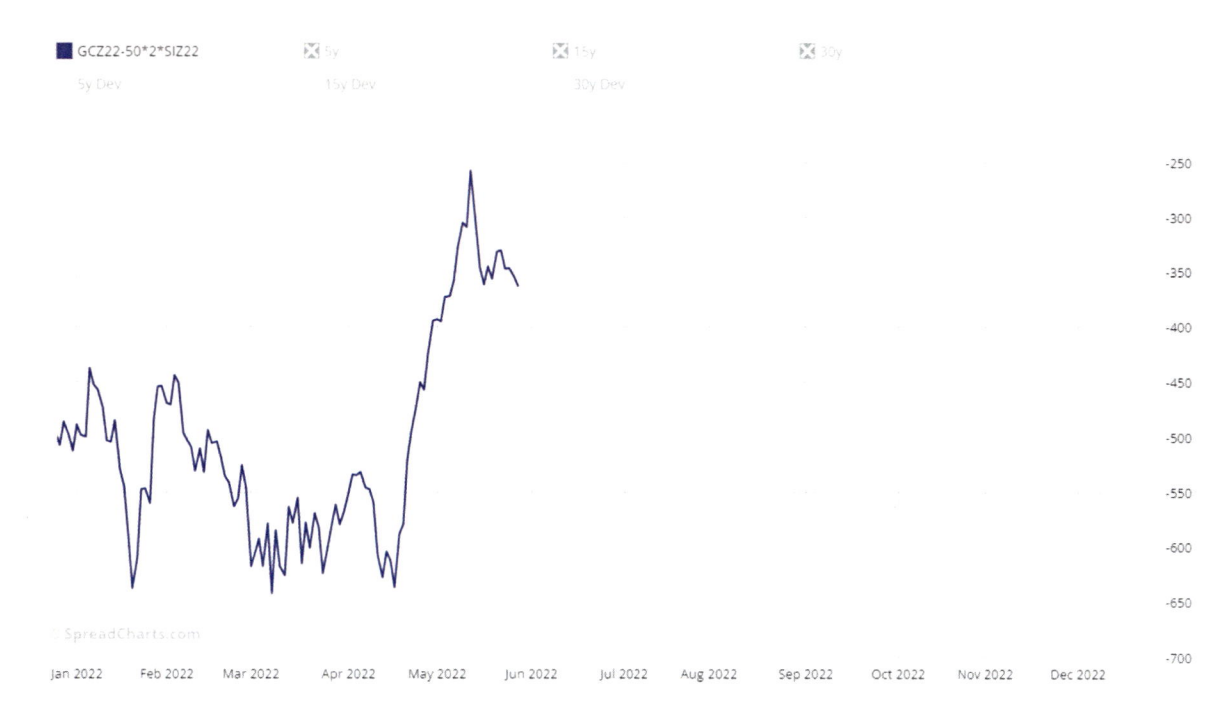

Figure 135 - GCZ22-50*2*SIZ22 spread chart (SpreadCharts.com)

This is the correct spread chart. However, one thing that especially those who work with these two metals know, the volatility of silver is usually much higher than that of gold. I now show you a study carried out by Weijie Jiang, a trader and friend with whom I have the pleasure of exchanging views via e-mail. Below in Figure 136 you can see the graph of the volatility study with a 1:1 ratio i.e., corresponding to the GCZ22-50*2*SIZ22 spread.

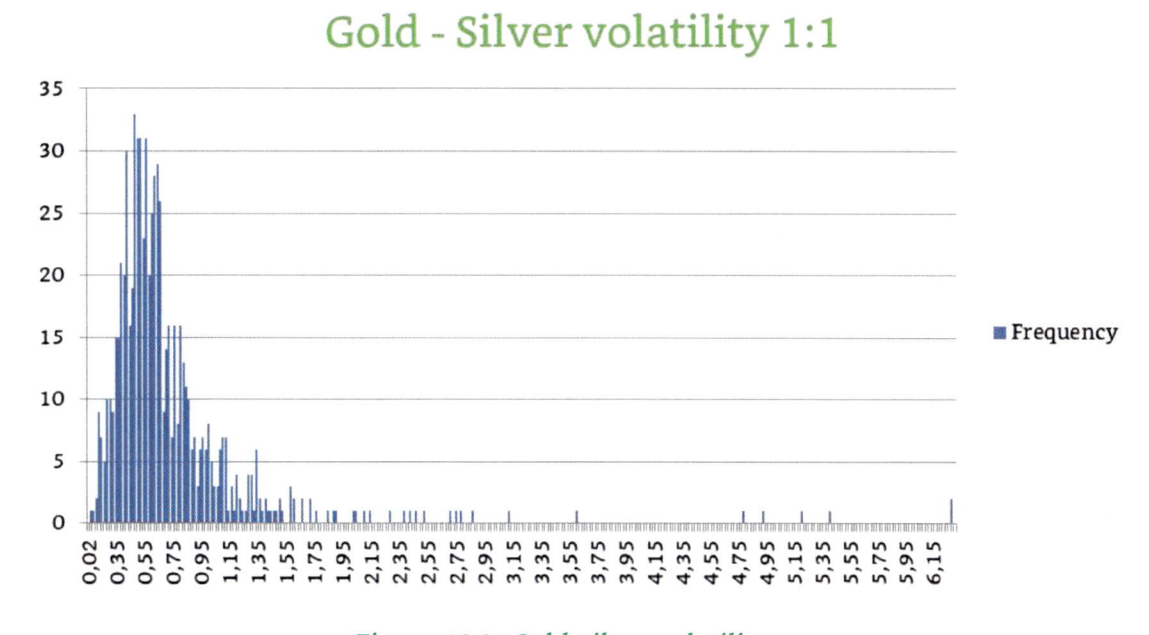

Figure 136 - Gold-silver volatility 1:1

Before explaining the meaning of those histograms, I will also show you the same

161

graph but with a 1:0.5 ratio that corresponds this time to the GCZ22-50*SIZ22 spread (Figure 137).

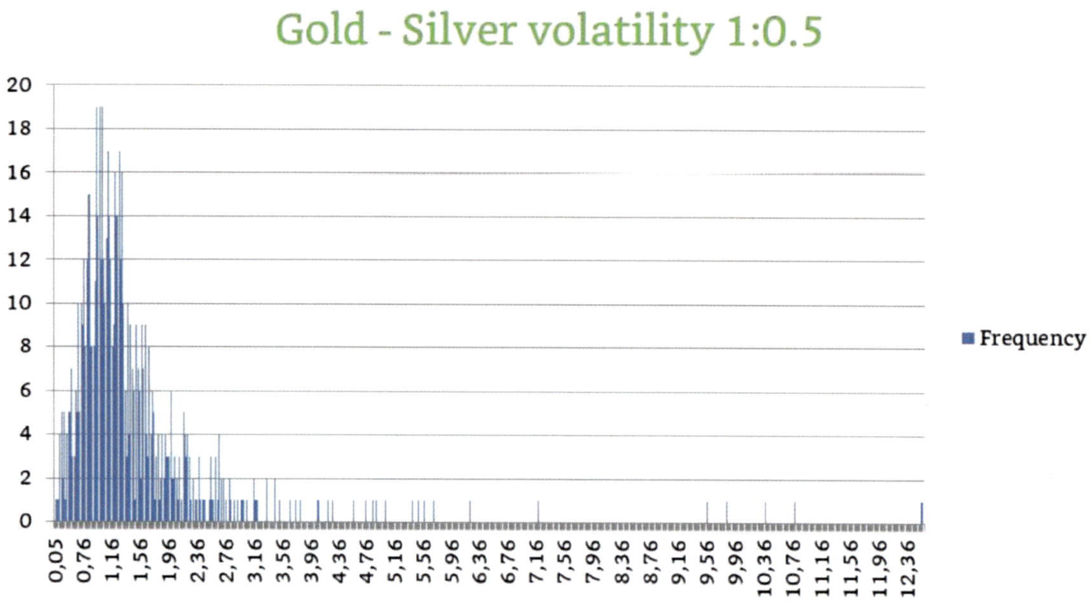

Figure 137 - Gold-silver volatility 1:0.5

The study calculates the daily volatility ratio between gold and silver. Each histogram represents a range of values within which the daily volatility ratios fall. The higher the column, the greater the number of daily ratios that fall within that specific range (frequency). All the charts presented in this chapter have been created using data from the past three years (2020-2022), thus providing an updated and relevant representation of the volatility dynamics between the two metals.

The ideal chart is one where the tallest columns are positioned around the value of 1 and its immediate surroundings. This is because the value of 1 represents the scenario in which the two futures contracts have the same volatility, a signal of perfect equilibrium. Looking at the two charts above, it is evident that the second configuration, with a 1:0.5 ratio, comes closer to this ideal condition.

In the first chart, which shows a 1:1 volatility ratio (Figure 136), the tallest columns, or those with the highest frequency, are within a range of 0.39 to 0.65. These values are clearly skewed towards the lower end relative to 1, indicating that the volatilities of the two futures contracts are quite different, with a clear predominance of silver's volatility.

In the second chart (Figure 137), the situation has improved significantly thanks to the 1:0.5 ratio, which halves silver's volatility. This adjustment has resulted in a much more balanced outcome. The tallest columns are now in the 0.76-1.28 range, with the peak right around 1 and the adjacent columns, indicating that the two volatilities are now much closer and balanced, creating an optimal condition for spread trading.

Observe how the chart changes using the GCZ22-50*SIZ22 spread (Figure 138).

Figure 138 - GCZ22-50*SIZ22 spread chart (SpreadCharts.com)

By comparing the charts of the two spreads, it immediately becomes clear that in the GCZ22-50SIZ22 spread in Figure 138, the impact of volatility is lower than in the GCZ22-502SIZ22 spread in Figure 135. This is evident not only from the smaller minimum/maximum range but also from the more linear trend of the spread.

Imagine two traders who, at the beginning of February, with a correct bullish outlook on gold relative to silver, entered a long position on the gold-silver spread, one on the GCZ22-502SIZ22 spread and the other on the GCZ22-50SIZ22 spread. The first trader was almost certainly stopped out, incurring a loss, while the second trader closed the trade with a good profit.

Let me give you another example. Drawing inspiration from a report, in one of my articles, I analysed the KCN22-SBN22 spread (https://tradingwithdavid.com/it/idea-di-trading-da-un-ratio/). I had an exchange of opinions with some traders about the number of contracts to use based on the volatility of the two commodities. I apply the same procedure as seen with the gold-silver spread.

The KCN22-SBN22 spread, constructed with SpreadCharts, is as follows:

375*KCN22-1120*SBN22

which minimised is:

KCN22-3*SBN22

In Figure 139 you can see the current chart.

*Figure 139 - KCN22-3*SBN22 spread chart (SpreadCharts.com)*

I do not do any analysis, all the reasons that led me to choose this combination of commodities and the spread considerations, as mentioned can be found in the relevant article on my site.

Of the two commodities, coffee generally has a higher volatility than sugar, so I apply the same volatility study as Weijie to assess its magnitude and impact on the spread. In Figure 140 you can see the graph of the volatility study with a 1:1 ratio, i.e., corresponding to the KCN22-3*SBN22 spread.

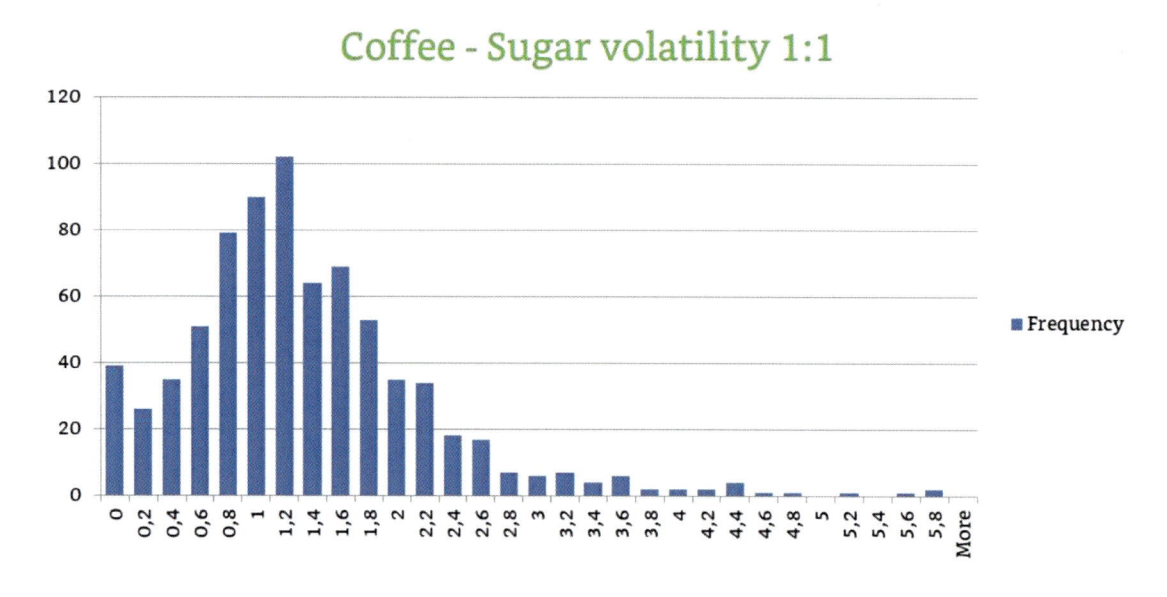

Figure 140 - Coffee-sugar volatility 1:1

164

In Figure 141, you can see the chart of the volatility study with a 1:1.33 ratio, i.e., corresponding to the KCN22-4*SBN22 spread.

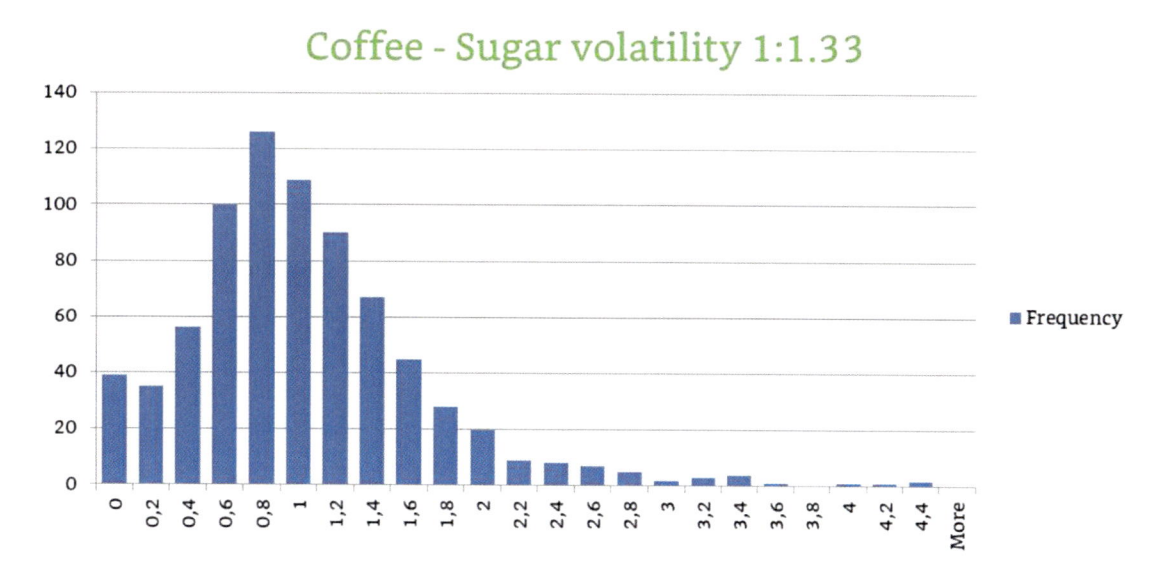

Figure 141 - Coffee-sugar volatility 1:1.33

The two charts above are very similar and differ only in a few nuances. In the first chart, the one with a volatility of 1:1 the three highest columns are 0.8 - 1 - 1.2 while in the one with a volatility of 1:1.33 they are 0.6 - 0.8 - 1. Thus, in the first, chart the volatility is slightly better distributed, however in the second the frequency (column height) is higher with as many as 4 columns (range 0.6/1.2) above 80. I will now show you the KCN22-4*SBN22 chart (Figure 142).

*Figure 142 - KCN22-4*SBN22 spread chart (SpreadCharts.com)*

The graphical difference of the two spreads is really minimal. Although coffee has a higher volatility than sugar, it is not particularly noticeable at the spread level. The KCN22-4*SBN22 spread may be preferable as it protects on those days where the volatility of coffee is much higher than that of sugar.

This can be seen in the two graphs in Figure 140 and Figure 141. The graph with volatility 1:1 has a maximum value of 5.8 (i.e., that column shows the number of days on which the volatility of coffee was almost 6 times that of sugar). The graph with volatility 1:33 has a maximum value of 4.4 (i.e., coffee had a volatility of almost 4.5 times that of sugar). So, with the KCN22-4*SBN22 spread there is more protection on those days when the volatility of coffee is very high.

At this point, you are surely thinking, "*yes, all very interesting but where do I find this information?*" Well, you do not find them, you have to build them. The data for each commodity, as seen in the chapter on Value-at-Risk, can be downloaded from Investing.com. To construct the graph, you need to have a good knowledge of Excel (or have a friend who does and can help you with this) and then use a simple formula that is the basis of Weijie's study.

For each day of the period, you are looking at (I use data from the last 3 years), you have to subtract the minimum from the maximum and then divide the result by the previous day's close. I take coffee as an example:

27 May 2022: high 229.90 - low 224.20

26 May 2022: close 226.60

The operation to be carried out is as follows:

(229.90 – 224.20) / 226.60 = 0.025200

Once you have done this for all the days under consideration and for both commodities, you must divide each daily value of the first commodity by that of the second as shown below:

27 May 2022: coffee 0.025200 – sugar 0.016888

The operation to be carried out is as follows:

0.025200 / 0.016888 = 1.49

All the results you get should then be represented in a histogram chart.

As you have seen, you can change the volatility by multiplying one of the two commodities by a parameter. In the case of the coffee-sugar spread, I multiplied the volatility of sugar by 1.33 in the following way:

27 May 2022: coffee 0.025200 – sugar 0.016888

The operation to be carried out is as follows:

0.025200 / (0.016888 * 1.33) = 1.12

You can see how the value has thus fallen closer to the ideal value of 1 (i.e., with the same volatility for both commodities). Why did I choose 1.33? Because that is the parameter that will change the number of contracts for that commodity. How? With a simple multiplication as shown below:

parameter * number of contracts = new number of contracts

In the example of the coffee-sugar spread, the number of sugar contracts is 3, so:

1.33 x 3 (sugar contracts) = 4 (new sugar contracts)

So, the study with a volatility of 1:1.33 corresponds to the KCN22-4*SBN22 spread. If you want to increase the number of sugar contracts to 5, you have to use the parameter 1.66. With a parameter of 2 the number of contracts increases to 6 and so on. Obviously, <u>the number of contracts must always be a whole number</u>.

With the gold-silver spread (GCZ22-50*2*SIZ22) using the parameter 0.5 in the silver volatility I get the following spread:

parameter * number of contracts = new number of contracts

In the example of the gold-silver spread, the number of silver contracts is 2, so:

0.5 x 2 (silver contracts) = 1 (new silver contracts)

And so, <u>the new spread will be as follows</u>:

GCZ22-50*SIZ22

Once you have changed the parameter and compared the histogram chart with the original (the one with 1:1 volatility) you will make your considerations and use the spread that gives you the best volatility ratio.

This is an aspect that is not explained in any course (like many of the ones you have seen in this book). It is something that requires work, patience and study, all things that most traders do not possess. Unfortunately, more and more the message goes out that if you follow what is explained, earning money from trading is easy.

Always remember: nowadays, in almost every industry, it is much easier to know how to sell yourself than to demonstrate real expertise. If you know how to present yourself and how to promote your services or products, you can make a lot of money, even if you have limited knowledge or offer something of low quality. Just take a look at what happens online every day. The glowing reviews you read? They are often fake, paid for. There are people and agencies whose job it is to write positive (or negative) reviews in exchange for money.

And those video testimonials? They are often performed by actors, sometimes even professionals, who can be hired by anyone. Personally, rather than convincing me to buy or subscribe, they only make me want to run in the opposite direction.

This trend of prioritising self-promotion over substance has become more widespread in recent years, especially with the rise of social media platforms. It's a reminder of how crucial it is to be discerning, as appearances can be deceiving. Many individuals are profiting from clever marketing rather than genuine expertise or value.

A second (and final) aspect of Intermarket spreads is the value of the two (or more) futures that make up the spread. I am talking about value, not price. Think of value as the total cost you would incur if the futures contract were to be delivered. This concept goes beyond just the market price, as it reflects the actual underlying worth of the assets involved. Let me show you this concept with an example. I take the ZSN22-ZLN22 spread with a current price of $17.50 for soybean and 80 cents for soybean oil, here is how I proceed:

The spread constructed on SpreadCharts is:

50*ZSN22-600*ZLN22

So, the calculation becomes:

50 * $1,750 – 600 * $80 = $87,500 - $48,000 = $39,500

One can clearly see that the values are unbalanced as the soybean contract is about twice as valuable as the soybean oil contract. So, it might be a good idea to sell more soybean oil contracts to better balance the spread. The result would be this equity spread:

$87500 / $48000 = $1.82 (number of soybean oil contracts)

50*ZSN22-600*1,82*ZLN22

Now the spread is balanced with the two futures having the same value. In Figure 143 you can sell the spread 50*ZSN22-600*ZLN22 and in Figure 144 the spread 50*ZSN22-600*1.82*ZLN22 (in this example I have not minimised the spread).

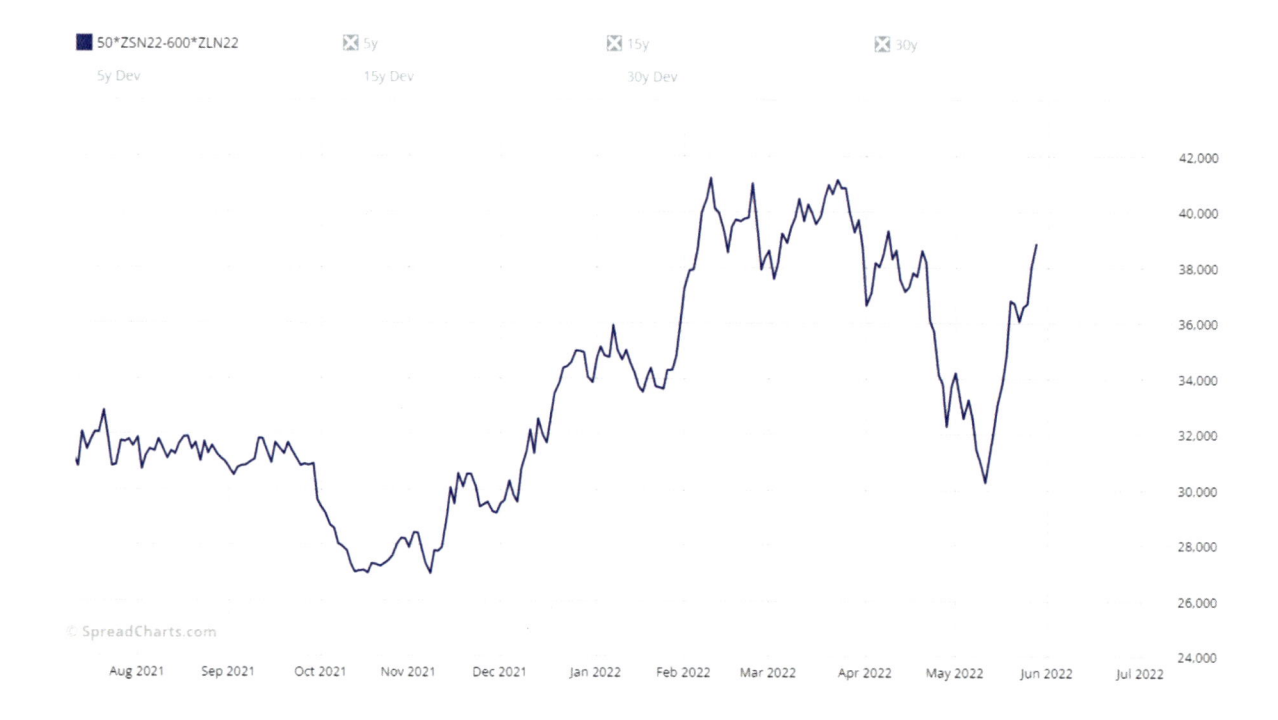

*Figure 143 - 50*ZSN22-600*ZLN22 spread chart (SpreadCharts.com)*

Figure 144 - 50*ZSN22-600*1,82*ZLN22 spread chart (SpreadCharts.com)

The equity spread is the correct form for analysing Intermarket spreads. If you plot a chart on SpreadCharts, the y-axis will correspond to the $ values, so you can easily see how your P/L will change depending on how the spread moves. Obviously, changing the number of contracts of one of the commodities that make up the spread will change the chart.

Keep in mind that what has been discussed is purely for analytical purposes. In practice, when trading on a platform, you can only buy whole contracts, so you cannot, for example, purchase 1.82 contracts. If the calculation results in a fractional number, you will need to round up or down and buy or sell whole contracts. In this specific case, you would buy 1 soybean contract and sell 2 (rounded from 1.82) soybean oil contracts (ZS-2*ZL). On platforms that require it, you will also need to enter the Unit Move.

Equating the value of the two futures is however something subjective, it depends on you, your way of trading, and seeing a spread.

That's really all; in these 24 chapters, I have explained every aspect of spread trading to you. Now, on a theoretical level, you have a complete understanding of this particular type of trading. The next chapter, the final conclusions.

FINAL COMMENTS

CHAPTER 25

You have come to the end of this course on commodities and spread trading. I would therefore like to conclude with some considerations that arise from my experience that I hope are useful, especially to those who are not familiar with trading.

Now you are probably thinking: "*I read the book, I know everything I need to know about Commodity spread trading, I am ready to start trading*". Not that simple!

Undoubtedly, reading this book has given you the knowledge about spread trading (and commodities), but what a book or course cannot give you, is experience. You need to develop a bit of experience, and you must understand the commodity market a lot more. Taking a theoretical course is one thing, applying it in the real market is another.

If you have never traded, not only with spread trading, but generally, and before you start using the real money that you worked so hard to get, you should do at least 25-30 trades on a demo platform. The number of these demo trades should drop to around 10-15 if you are already trading, but just not with spread trading.

Only after this will you be able to start trading on a real platform, but only with Intramarket spreads; these are more comfortable for you and have a maximum margin of $ 400-500. Once you have gained more experience, I would then recommend that you trade intermarket spreads.

Experience cannot be taught; it builds over time and from mistakes. It is much better when mistakes are made in such a way that they do not lead to a loss of money. Like most traders, I started losing some of my savings. I made errors that led me, in time, to understand the proper way to trade. If you can get the same experience without losing money, however, this would be far better.

As to making mistakes, let's see the most common ones, at least initially, and that you have to avoid doing. As mentioned, it is imperative to diversify your investments, and should be very careful to get it right.

A first consideration: if there is more than one spread with the same commodity (e.g., corn) recommended by the statistical databases, I always prefer an Intramarket spread to an Intermarket one. The reason is that it has a lower margin and allows me to open more trades against the only one of an Intermarket spread. This enables me to get a better management of a position.

So, if SeasonAlgo recommends the spreads, corn/corn (different deliveries) and corn/wheat, I do not trade both of them but just corn/corn. By the same margin of corn/wheat, I can trade four or five contracts of corn/corn.

Now, two mistakes that you should avoid. The first is to never be overexposed with a single commodity. For example, if the statistical database recommends the (bearish) spreads corn/soybean and wheat/soybean, by selling both of them, you would be long with two positions on soybean. Better to pick one and diversify the portfolio by choosing another spread (e.g., on meats or metals).

A second mistake to avoid is to be both long and short on the same commodity. For example, the statistical database recommends you the (bullish) spreads corn/wheat and wheat/soybean, by buying both of them, it would mean being long and short on the wheat and would not make much sense.

Even in this case, you have to choose one of them, and then, if possible, diversify your portfolio with a spread in another industry (naturally, if your money management allows it).

Now, let's see some considerations on the operational level. In Intermarket spreads, you should always bear in mind the value of the futures contracts that make up the spread because they can have very different values.

An example to get this completely clear. Moore Research recommends the intermarket spread HEM18-LEV18; it means buying the lean hogs futures delivery June 2018, and selling the live cattle futures delivery October 2018.

Currently, the price of the two futures is $ 79.000 for the lean hogs futures delivery June 2018, and $ 114.600 for the live cattle futures delivery October 2018. If, for example, both the futures increase their prices by one percentage point, your spread loses. This is because 1% on $ 79.000 (the futures purchased) is less than 1% on $ 118.100 (the futures sold).

Therefore, always bear in mind the value of the two futures that make up the spread. Not only, but you should also consider that the more the deliveries of the legs of a spread are far away, the more they are distant, meaning that the price of the spread is more likely to be volatile.

You must, then, also keep in mind that, regardless of the type of spread (Intramarket, Intermarket or Inter-Exchange), the earliest delivery will always react more to a piece of news or data than the farthest one.

In addition, good news or data will have the same impact on both the futures, but a bit more for the one with the earliest delivery. For example, if you are long on the spread ZCH18-ZCM18 (buying corn futures contract delivery in March 2018 and selling corn futures contract delivery in June 2018), a drought will affect positively both the futures, but a bit more the delivery March 2018 because less time is left on the expiry of the contract. Moreover, volumes will be focused more on the earliest delivery than the following.

Another factor to keep in mind, the impact that currencies might have on a commodity market are, and in particular, those of emerging countries. Of those countries that often produce, import and export commodities (just think of coffee and Brazilian Real), and you know very well that commodities are quoted in dollars.

A strong dollar puts a lot of pressure on commodities, and this creates problems for American producers because they have more difficulties in exporting than before, due to the strength of their currency.

Currencies that can influence commodity markets are those of emerging countries that are strong producers such as Brazil (Real) that besides coffee, along with Argentina (Peso) produce about 48% of the world's soybean. India (Rupee) the largest producer of cotton. Russia (Ruble) the largest exporter of wheat in the world (source USDA). China (Yuan) besides being a strong producer of commodities is the largest importing country [data for 2018].

With their currencies, which have heavily depreciated against the US dollar, these countries could increase exports abroad, putting further pressure on commodity prices.

This is the main reason (but not the only reason) why the prices of several commodities were at levels of production costs, or even below, from 2016 to May 2019.

The currencies of emerging countries are something that you always have to evaluate when you do your analysis. Similarly, you need to read the various reports released in order to have an updated view on commodities. You will find listed, with their internet sites, in Appendix E.

Holiday periods are another factor to take into account when you trade. They are periods in which the volume decreases considerably, and violent movements may occur. For this reason, I never trade in Summer (about from July 20 to August 20), and during the Christmas season (about from mid-December to the first week of January).

Everything you have seen in this book is not suitable for 'all seasons', since you always have to evaluate the historical moment you are living in. In some situations, it is not unusual to see movements, in short to medium term, that are completely devoid of logic.

This is what has been happening in the markets since the end of February 2020 with the 'Covid-19' crisis. Everything seems unaligned. Any connection with fundamentals and reality evaporates like a mist hit by the sun when markets collide with the general hysteria of traders, or the need to recover heavy losses from Hedge Funds. Everything loses meaning.

So, do not be surprised if you see the S&P 500 index collapse, with gold falling, as shown in the chart in Figure 145, in periods like this anything could happen. After all, it is not an ordinary financial crisis, but due to a pandemic.

Figure 145 - S&P 500 Index and Gold Futures (TradingView.com)

What has happened in this case is very simple. Hedge Funds were overexposed in the stock markets. With the collapse of the S&P 500, they suffered heavy losses and to cover them, they closed precipitously all their gaining assets, including gold.

My last tip: markets do not give away money. If there are situations that lead you to think so, be very careful. The reality is, there is no effortless money in the markets.

I hope I have managed to provide you with straightforward and positive guidance in commodity market analysis and the fundamentals for understanding spread trading. Now you should keep learning and gain practical experience. Spread trading is a great way to trade but it is not as easy as it may seem, and you cannot succeed at it simply by reading a book or following a course.

Never forget that the statistical databases, Moore Research and SeasonAlgo, are not everything you need to know. They are unquestionably important; they add weight to your analysis but not alone.

If you want to know my methods step by step based on what I have explained in this book, I suggest you read my second book: "*Spread trading – The Correct Method of Analysis*".

On my website https://tradingwithdavid.com, you will find articles, analyses, and much more educational material. My other books on trading and financial markets are available for purchase on Amazon: https://amazon.com/author/davidcarli.

I conclude by thanking from the bottom of my heart Hannah for her efforts in proofreading this book into English, she was very kind and professional. You can contact her through her email: hannahhermes@gmail.com.

I am not a fan of social networks; however, you can also follow me on:

- X: https://x.com/tradingwdavid;

- LinkedIn: https://www.linkedin.com/in/davidcarli/;
- YouTube: https://www.youtube.com/@tradingwithdavid, where you will find many videos explaining various aspects of trading;
- TradingView: https://www.tradingview.com/u/TradingwDavid.

Before you go, there is one last thing.

If you enjoyed this book or found it useful, I would be very grateful if you would post a short review on Amazon. Your support does make a difference, and I read all the reviews personally so I can get your feedback and make this book even better.

Thanks in advance for your support! I really hope that what you have read will help you in your trading.

Happy Trading to you all!

APPENDIX

Commodity Summary

Appendix A

~

In the table below, you find a summary of the most important commodities treated with some data that will interest your trading.

Commodity	Ticker	Exchange	Trading Hours
Corn	ZC	CBOT	Monday – Friday, 2:00 – 14:45 e 15:30 – 20:20
Soft Red Wheat	ZW	CBOT	Monday – Friday, 2:00 – 14:45 e 15:30 – 20:20
Hard Red Wheat	KE	KCBOT	Monday – Friday, 2:00 – 14:45 e 15:30 – 20:20
Spring Wheat	MW	GME	Monday – Friday, 2:00 – 14:45 e 15:30 – 20:20
Oats	ZO	CBOT	Monday – Friday, 2:00 – 14:45 e 15:30 – 20:20
Soybean	ZS	CBOT	Monday – Friday, 2:00 – 14:45 e 15:30 – 20:20
Soybean Meal	ZM	CBOT	Monday – Friday, 2:00 – 14:45 e 15:30 – 20:20
Soybean Oil	ZL	CBOT	Monday – Friday, 2:00 – 14:45 e 15:30 – 20:20
Live Cattle	LE	CME	Monday – Friday, 15:30 - 20:05
Feeder Cattle	GF	CME	Monday – Friday, 15:30 - 20:05
Lean Hogs	HE	CME	Monday – Friday, 15:30 - 20:05
Cotton	CT	NYBOT	Sunday – Friday, 3:00 – 20:20
Cocoa	CC	NYBOT	Monday – Friday, 10:45 - 19:30
Coffee	KC	NYBOT	Monday – Friday, 10:15 - 19:30
Orange Juice	OJ	NYBOT	Monday – Friday, 14:00 - 20:00
Sugar	SB	NYBOT	Monday – Friday, 9:30 - 19:00
Lumber	LB	CME	Monday – Thursday, 15:00 - 22:00, Friday: 15:00 - 19:55
Gold	GC	NYMEX	Monday – Friday, 00:00 - 23:00

Silver	SI	NYMEX	Monday – Friday, 00:00 - 23:00
Platinum	PL	NYMEX	Monday – Friday, 00:00 - 23:00
Palladium	PA	NYMEX	Monday – Friday, 00:00 - 23:00
Copper	HG	NYMEX	Monday – Friday, 00:00 - 23:00
WTI Crude Oil	CL	NYMEX	Monday – Friday, 00:00 - 23:00
Brent Crude Oil	CB	ICE	Monday – Friday, 02:00 - 23:00
Gasoline	RB	NYMEX	Monday – Friday, 00:00 - 23:00
Heating Oil	HO	NYMEX	Monday – Friday, 00:00 - 23:00
Natural Gas	NG	NYMEX	Monday – Friday, 00:00 - 23:00

Table 2 - Commodities data

EXCHANGES:

CBOT = Chicago Board of Trade - KCBOT = Kansas City Board of Trade - MGE = Minneapolis Grain Exchange - CME = Chicago Mercantile Exchange - NYBOT = New York Board of Trade - ICE = Intercontinental Exchange - NYMEX = New York Mercantile Exchange

THE UNIT MOVE

APPENDIX B

In the table below, you will find the tick value and Unit Move of the most important traded commodities.

Commodity	Ticker	Tick	Tick Value	Unit Move
Corn	ZC	0.25	$12.50	$50.00
Soft Red Wheat	ZW	0.25	$12.50	$50.00
Hard Red Wheat	KE	0.25	$12.50	$50.00
Spring Red Wheat	MW	0.25	$12.50	$50.00
Oats	ZO	0.25	$12.50	$50.00
Soybean	ZS	0.25	$12.50	$50.00
Soybean Meal	ZM	0.10	$10.00	$100.00
Soybean Oil	ZL	0.01	$6.00	$600.00
Live Cattle	LE	0.025	$10.00	$400.00
Feeder Cattle	GF	0.025	$12.50	$500.00
Lean Hogs	HE	0.025	$10.00	$400.00
Cocoa	CC	1.00	$10.00	$10.00
Coffee	KC	0.0005	$18.75	$37,500.00
Cotton	CT	0.0001	$5.00	$50,000.00
Orange Juice	OJ	0.05	$7.50	$750.00
Sugar	SB	0.0001	$11.20	$112,000.00
Lumber	LB	0.10	$11.00	$110.00
Gold	GC	0.10	$10.00	$100.00

Silver	SI	0.005	$25.00	$5,000.00
Platinum	PL	0.10	$5.00	$50.00
Palladium	PA	0.05	$5.00	$100.00
Copper	HG	0.0005	$12.50	$25,000.00
WTI Crude Oil	CL	0.01	$10.00	$1,000.00
Brent Crude Oil	CB	0.01	$10.00	$1,000.00
Gasoline	RB	0.0001	$4.20	$42,000.00
Heating Oil	HO	0.0001	$4.20	$42,000.00
Natural Gas	NG	0.001	$10.00	$10,000.00

Table 3 - Lo Unit Move

FND e LTD

APPENDIX C

Below, you can find the table with the First Notice Day and the Last Trading Day of all the most important commodities treated.

Commodity	FND	LTD
Corn	Last business day of month preceding contract month	The business day prior to the 15th calendar day of the contract month
Soft Red Wheat	Last business day of month preceding contract month	The business day prior to the 15th calendar day of the contract month
Hard Red Wheat	The business day preceding the first business day of the liquidating month	The business day prior to the 15th calendar day of the contract month
Spring Red Wheat	Last business day of month preceding contract month	The business day prior to the 15th calendar day of the contract month
Oats	Last business day of month preceding contract month	The business day prior to the 15th calendar day of the contract month
Soybean	Last business day of month preceding contract month	The business day prior to the 15th calendar day of the contract month
Soybean Meal	Last business day of month preceding contract month	The business day prior to the 15th calendar day of the contract month
Soybean Oil	Last business day of month preceding contract month	The business day prior to the 15th calendar day of the contract month
Live Cattle	Not applicable (cash-settled contract)	Last business day of the contract month
Feeder Cattle	Not applicable (cash-settled contract)	Last Thursday of the contract month with exceptions for November and other months
Lean Hogs	Not applicable (cash-settled contract)	10th business day of the contract month

Cotton	Twelve business days from the end of the spot month	Seventeen business days from the end of the spot month
Cocoa	Ten business days prior to the first business day of the delivery month	One business day prior to last notice day
Coffee	Seven business days prior to the first business day of the delivery month	One business day prior to last notice day
Orange Juice	First business day of the contract month	14th business day prior to the last business day of the month
Sugar	First business day of the contract month	Last business day of the month preceding delivery month
Lumber	Business day after last trading day	Business day preceding the 16th calendar day of the contract month
Gold	Last business day of month preceding contract month	3rd last business day of the delivery month
Silver	Last business day of month preceding contract month	3rd last business day of the delivery month
Platinum	First business day of the contract month	The 4th business day prior to the end of the delivery month
Palladium	First business day of the contract month	The 4th business day prior to the end of the delivery month
Copper	Last business day of month preceding contract month	3rd last business day of the month
WTI Crude Oil	Second business day after last trading day	The 3rd business day prior to the 25th calendar day of the month preceding the delivery month
Brent Crude Oil	The last Business Day of the second month preceding the relevant contract month	The last Business Day of the second month preceding the relevant contract month
Gasoline	2-5 days after last trading day	The last business day of the month preceding the delivery month
Heating Oil	Second business day after last trading day	The penultimate US business day of the month preceding the delivery month
Natural Gas	Business day after last trading day	Three business days prior to the first day of the delivery month

Table 4 - FND and LTD

MONTH SYMBOLS

APPENDIX D

~

Below, you can find the table with the futures contract symbols.

Month	Symbol
January	F
February	G
March	H
April	J
May	K
June	M
July	N
August	Q
September	U
October	V
November	X
December	Z

Table 5 - Futures Contract Symbols

COMMODITY REPORTS

APPENDIX E

Below you find the most important Commodity Reports. Click on the report's name to open the relative web page.

Grains

The World Agricultural Supply and Demand Estimates (WASDE) is a monthly report that provides the USDA's comprehensive forecasts of supply and demand for major U.S. and global crops and U.S. livestock. The report gathers information from several statistical reports published by USDA and other government agencies and provides a framework for additional USDA reports. It is published around the 10th of each month. Link: https://www.usda.gov/oce/commodity/wasde.

The USDA releases the Prospective Plantings report once a year at the end of March. The report is sometimes referred to as the Planting Intentions report, and it is based on a survey the USDA conducts with farmers around the country on how many acres they expect to plant of each crop. The Prospective Plantings missive provides the market with a solid expectation of the size of each crop for the coming crop year. The report is a projection; farmers still need to plant, tend and harvest crops. Link: https://usda.library.cornell.edu/concern/publications/x633f100h.

The Grain Stocks is issued four times a year and contains stocks of corn, soybean, all wheat, oats, and other crops, by States and the U.S. and by position (on-farm or off-farm storage); includes number and capacity of off-farm storage facilities and capacity of on-farm storage facilities. Link: https://usda.library.cornell.edu/concern/publications/xg94hp534.

The Grain: World Markets and Trade is published around the 10th of each month and includes data on U.S. and global trade, production, consumption, and stocks, as well as analysis of developments affecting world trade in grains. Covers wheat, rice and coarse grains (corn, barley, sorghum, oats and rye). Link: https://usda.library.cornell.edu/concern/publications/zs25x844t.

The Crop Production is a report published monthly and shows for each crop the area sown, area harvested, soil yield and total production in the United States. Link: https://usda.library.cornell.edu/concern/publications/tm70mv177.

Issued weekly during the growing season (April to November), the Crop Progress lists planting, fruiting, and harvesting progress and the overall condition of selected crops in major producing states. During the months of December through March, the report is issued monthly titled State Stories. Link: https://usda.library.cornell.edu/concern/publications/8336h188j.

The Outlook for U.S. Agricultural Trade is a quarterly report that examines the annual U.S. international agricultural trade. A global economic outlook is provided with an emphasis on the effect on the U.S. economy and trade. Imports and exports over the past fiscal year are analysed on a commodity basis as well as on a regional basis. Importation and exportation forecasts are provided as well as an analysis on the accuracy of past forecasts. Link: https://usda.library.cornell.edu/concern/publications/6m311p28w.

Acreage is an annual report that presents acreage by planted and/or harvested areas by the state for corn, soybeans, wheat, oats, barley, rye, sorghum, rice, peanuts, sunflower, flaxseed, canola, rapeseed, safflower, mustard seed, cotton, dry beans, potatoes, sweet potatoes, sugar beets, alfalfa hay, tobacco, and sugarcane. Link: https://usda.library.cornell.edu/concern/publications/j098zb09z.

The Oilseeds: World Markets and Trade is a monthly report and includes data on U.S. and global trade, production, consumption and stocks, as well as analysis of developments affecting world trade in oilseeds. Link: https://www.fas.usda.gov/data/oilseeds-world-markets-and-trade.

The Wheat Outlook is a monthly report that examines the U.S. and global wheat industry. Aggregate U.S. wheat production is reported by season, wheat variety and region. Prices, supply, and stocks are also reported with historical context. Global wheat production, use, stocks, and trade are included as an aggregate and on a country-by-country basis. Link: https://usda.library.cornell.edu/concern/publications/cz30ps64c.

The Feed Outlook examines the season-average price, production, supply, use, and trade for feed grains in major exporting and importing countries. The report focuses on corn but covers sorghum, barley, oats, hay, and wheat as well. Contains future projections of production, supply, use, and trade made based on weather conditions and current agricultural and industrial developments. Link: https://usda.library.cornell.edu/concern/publications/44558d29f.

The Oil Crop Outlook report examines the annual and recent monthly supply, use, and pricing of oil crops (primarily soybeans and products) and animal fats. Also included are current and projected crop stocks and supply and demand prospects of major importing and exporting countries. This report includes the following: soybean, rapeseed, sunflower seed, canola, cottonseed, peanuts, flaxseed, lard, tallow. Link: https://usda.library.cornell.edu/concern/publications/j098zb08p.

The Winter Wheat and Canola Seedings is an annual report that includes data on the annual seeded acreage of winter wheat, durum wheat, and canola seedlings. Data is presented on a national basis and on a state-by-state basis with historical context given for the current year's seeded acreage. Link: https://usda.library.cornell.edu/concern/publications/z890rt24s.

The Agricultural Prices is a monthly file that contains prices received by farmers for principal crops, livestock and livestock products; indexes of prices received by farmers; feed price ratios; indexes of prices paid by farmers; and parity prices. Link: https://usda.library.cornell.edu/concern/publications/c821gj76b.

Meats

The most important report is the World Agricultural Supply and Demand Estimates (WASDE) that contains the forecasts of supply and demand for U.S. livestock (it is published around the 10th of each month). Link: https://www.usda.gov/oce/commodity/wasde.

The Cattle on Feed contains the monthly total number of cattle and calves on feed, placements, marketing, and other disappearances; by class and feedlot capacity for selected states; a number of feedlots and fed cattle marketing by size groups for selected states. Link: https://usda.library.cornell.edu/concern/publications/m326m174z.

The Livestock, Dairy and Poultry report gives information, focusing on current and forecast production, prices, and trade for each of the sectors. Link: https://usda.library.cornell.edu/concern/publications/g445cd121.

The Hogs and Pigs, issued four times yearly, presents data on the U.S. pig crop for 16 major states in the U.S., including inventory number by class, weight group, farrowing, and farrowing intentions. Link: https://usda.library.cornell.edu/concern/publications/rj430453j.

The Livestock Slaughter is a monthly full-text file and contains the number of head, live weight, dressed weight of cattle, calves, sheep, lambs, hogs and pigs slaughtered in commercial plants and number by class in federally inspected plants by regions as well as red meat production by species by states and U.S. Link: https://usda.library.cornell.edu/concern/publications/rx913p88g.

The Livestock and Poultry: World Markets and Trade is a quarterly report and includes data on U.S. and global trade, production, consumption and stocks, as well as analysis of developments affecting world trade in livestock and poultry. Covers beef and veal, cattle, pork, swine and chicken meat. Link: https://www.fas.usda.gov/data/livestock-and-poultry-world-markets-and-trade.

The United States and Canadian Cattle is a result of a joint effort by Statistics Canada and NASS to release the number of cattle and calves by class and calf crop for both countries within one publication. Published twice a year in late winter (March) and summer (August). Link: https://usda.library.cornell.edu/concern/publications/474299142.

The United States and Canadian Hogs is a result of a joint effort by Statistics

Canada and NASS to release the total hogs, breeding, market hogs, sows farrowed, and pig crop for both countries within one publication. Published twice a year in late winter (March) and summer (August). Link: https://usda.library.cornell.edu/concern/publications/7h149p85x.

Softs

Cocoa: The Quarterly Cocoa Grind is a quarterly report for cocoa traders and others in the industry. Supplied by NCA for the ICE Futures U.S, the report measures the number of cocoa beans that have been ground during the reporting period in North America. About 10 chocolate processors contribute their data to the report. Link: https://candyusa.com/cocoa-grinds-report/.

Coffee: The Coffee: World Markets and Trade is a biannual report issued by the Foreign Agriculture Service (FAS) in June and December. It includes data on U.S. and global trade, production, consumption and stocks, as well as analysis of developments affecting world trade of coffee. Link: https://usda.library.cornell.edu/concern/publications/m900nt40f.

The Monthly Coffee Market is a report published monthly by the International Coffee Organisation (ICO) and provides data and estimates on world coffee production, prices, imports and exports. Link: https://www.ico.org/Market-Report-21-22-e.asp (the link changes every year, just change the years and go from 21-22 to 22-23 and so on, the same for accessing past reports, 20-21, 19-20 etc.).

Cotton: as for Grains, the most important reports are the WASDE and the Prospective Plantings. You can find everything on the Weekly Cotton Market Review that is published every week by the USDA. This report summarises all the USDA's information on cotton, including world prices, export sales, crop conditions, weather and more. Link: https://usda.library.cornell.edu/concern/publications/w9505044z?locale=en.

The Cotton: World Markets and Trade is published around the 10th of each month and includes data on U.S. and global trade, production, consumption, and stocks, as well as analysis of developments affecting world trade in cotton. Link: https://usda.library.cornell.edu/concern/publications/kp78gg36g.

The Cotton Ginnings is published fortnightly from September to January and monthly in February, March and August by the National Agricultural Statistics Service (NASS). It reports data on cotton production in the United States. Link: https://usda.library.cornell.edu/concern/publications/q524jn76v.

The Cotton System Consumption and Stocks is a monthly report that is part of the Current Agricultural Industrial Reports (CAIR) program. The report provides monthly and annual totals for extra-long-staple cotton and manmade fibres consumption, as well as ending stocks and monthly spindle activity on the U.S. cotton system. Link: https://usda.library.cornell.edu/concern/publications/ng451h506.

The Cotton and Wool Outlook report examines the latest USDA cotton projections for the production, supply, demand, and global ending stocks in the United States as well as in major exporters and importers of cotton and wool. Also includes tabular data on raw fibre and textile imports, exports, and prices. Link: https://usda.library.cornell.edu/concern/publications/n870zq801?locale=en.

Sugar: WASDE is the most important report. Another important report is Sugar: World Markets and Trade. This biannual report, issued by the Foreign Agriculture Service (FAS) in May and November, includes data on U.S. and global trade, production, consumption and stocks, as well as analysis of developments affecting world trade in sugar. Link: https://usda.library.cornell.edu/concern/publications/z029p472x.

The Sugar and Sweeteners Outlook report provides an outlook on domestic and global sugar production, use, and stocks. Annual domestic production of sugar is estimated for the current year and forecasted for the next fiscal year and compared with annual sugar use and annual importation. International production and use of sugar (especially that of Mexico's) are also estimated for the current year and forecasted for next year. International imports and exports are estimated on a country-by-country basis, with analysis for notable policy changes. Also included are international and global ending stocks of sugar and how they measure against production and use. Link: https://usda.library.cornell.edu/concern/publications/pv63g024f?locale=en.

With the Sugar and Sweeteners Yearbook Tables the ERS analysts track U.S. and international sugar and sweetener production, consumption, and trade. They also monitor and analyse U.S. sweetener policy and events that affect the domestic, Mexican, and other international sweetener markets. Link: https://www.ers.usda.gov/data-products/sugar-and-sweeteners-yearbook-tables/.

Orange Juice: the Citrus: World Markets and Trade is a biannual report, published in January and July, which includes data on U.S. and global trade, production, consumption and stocks, as well as analysis of developments affecting world trade in citrus. Covers fresh oranges, orange juice, tangerines/mandarins, lemons and limes, and grapefruit. Link: https://usda.library.cornell.edu/concern/publications/w66343603.

Energy

Crude Oil: A Weekly Petroleum Status Report is released by the Energy Information Administration (EIA) and provides timely information on supply and selected prices of crude oil and principal petroleum products. Link: https://www.eia.gov/petroleum/supply/weekly/.

Also important is the Monthly Oil Market Report (MOMR) issued by OPEC which covers major issues affecting the world oil market and provides an outlook for crude oil market developments for the coming year. The report provides a detailed analysis of key developments impacting oil market trends in world oil demand and supply as well as the oil market balance. Link: https://www.opec.org/opec_web/en/publications/338.htm.

The Short-Term Energy Outlook is published monthly by the Energy Information

Administration (EIA) and reports short-term forecasts of production, consumption, and price trends for each energy source in the United States. Link: https://www.eia.gov/outlooks/steo/.

The Monthly Energy Review is a report published by the Energy Information Administration (EIA) with recent and historical energy statistics. This publication includes total energy production, consumption, stocks, and trade; energy prices; overviews of oil, natural gas, coal, electricity, nuclear power, renewable energy, and carbon dioxide emissions; and conversion values of data units. Link: https://www.eia.gov/totalenergy/data/monthly/.

The International Energy Agency's Oil Market Report (OMR) is one of the world's most authoritative and timely sources of data, forecasts and analysis on the global oil market. The report is monthly and charged but you can read the very interesting highlights for free. Link: https://www.iea.org/topics/oil-market-report.

The OPEC's Annual Statistical Bulletin (ASB) contains about 100 pages of tables, charts and graphs detailing the world's oil and gas reserves, crude oil and product output, exports, refining, tankers, plus economic and other data. Link: https://opec.org/opec_web/en/publications/202.htm.

This Week in Petroleum provides insights into the energy market, as well as data on oil and other liquids. Link: https://www.eia.gov/petroleum/weekly/index.php.

Gasoline: The Weekly Petroleum Status Report, Monthly Oil Market Report, Short-Term Energy Outlook and Monthly Energy Review.

Heating Oil: The Weekly Petroleum Status Report, Monthly Oil Market Report, Short-Term Energy Outlook and Monthly Energy Review.

Natural Gas: The Weekly Natural Gas Storage Report is a weekly report containing estimates of natural gas in underground storage for the United States and five regions of the United States released each Thursday at 10:30 a.m. at the EIA website, except for certain weeks with Federal holidays. The report contains estimates of storage for the current and prior week and comparisons to previous periods. Link: https://ir.eia.gov/ngs/ngs.html.

The Natural Gas Weekly Update reports news, production data and stocks of natural gas in the United States. Link: https://www.eia.gov/naturalgas/weekly/.

The Natural Gas Monthly, released by EIA, highlights activities, events, and analyses of interest to public and private sector organisations associated with the natural gas industry. Volume and price data are presented each month for natural gas production, distribution, consumption, and interstate pipeline activities. Producer-related activities and underground storage data are also reported. Link: https://www.eia.gov/naturalgas/monthly/.

The Short-Term Energy Outlook, Monthly Energy Review, and Annual Statistical Bulletin (ASB).

Metals

You will find interesting resources in the table in Appendix F.

Weather

The Weekly Weather and Crop Bulletin is released by 4:00 p.m. on the second workday of each week. The Bulletin includes the National Summary, State Stories, current data for weather, temperature and precipitation and international agricultural weather. The full report is jointly published by the National Oceanic and Atmospheric Administration of the U.S. Department of Commerce, the National Agricultural Statistics Service, and the World Agricultural Outlook Board. Link: https://usda.library.cornell.edu/concern/publications/cj82k728n.

I have included for each report the link where you can go to read and download it. However, for your convenience, you can find all these reports on my website under the category Commodity Reports, along with the Commodity Reports Calendar.

WEB RESOURCES

APPENDIX F

Below, you will find a summary of all the resources you have seen in this book, along with many others that will help you in your analysis.

Website	Link
Platforms	
Interactive Brokers	https://www.interactivebrokers.com/en/home.php you can request a demo.
TradingView	https://www.tradingview.com
ProRealTime	https://www.prorealtime.com
Databases	
Moore Research	https://www.mrci.com, 14-day free trial.
SeasonAlgo	https://www.seasonalgo.com, free access to the software, but limited to corn only.
SpreadCharts	https://spreadcharts.com, free access to the app.
Exchanges	
CME Group	https://www.cmegroup.com
ICE	https://www.theice.com/index
MGEX	http://www.mgex.com
Reports	
C.O.T. Report	https://www.cftc.gov
Financial Websites	
Barchart	https://www.barchart.com
Finviz	https://www.finviz.com/futures.ashx
Investing	https://www.investing.com
Index Mundi	https://www.indexmundi.com/

Grains

AGWeb	https://www.agweb.com
Int.l Grains Council	https://www.igc.int/en/default.aspx
Costs and Returns	https://www.ers.usda.gov/data-products/commodity-costs-and-returns
NASS Publications	https://www.nass.usda.gov/Publications/
ERS Publications	https://www.ers.usda.gov/Publications/
FAS Publications	https://www.fas.usda.gov/data
USDA Agency Reports	https://www.usda.gov/media/agency-reports

Meats

Cattle Range	https://www.cattlerange.com
Livestock Slaughter	https://usda.library.cornell.edu/concern/publications/rx913p88g
Livestock and Poultry	https://www.fas.usda.gov/data/livestock-and-poultry-world-markets-and-trade
Daily Livestock Report	https://dailylivestockreport.com/
The Pig Site	https://www.thepigsite.com/

Softs

Int.l Cocoa Org. (ICCO)	https://www.icco.org/
Int.l Coffee Org. (ICO)	https://www.ico.org/trade_statistics.asp
Vanderbilt Institute	https://www.vanderbilt.edu/ics/
Coffee Search	http://www.coffeeresearch.org/
Unica	https://unica.com.br/en/
The Sugar Association	https://www.sugar.org/

Energy

Oil Price	https://oilprice.com
What drives prices?	https://www.eia.gov/finance/markets/crudeoil/
Energy Explained	https://www.eia.gov/energyexplained/
Energy KIDS	https://www.eia.gov/kids/

Metals	
World Gold Council	https://www.gold.org/goldhub/research/library
London Bullion Market	https://www.lbma.org.uk/
Silver Institute	https://www.silverinstitute.org/
Platinum Investment	https://platinuminvestment.com/
Pgm Market Report	http://www.platinum.matthey.com/services/market-research/pgm-market-report
Int.l Platinum Assoc.	https://ipa-news.de/index/platinum-group-metals/
LPPM	https://lppm.com/
Copper Study Group	https://icsg.org/selected-copper-statistics/
Copper Association	https://www.copper.org/resources/market_data/
IWCC	http://www.coppercouncil.org/iwcc-statistics-and-data
NYMEX Delivery Notices	https://www.cmegroup.com/clearing/operations-and-deliveries/nymex-delivery-notices.html
Weather	
Weather Channel	https://weather.com
Drought Monitor	https://droughtmonitor.unl.edu
Follow me	
Website	https://tradingwithdavid.com
X	https://x.com/tradingwdavid
LinkedIn	https://www.linkedin.com/in/davidcarli/
YouTube	https://www.youtube.com/@tradingwithdavid
TradingView	https://www.tradingview.com/u/TradingwDavid
Resources	
Economic Calendar	https://www.forexfactory.com/
	https://tradingwithdavid.com/economic-calendar

Table 6 - Web Resources

Commodity Glossary

Appendix G

Actuals: commodities on hand, ready for shipment, storage, or manufacture.

Arbitrage: simultaneous purchase and sale of the same quantity of the same commodity in two different markets, either in the same country or in different countries. Used to take advantage of perceived mispricing.

Ask: the price a seller is willing to accept for a security, which is often referred to as the offer price.

At the market: an order to buy or sell at the best price obtainable at the time the order reached the trading pit or ring.

Backwardation: a futures market in which the relationship between two delivery months of the same commodity is abnormal. The opposite of Contango.

Basis: the price difference over or under a designated future at which a commodity of a certain description is sold or quoted.

Basis contract: a forward contract in which the cash price is based on the basis relating to a specified futures contract.

Bear/Bearish: a market trending downward, or a person who expects prices to go lower.

Bid: an offer made by an investor, a trader to buy a security, commodity or currency.

Board of Trade: designated by the CFTC to trade futures or options contracts on a particular commodity. Commonly used to mean any exchange on which futures are traded.

Bollinger Bands: an indicator that allows users to compare volatility and relative price levels over a period of time. The indicator consists of three bands: a Simple Moving Average (SMA) usually at the 20-period, an SMA+2 standard deviation and an SMA-2 standard deviation. They are designed to encompass the majority of a security's price action.

Break: a quick, extensive decline in prices.

Broker: a person paid a fee or commission for executing the buy or sell orders of a customer.

Bulge: a rapid advance in prices.

Bull/Bullish: a market trending upward; on a person who expects prices to go higher.

Buy on close: to buy at the end of a trading session at a price within the closing range.

Buy on opening: to buy at the beginning of a trading session at a price within the opening range.

Carrying broker: a member of a futures exchange, usually a clearinghouse member, through which another firm, broker or customer chooses to clear all or some trades.

Carryover: last year's ending stocks of a storable commodity.

Cash commodity: the actual physical product, as distinguished from the 'future'.

CFTC: Commodities Futures Trading Commission. The independent body that oversees all futures trading in the United States.

Charting: the use of graphs and charts in the technical analysis of futures markets to plot price movements, volume, open interest or other statistical indicators of price movement.

Clearinghouse: an agency or separate corporation of a futures exchange that is responsible for settling trading accounts, collecting and maintaining margin monies, regulating delivery and reporting trade data (i.e., CME Clearing is the clearinghouse for CME).

Close: the period at the end of the trading session officially designated by the exchange during which all transactions are considered made 'at the close'.

Closing price or range: the price or price range recorded during the period designated by the exchange as the official close.

Commission: for futures contracts, the one-time fee charged by a broker to cover the trades a client makes to open and close each position. It is payable when the client exits the position. Also called a round-turn.

Commodity: the underlying instrument upon which a futures contract is based.

Commodity exchange: an exchange that lists designated futures contracts for the trading of various types of derivative products and allows the use of its facilities by traders. Must comply with rules set forth by the Commodity Futures Trading Commission (CFTC).

C.O.T. Report: Commitments Of Traders. A weekly report from the CFTC, providing a breakdown of each Tuesday's open interest for markets in which 20 or more traders hold positions equal to or above the reporting levels established by the CFTC. Open interest is broken down by aggregate Commercial, Non-Commercial, and non-reportable holdings.

Contango: futures market in which prices in succeeding delivery months are progressively higher. The opposite of Backwardation.

Contract grades: those grades of a commodity that have been officially approved by an exchange as a deliverable in settlement of a futures contract.

Contract month: the month in which delivery is to be made in accordance with the terms of the futures contract.

Convergence: the tendency for prices of physical commodities and futures to approach one another, usually during the delivery month.

Correlation: a statistical measure of how two commodities, or the same commodity in two different periods, move in relation to each other. A measure of 1 means the commodities are highly correlated and move in conjunction. A measure of 0 (zero) means the commodities are not at all correlated and do not move in conjunction. A measure of -1 means the commodities are inversely correlated.

Cover: the cancellation of a short position in any future by the purchase of an equal quantity of the same future.

Crop year: period from the harvest of a crop to the corresponding period in the following year, as used statistically. The U.S. wheat crop year begins June 1 and ends May 31; cotton, August 1 to July 31; varying dates for other commodities.

CTA: Commodity Trading Advisor. A person who, for compensation or profit, directly or indirectly advises others as to the advisability of buying or selling futures or commodity options. Providing advice includes exercising trading authority over a customer's account. A CTA may be required to be registered with the CFTC.

Day order: order at a limited price is understood to be good for the day only unless expressly designated as an open order or good till cancelled order.

Day trader: a speculator who will normally initiate and offset a position within a single trading session.

Default: the failure to perform on a futures contract as required by exchange rules, such as a failure to meet a margin call or to make or take delivery.

Delivery: the tender and receipt of the actual commodity, or warehouse receipts covering such commodity, in settlement of a futures contract.

Delivery month: a specified month within which delivery may be made under the terms of a futures contract.

Delivery notice: a notice of a clearing member's intention to deliver a stated quantity of a commodity in settlement of a futures contract.

Demand: the quantity of a commodity that buyers are willing to purchase in the market at a given price.

Derivative: a financial instrument, traded on or off an exchange, the price of which is directly dependent upon the value of one or more underlying securities, equity indices, debt instruments, commodities, other derivative instruments, or any agreed-upon pricing index or arrangement. Derivatives involve the trading of rights or obligations based on the underlying product but do not directly transfer that product. They are generally used to hedge risk.

Differentials: the premiums paid for the grades better than the basic grade and the discounts allowed for grades lower than the basic grades. These differentials are fixed by the contract terms on most exchanges.

Discount: (1) the amount a price would be reduced to purchase a commodity of lesser grade. (2) Sometimes used to refer to the price differences between futures of different delivery months, as in the phrase 'July is trading at a discount to May', indicating that the price of the July future is lower than that of May. (3) Applied to cash grain prices that are below the futures price.

Divergence: an action by one indicator moving not in conjunction or agreement with the price or another indicator, but rather counter to or short of it. Such non-confirmations often signal reversals.

Double top/bottom: a chart formation that signals a possible price trend reversal. In a point and figure chart, double tops and bottoms are used to buy and sell signals.

Downtrend: a price trend characterised by a series of lower highs and lower lows.

Electronic order: an order placed electronically (without the use of a broker) either via the Internet or an electronic trading system.

Electronic trading system: systems that allow participating exchanges to list their products for trading electronically. These systems may replace, supplement or run alongside the open outcry trading.

Equity: (1) the value of a futures trading account if all open positions were offset at the current market price. (2) An ownership interest in a company, such as stock.

Farm prices: the prices received by farmers for their products, as published by the U.S. Department of Agriculture, as of the 15th of each month.

FCM: Futures Commission Merchant. An individual or organisation which solicits or accepts orders to buy or sell futures contracts or commodity options and accepts money or other assets from customers in connection with such orders. An FCM must be registered with the CFTC.

Floor broker: an individual who is registered with the CFTC to execute orders on the floor of an exchange for the account of another. He/she receives a fee for doing so by clearing members or their customers.

FND: First Notice Day. The first day on which transferable notices can be issued for delivery in a specified delivery month.

FOB: Free On Board. Usually covers the cost of putting commodities on board whatever shipment conveyance is being used.

Forward contract: a private, cash-market agreement between a buyer and seller for the future delivery of a commodity at an agreed price. In contrast to futures contracts, forward contracts are not standardised and not transferable.

FPD: First Position Day, is the initial day on which the investor who is short a commodity futures contract may notify the clearing corporation of an intention to deliver the commodity.

Fundamental analysis: the study of supply and demand information to aid in anticipating futures price trends.

Futures contract: an obligation to deliver or to receive a specified quantity and grade of a commodity during a designated month at the designated price. Each futures contract is standardised and specifies commodity, quality, quantity, delivery date and settlement.

Globex: an international electronic trading system for futures and options that allows participating exchanges to list their products for trading after the close of the exchanges' open outcry trading hours. Developed by Reuters Limited for use by the Chicago Mercantile Exchange (CME), Globex was launched on June 25, 1992, for certain CME contracts.

Grades: various qualities according to accepted trade usage.

Grading certificates: certificates attesting to the quality of a commodity graded by official inspectors, testers, graders, and so on.

Growths: description of a commodity according to areas of growth; refers to the country, district, or place of Semis manufacture.

GTC: Good Till Cancelled. Usually refers to open orders to buy or sell at a fixed price.

Hedge: a sale of any commodity for further delivery on or subject to the rules of any futures market to the extent that such sales are offset in quantity by the ownership or purchase of the same cash commodity; or, conversely, purchases of any commodity for future delivery on or subject to the rules of any futures market to the extent that such purchases are offset by sales of the same cash commodity.

High: the highest price of the day/week/month for a particular futures contract.

Initial margin: the amount a futures market participant must deposit into a margin account at the time an order is placed to buy or sell a futures contract.

Introducing Broker (IB): a firm or individual that solicits and accepts commodity futures orders from customers but does not accept money, securities or property from the customer. All Introducing Brokers must be registered with the CFTC.

Leverage: the ability to control large dollar amounts of a commodity with a comparatively small amount of capital.

Life of delivery: the period between first and last trade in any futures delivery contract.

Limited order: an order given to a broker by a customer that has some restrictions upon its execution, such as price or time.

Liquidation: a transaction made in reducing or closing out a long or short position, but more often used by the trade to mean a reduction or closing out of a long.

Liquidity/Liquid market: a characteristic of a security or commodity market with enough units outstanding and enough buyers and sellers to allow large transactions without a substantial change in price.

Long: (1) the buying side of an open futures contract. (2) A trader whose net position in the futures market shows an excess of open purchases over open sales.

Lot: usually any definite quantity of a commodity of uniform grade; the standard unit of trading in the futures market.

Low: the lowest price of the day/week/month for a particular futures contract.

LTD: Last Trading Day. The last day on which trading may occur in a given futures contract.

Maintenance margin: a set minimum amount (per outstanding futures contract) that a customer must maintain in his margin account to retain the futures position.

Margin: an amount of money deposited by both buyers and sellers of futures contracts and by sellers of options contracts to ensure the performance of the terms of the contract (the making or taking delivery of the commodity or the cancellation of the position by a subsequent offsetting trade). The margin in commodities is not a down payment, as for securities, but rather a performance bond.

Margin call: demand for additional funds, or equivalent, because of adverse price movement or some other contingency.

Mark-to-Market: to debit or credit on a daily basis a margin account based on the close of that day's trading session. In this way, buyers and sellers are protected against the possibility of contract default.

Market order: an order for immediate execution at the best available price.

Maturity: period within which a futures contract can be settled by delivery of the actual commodity; the period between the first notice day and the last trading day of a commodity futures contract.

Maximum price fluctuation: the maximum amount the contract price can change up or down, during one trading session, as stipulated by exchange rules. Consult CME Clearing contract specifications for specific price limit information.

Mediation: a voluntary process in which the parties to a futures-related dispute work with a neutral third party to find a mutually acceptable solution.

Moving averages: a type of technical analysis using the averages of settlement prices.

Nearby: the futures contract closest to expiration.

Net asset value: the value of each unit of participation in a commodity pool. Basically, a calculation of assets minus liabilities plus or minus the value of open positions when marked to the market, divided by the total number of outstanding units.

Net performance: an increase or decrease in net asset value exclusive of additions, withdrawals and redemptions.

Net position: the difference between the open contracts long and the open contracts short held in any one commodity by any individual or group.

NFA: National Futures Association. Authorised by Congress in 1974 and designated by the CFTC in 1982 as a 'registered futures association', NFA is the industry-wide self-regulatory organisation of the futures industry.

Offer: the quantity of a commodity that sellers are willing to sell in the market at a given price.

Offset: (1) to remove a position from an account by establishing a position opposite an existing position, making or taking delivery, or exercising an option (i.e., selling if one has bought, or buying if one has sold). (2) To report reductions of a firm's inventory of open long purchase dates to CME Clearing.

On opening: a term used to specify execution of order during the opening.

Open: the period at the beginning of the trading session officially designated by the exchange during which all transactions are considered made 'at the opening'.

Open contracts: contracts that have been bought or sold without the transaction having been completed by subsequent sale, or repurchase, or actual delivery or receipt of the commodity.

Open interest: the total number of futures contracts long or short in a delivery month or market that has been entered into and not yet liquidated by an offsetting transaction or fulfilled by delivery Also known as Open Contracts or Open Commitments. Each open transaction has a buyer and a seller, but for calculation of open interest, only one side of the contract is counted.

Open order: an order that is good until cancelled.

Opening price or range: the price or price range recorded during the period designated by the exchange as the official opening.

Option: the right, but not the obligation, to sell or buy the underlying (in this case, a futures contract) at a specified price on or before a certain expiration date. There are two types of options: call options and put options. Each offers an opportunity to take advantage of future price moves without actually having a futures position.

Out trade: a trade which cannot be cleared by a clearinghouse because the data submitted by the two clearing members involved in the trade differs in some respect. All out trades must be resolved before the market opens the next day.

Overbought: a technical opinion that the market price has risen too steeply and too fast in relation to underlying fundamental factors.

Oversold: a technical opinion that the market price has declined too steeply and too fast in relation to underlying fundamental factors.

Pit: an octagonal platform on the trading floor of an exchange, consisting of steps upon which traders and brokers stand while executing futures trades.

Point: the minimum unit in which changes in futures price may be expressed. Minimum price fluctuation may be in multiples of points.

Position: an interest in the market in the form of open commitments.

Position trader: a trader who either buys or sells contracts and holds them for an extended period of time, as distinguished from a day trader.

Premium: (1) the price paid by the purchaser of an option to the grantor (seller). (2) The amount by which a cash commodity price trades over a futures price or other cash commodity price.

Price: price to which the given instrument should be traded in an order or a trade. Also called limit.

Price order: an order to sell or buy at a certain price or better.

Price limit: the maximum advance or decline, from the previous day's settlement price, permitted for a futures contract in one trading session. Also referred to as Maximum Price Fluctuation.

Primary markets: when used in connection with foreign-produced commodities, refers to the country of production. In domestic commodities, refers to centres that receive commodities directly from country shippers.

Purchase and sale statement (P&S): a statement sent by a commission merchant to a customer when his or her futures position has been reduced to close out. It shows the amount involved; the price at which the position was acquired and reduced or closeout, respectively; the gross profits or loss; the commission charged; and the net profit or loss on the transaction.

Pyramiding: the use of unrealised profits on existing futures positions as margin to increase the size of the position, normally in successively smaller increments.

Quotation: the actual price or the bid or ask price of either cash commodities or futures or options contracts at a particular time.

Range: the difference between the high and the low price of the future during a given period.

Reaction: the downward tendency of a commodity after an advance.

Realising: when a profit is realised either by a liquidating sale or the repurchase of a short sale.

Reportable positions: the number of open contracts specified by the CFTC when a firm or individual must begin reporting total positions by delivery month to the authorised exchange and/or the CFTC.

Resting order: an instruction to buy or sell at figures away from the current level.

Ross, Joe: An American trader known for inventing several chart patterns in technical analysis and trading techniques. The most famous is the 1-2-3 high or low and the Ross Hook.

Round lot: the trading unit in which the major portion of trading occurs on those exchanges that make provisions for trading in two different units; prices of transactions in such units are only registered as official quotations.

Round turn: the execution for the same principal of a purchase transaction and a sales transaction that offset each other.

Round turn commission: the cost to the customer for executing a futures contract which is charged only when the position is liquidated.

RSI: Relative Strength Index. A momentum indicator developed by noted technical analyst Welles Wilder that compares the magnitude of recent gains and losses over a specified time period to measure speed and change of price movements of a security.

Scalping: for floor traders, the practice of trading in and out of contracts throughout the trading day in hopes of making a series of small profits.

Seasonality: characteristic of a time series in which the data experience regular and predictable changes that recur every calendar year. Any predictable change or pattern in a time series that recurs or repeats over a one-year period can be said to be seasonal.

Segregated account: a special account used to hold and separate customers' assets from those of the broker or firm.

Settlement price: the official daily closing price of a futures contract, set by the exchange for the purpose of settling margin accounts.

Short: (1) the selling of an open futures contract. (2) A trader whose net position in the futures market shows all excess of open sales over open purchases.

Speculator: an individual who does not hedge, but who trades in commodity futures or options with the objective of achieving profits through the successful anticipation of price movements. The speculator has no interest in taking delivery.

Spot commodity: the actual physical commodity, as distinguished from the futures.

Spot price: the price at which the spot or cash commodity is selling. In grain trading, it is called the 'cash' price.

Spread: usually refers to a simultaneous purchase of a contract and sale of another. Spreads can be transacted between contracts with the same underlying commodity, but different months; the same month but different commodities; or the same month and commodity but traded on different exchanges.

Stop order: an order specifying a price at which it is activated and becomes a limit order. A buy stop is entered above the current market and becomes a limit order when the commodity trades at or above the specified stop trigger price. A sell stop is entered below the current market. It becomes a limit order when the commodity trades at the stop price or below. The stop can immediately execute up to the limit price.

Supply: the quantity of a commodity that producers are willing to provide to the market at a given price.

Swap: in general, the exchange of one asset or liability for a similar asset or liability for the purpose of lengthening or shortening maturities, or raising or lowering coupon rates, to maximise revenue or minimise financing costs.

Target price: an expected selling or buying price.

Technical analysis: the study of historical price patterns to help forecast futures prices.

Tick: the smallest increment of price movement for a futures contract. Also referred to as Minimum Price Fluctuation.

Ticker: letters that identify a stock or a commodity traded. A short and convenient way of identifying them.

Tick value: the cash value of one tick (one minimum price movement).

Trader: (1) a person who takes positions in the futures market, usually without the intention of making or taking delivery. (2) A member of the exchange who buys and sells futures and options through the floor of the exchange.

Trailing stop: a stop order that follows your trade around and closes it out when the price has moved a certain amount from the highest level since the inception of the trade.

Uptrend: a price trend characterised by a series of higher highs and higher lows.

Unit move: the dollar value of 1 point of the future movement.

Variation margin: additional margin required to be deposited by a clearing member firm to the clearinghouse during periods of great market volatility or in the case of high-risk accounts.

Volatility: an annualised measure of the fluctuation in the price of a futures contract. Historical volatility is the actual measure of the future price movement of the past. Implied volatility is a measure of what the market implies, it is, as reflected in the option's price,

Volume: represents a simple addition of successive futures transactions. (A transaction consists of a purchase and a matching sale).

Warehouse: a firm operating a private wire to its own branch offices or to other firms.

Yield: a measure of the annual return on investment.

Yield curve: a graphic representation of market yield for fixed income security plotted against the maturity of the security.

Made in the USA
Las Vegas, NV
01 March 2025